Haunted by Waters

American Land and Life Series

Wayne Franklin,

series editor

Haunted by Waters

A Journey through Race and Place
in the American West

ROBERT T. HAYASHI

Foreword by

Wayne Franklin

University of Iowa Press

Iowa City

University of Iowa Press, Iowa City 52242
Copyright © 2007 by the University of Iowa Press
www.uiowapress.org
All rights reserved
Printed in the United States of America

Design by Omega Clay

The University of Iowa Press is a member of Green Press Initiative and is committed to preserving natural resources.

Printed on acid-free paper

LCCN: 2007923928
ISBN-13: 978-1-58729-610-9
ISBN-10: 1-58729-610-1

07 08 09 10 11 C 5 4 3 2 1

In Memory of
Teruo Terry Hayashi, M.D.

Parted by circumstance,
Grant each your indulgence
That we may meet in dreams
For talk, for dalliance,
By warm hearths, by cool streams.

W. H. AUDEN

CONTENTS

FOREWORD

Wayne Franklin

We are all haunted by waters—and by water. I suspect that the abundance and relative purity of this simple but almost universal compound helps explain why. Not that we encounter water in potable form in our daily experience. Far from it. The by now nearly ubiquitous little plastic *vade mecums* of spring water or filtered water or god-knows-what that have become our fetishes attest to how rarely we expect to find the real thing as we make our way through the world. Yet even when we encounter it in a less than ideal form, murky or even turbid, perhaps with a slick on it, water remains almost always recognizably itself. It has the strange power of absorbing other things, disguising them or even hiding them in the process, without profoundly altering its own magical liquidity. It has no real shape, is restless in its Newtonian quest for lower ground, and cycles endlessly through profound physical changes that nevertheless tend to purify it. It is a rare thing to find a substance that, while constantly on the move, all the while endures—and returns.

So water threads its way through our minds and imaginations, as through the valleys of the earth, with a down-cutting, erosive insistence. And it carries a peculiar burden as it passes. In nature writing, at least since the time of Henry David Thoreau's *A Week on the Concord and Merrimack Rivers* (1849), it is not always *there* merely as a fact of the world. It also takes on a profound role as the bearer of memories. Some of this symbolic meaning we may certainly ascribe to the way that water, always changing even in a puddle, images time. But part of it, certainly in American nature writing, has to do with Thoreau's potent example. The two-week river trip chronicled in Thoreau's book took place in late August and early September, 1839. Thoreau and his slightly older brother John, to whom he was very close, began the trip by passing down their slow-moving home river to the place where it lost itself in the more vigorous Merrimack at the recently founded mill city of Lowell, Massachusetts. (They traveled in a rowboat they had made themselves, a modest dory-like vessel named the *Musketaquid*, after the Indian name for the Concord. Eventually the boat was purchased by their sometimes fellow townsman Nathaniel Hawthorne, who in turn gave it to Henry Thoreau's good friend, poet William Ellery Channing, thus making it the most literary of American small craft.) Once afloat on the Merrimack, the Thoreau brothers turned upstream and rowed against the current until, having passed through another mill city, Manchester, they beached the boat because the water route was too tough above there. Instead, the travelers continued by foot and by stage to Mount Washington, which they ascended before returning to their boat and hurrying home. They reached Concord again just as the first chill of autumn was descending.

This was no great Homeric voyage, no Lewis and Clark venture, but a relatively domestic passage amid cultivated fields and villages (partly by means of canal locks on both rivers) as well as through industrial sites notable for the way they were forever altering American society. We know about it only because Thoreau insisted on writing about it—and later wrote about an even less adventurous experience, solitary this time, that he contrived to have on the shores of a sleepy pond just outside the bustling village of Concord. How and why he wrote about the river trip illuminates the sorts of freight that water has come to bear in American literature. Thoreau jotted down now-lost field notes during the trip itself, later copying and reconstructing and extending them in his journal in the period from 1840 to 1844. About the latter year, Thoreau began to think of the trip as worthy of a more extended treatment. When he went to live at Walden Pond in 1845, writing the river book was the most pertinent part of the "private business" that drove him to take up residence there. He wrote two drafts of the book while at Walden, in between hoeing beans, contemplating the deep pond, keeping his journal, and running off to, among other places, Maine. Eventually the book was published in May, 1849, almost a decade after the trip.

That long interval helps explain why Thoreau wedded water to memory. There would be in most of his writings a considerable gap between when he did something and when he at last published an account of it—*Walden* itself, most famously, went through eight versions between 1846 and 1854, when it finally appeared in print. But in the case of *A Week on the Concord and Merrimack Rivers*, the delay was deeply emotional as well. On New Year's Day, 1842, Thoreau's brother John accidentally cut the tip of one finger while stropping his razor. On January 11, having developed lockjaw, he died in the arms of the relative who had been his tireless nurse through a dreadful ordeal—Henry. The impact on Henry was so profound that within less than two weeks he himself was exhibiting the physical symptoms of lockjaw, and although these soon passed, he was incapacitated and emotionally numb for weeks. For years afterward, on the anniversary of John's death, Henry was visited with tragic dreams.

So A Week on the Concord and Merrimack Rivers, which took Thoreau so long to finish, became an unspoken elegy to his brother. John is barely mentioned, never directly seen or described, but his presence is felt throughout —in the fragility of the book's emotional tenor, its focus on fleeting natural details (such as the momentary play of light or the evanescent mistiness of the air), or its overt interest in the historical tales associated with the scenes through which the Musketaquid passes (among others, the bloody legend of Hannah Dustan). John Thoreau is the presence in the landscape that is now absent, the person whose death seems expressed in the changes constantly cycling through nature and human experience. Even the moment of the brief trip, begun in the heat of August but concluded in the fall, marks the young man's bitter loss.

Ralph Waldo Emerson, Thoreau's mentor and friend, once asked, "Who looks upon a river in a meditative hour, and is not reminded of the flux of all things?" The insight is an ancient one, traceable to the Greek philosopher Heraclitus. And other of Thoreau's contemporaries pondered water—most notably Herman Melville, whose most famous narrator speaks of the eternal wedding of "water and meditation" (among its varied themes, the ocean tale told by the lucky survivor Ishmael is about many kinds of loss). Yet Thoreau it was who, borne downstream in his own life by the flood of feeling released by the loss of John and his own unworthiness as a survivor, made the union truly permanent. One finds his influence in Goodbye to a River, the lamentation that Texas writer John Graves eloquently penned on the eve of the damming (and damning) of the Brazos. And also, more profoundly even, one finds it in the book that supplies Robert Hayashi with his lyrical inspiration—Norman Maclean's long prose poem, "A River Runs through It." The latter is the most pertinent model for Hayashi, but also the most pertinent proof of Thoreau's real accomplishment in what remains, otherwise, the drifting, surficial narrative of A Week on the Concord and Merrimack Rivers. In his plumbing of emotional depths, Thoreau set an agenda for others long after himself. Maclean thus wrote, decades after the tragic loss of his own brother Paul, a moving testament to Paul's grace as a fly fisherman. Anyone who has read and enjoyed Maclean's narrative knows that this is not simply a sports story. It concerns itself with the mysteries of difference and kinship, with what made Paul so ideal an embodiment of the Maclean family's passion for fishing, and at the same time so self-destructively foreign to his kin.

In the case of *Haunted by Waters*, which concerns Hayashi's westward search for understanding, the loss audible in those words beneath the river is incalculably large. Thoreau was fond of asserting that the deepest moral lessons of experience, if one attended to them, were present in one's first encounter with any big truth—that being open to the full reality of a tough situation would make re-exposure unnecessary. As he put the idea in describing a shipwreck that took the lives of more than a hundred Irish emigrants in *Cape Cod*, "A man can attend but one funeral in the course of his life, can behold but one corpse." Even if we know what he means here—that for him cradling John in 1842 was all *he* needed to know about death—we should demur on the larger point. For Hayashi, the lessons of Minidoka and the other Japanese American "internment camps"— *camps!*—or of the Asian American experience of the West in general, can never be written off as moral overload. It is indeed the precise telling of the record of so many individual griefs and injuries that is required. His own insistence on coming to terms with the particular places of his family's experience, and the broader landscape of ethnic difference and mistreatment in the West, is salutary and sanative. We need these stories, these words.

Haunted by Waters is essential truth but also fine prose. At one point, Hayashi jokes about the sometime tourist fisherman who has a thousand-dollar rod but a ten-cent cast. I can only imagine how much went into the purchase of Hayashi's own equipment as a writer, but it is clear on page after page that his cast is priceless. Borrowing a title from so perfect a book as Maclean's takes courage; it also requires the ability to deliver on the underlying presumption, and that ability Robert Hayashi indisputably has. Despite—and because of—its vital concern with race and place in the American West, this is a delicious, satisfying, haunting book.

ACKNOWLEDGMENTS

This project was born in serendipity and continued to offer me unexpected rewards as I worked on it over the last several years. It led me down many dusty gravel roads in Idaho, to archives across the country, and into relationships that were its greatest rewards.

I wish to thank my mentors: Judith Davidov, whose unwavering support allowed me always to write with my ear; Joe Skerrett for his pithy insights and the many wonderful meals we have shared; David Glassberg for convincing a poet that he could write history; and Jules Chametzky for being the all-around mensch that he is.

I also owe the many Idahoans who welcomed me and aided in my research: the Idaho Japanese American Citizens League (JACL) chapters, Masa and Midori Tsukamoto, Mary Fujii Henshall and her family, and Alan Virta and Mary Carpenter-Hepworth at Boise State University's Special Collections Department. Thanks also to Robert Sims, Priscilla Wegars, and the staff at the Idaho State Historical Society, who streamlined my searching and answered all of my obvious questions. I also wish to thank the staff of the National Archives, the Bancroft Library, Twin Falls Public Library, and the College of Southern Idaho Library. For granting permission to reprint works, I thank Philip White, Rutgers University Press, Brooding Heron Press, Lonny Kaneko, Phyllis Okada Kacher, Kay Yokoyama, Jane Shaw Karlson, Steve Earle, and the Nez Perce Tribe. Also, a big mahalo to the staff of the National Park Service's Pacific West Region, especially Neil King, Anna Hosticka Tamura, and Frank Hays. For their help in tracking down permissions, my thanks to Wing Tek Lum, Joanna Lau, Kats Fujita, Mary Masugi, and Vicki Blackwell. Finally, for sharing fishing advice and stories, thanks to Clayne Baker, the folks at the Idaho Angler, the Riverkeeper, Silver Creek Outfitters, and the Bent Rod.

Holly Carver has proven herself a writer's best friend, embracing my work's unique character and helping guide me through a daunting process. I also want to thank Wayne Franklin and the outside reviewer for their generous comments and everyone at Iowa who had a hand in this project.

Lastly, I wish to thank my family for their love and support, especially my mother for all that she has provided me, her dilling. Thanks always to Angelo Robinson, Albert Turner, and Leanne White, who helped me get through those long graduate school years, and to Fred Siewers for memories made on Western waters. Finally, I owe the most to my wife, Wendy Bergoffen, who has read numerous revisions, offered insightful suggestions, tolerated my quirky mania, and in general, been the best partner in life that one could imagine.

"Answer the Call" by Mas Okada, from Hunt Hi-Lites, October 1, 1943, used by permission of Phillis Okada Kacher.

"Family Album" by Lonny Kaneko, from Coming Home from Camp (Waldron, Washington: Brooding Heron Press, 1984), used by permission of the publisher.

"In the Outhouse" by Mitsuye Yamada, from Camp Notes and Other Poems (Piscataway, NJ: Rutgers University Press, 1998), used by permission of the publisher.

Lines from "Seed" by Philip White, from Harvest: Contemporary Mormon Poems edited by Eugene England and Dennis Clark (Salt Lake City: Signature Books, 1989), used by permission of Philip White.

Quotations from personal interviews with Masa and Midori Tsukamoto used by permission of Masa and Midori Tsukamato.

Selections from Japanese American Evacuation and Resettlement Records, BANC MSS 67/14, used by permission of the Bancroft Library, University of California, Berkeley.

Untitled poems by Henry H. and Fumiko Fujii used by permission of Ed Fujii.

Untitled tanka poem by Sojin Takei, from Poets behind Barbed Wire, edited by Jiro Nakano and Kay Nakano (Honolulu: Bamboo Ridge Press, 1984), used by permission of the publisher.

Haunted by Waters

INTRODUCTION

... we imagine love
by the memory of it

and begin not in beginnings
but, first, in the teachings granted us

by those ancestral mothers and fathers
that we cannot fail

we cannot fail
this earth,
this arduous earth.

PHILIP YELLOWHAWK MINTHORN,
"This Earth"

In 2001, the U.S. Board on Geographic Names changed the name of a small mountain just outside of Pocatello, Idaho, from Chink's Peak to Chinese Peak. For three years, local Idaho groups had lobbied for the change, led by the Japanese American Citizens League Pocatello-Blackfoot chapter, which received the support of a broad coalition that included the Organization of Chinese Americans, the Anti-Defamation League, the Indian American Center for Political Awareness, the Mexican American Legal Defense Fund, the National Association for the Advancement of Colored People, and the Wilderness Society. Other Idaho groups, including the Idaho Geographic Names Advisory Council, protested what they saw as an unwarranted erasure of Idaho history and another example of unchecked political correctness. That same year the Idaho State Senate voted to remove the word *squaw* from all Idaho place-names, a gesture meant to illustrate the body's sensitivity to its Native American constituents. The Idaho legislature was following the lead of such states as Montana and Oklahoma, which had already enacted similar legislation. This recent sanitizing of the Western landscape, however, only addresses the most obvious signs of the history I explore here: the connection between race and place in the symbolic space of American democracy—the storied mountains, sage desert flats, and wild rivers of the West.

Despite the increasing amount of scholarship focused on the environment of the American West and its cultural representations, studies exploring the role racial minorities have played in shaping and defining the Western landscape remain rare. This absence is part of a larger failure to investigate the experiences of racial minorities in relation to American environmental history, as noted, for instance, by Carolyn Merchant in a recent presidential address to the American Society for Environmental History. Merchant noted, "We especially need more research on the roles of African Americans in the southern and western U.S. environment and in early urbanization and more research on Asian and Hispanic perceptions of nature."[1] Similar charges from literary scholars about the lack of attention to minority aesthetic representations of place echo her remarks.[2] In discussions of the environmental or cultural history of Western places, racial and ethnic minorities remain background figures, and their experiences remain isolated; if they are discussed, it is usually in contrast to white Americans.

What definitions of place have these people held, and how have these individuals imagined, encountered, and shaped the Western American landscape and its meaning? *Haunted by Waters: A Journey through Race and Place in the American West* provides an opportunity to view the American West from a different perspective by following these lines of inquiry. It presents the experiences and writings of some of these individuals and explores environmental history in relation to the formation of racial identity. In recent years, the groundbreaking work on racial formation, notably by Michael Omi and Howard Winant, illuminates the multifaceted manner in which American social institutions construct racial identity. The authors argue that social institutions shape and organize identities along racialized categories via "racial projects" and that the discovery and settlement of the New World by Europeans was an unparalleled consolidation of racial identities that relied increasingly on scientific rationale.[3] I argue here that ideas about environment are part of the ideological and material framework of this process and, moreover, that ideas about race and place have been intertwined in a kind of Gordian knot in the development of the American West.[4]

Race has influenced not only how Americans envisioned and represented the West but also how they shaped it. Yet, it is a process characteristically represented as a "natural" one that obscures its founding in subjective biases, in imagined realms, which often have little in common with either the environmental or racial reality of the West. Environmental historians, such as Carolyn Merchant and William Cronon, have explored how the power to control definitions of place and dominant modes of their representation naturalizes the manipulation of environments and people.[5] I analyze how the unnatural development of one section of the West— Idaho—was similarly portrayed. With the spread of European and later American influence across the continent, a dominant way of imagining and manipulating the earth followed. Merchant has outlined how the conjoined strands of Western civilization's concepts of gender, science, and nature led to a dynamic and rapid change in one American locale—New England. It was made, in a sense, a new world for its inhabitants—human, vegetable, and mineral. This process had grave consequences for white and especially Indian women, in both the material and ideological realms. I focus on the spread of similar paradigms, Jeffersonian agrarianism and democracy across the West, and how they represented a similar revolution that ordered the human and natural world in a process of ideological, aesthetic, and material control. However, unlike other scholars working in environmental history, I am interested not only in the various ideological and material manifestations of this legacy but how they have operated in defining and policing racial identity over the last two centuries.

In America, specific ethnic identities of nonwhites, such as Japanese Americans, have been impacted by and often risked erasure due to the institutionalization of broad racial categories. Since racial identity formation is a political project that confers social order and privilege, these identities then have consequences for how individuals and groups relate to and interact with the environment and the cultural ideologies that surround it. For instance, Japanese Americans have had to negotiate the consequences of a general racial category, as "mongolians," "Orientals," or "Asians," and that has materially affected their experiences in America, how fully they could participate in Jefferson's imagined agrarian West and its democratic promise.[6] And while racial identity may be more ascribed than ethnic identity, ethnicity too is powerfully shaped from the outside. At times their specific classification as people of Japanese ethnicity has dominated the experience of Japanese Americans in the United States and their identity within society. The World War II labeling of all ethnic Japanese as potential disloyals and their subsequent segregation and removal from the larger Asian American populace is a dramatic example. Moreover, ethnic identities evolve, as groups both negotiate panethnic categories and work to self-define their identity in relation to the dominant society, especially in terms that are advantageous, as Japanese Americans have done in the post–World War II years. Because of this dialectic quality of ethnicity and race, I include Mormon history in my discussion, for Mormons can be seen as inhabiting a unique group identity, one sometimes defined by the larger society as not fully "white."[7] I hope to expand the historical understanding of unique minority identities by viewing them as separate neither from racial categories nor from the ethnic identity narratives that are salient parts of how ethnic groups apprehend the American environment.

My frequent use of legal materials is a means to connect materially these usually separate inquiries of identity and environment and is informed by recent contributions to critical race studies. As Ian F. Haney Lopez notes, "Racial categories are in one sense a series of abstractions, but their constant legal usage makes these abstractions concrete and material."[8] A longitudinal look at how laws manifested a coupling of ideas about environment, race, and democracy deconstructs the traditional mythos of the pioneering West, as American Indians, Asians, and Mormons experienced, represented, and shaped the American West in various and interconnected ways. In some instances, they echoed a dominant vision, while at other times they provided alternative plans for Western development, including resource use and race relations.

Since ideologies of race were central to the development of American places, they are vectors by which we can retrace the history of these locales. Unraveling the intertwining legacy of race and place in the development of America can illuminate the physical and racial geography of today. Race is central to a full understanding of American places—the names we know them by, the stories told about them, and who is considered the native and who the foreigner in them. It is relevant not only in hindsight as we examine the current environmental legacy of discriminatory social policies of the past. Environmental justice is a valuable attempt to address the historical inattention to minorities in relation to our understanding of the environment but is focused mainly on current environmental hazards and the prevention of future ones affecting communities of color. This orientation can reinforce an ahistorical perspective by looking at race and environment within a limited time frame and in light of only a select set of concerns. As Julie Sze notes, "The current singular emphasis on public policy and on remediation of environmental harms necessarily narrows environmental justice as an analytic frame because it truncates theory and action/practice."[9] The same will to claim, control, and rename America's geographic space defines the modalities of shaping its social space. But, as processes traditionally seen as natural and separate, their intertwined roots remain obscured. Other histories, too, remain unrecognized, not signified by a place-name, such as Jap Creek—another spot still on the Idaho map.

I have tried in this book to reconnect such histories of the West to the West, its places, to create a fuller picture of its past or, at least, to offer one deep and suggestive slice across its topography. Although I focus on but one Western locale, the territory constituting the present-day state of Idaho, as a grounding site for my exploration, I also infer similar stories within the larger geographic and social space of the American West. By focusing on a limited space and critically analyzing the cultural representations and governmental policies informing its development as a case study, I detail how the vision of an agrarian and all-white West became an assumed natural blueprint for its development. However, I do not discount the obviously specific conditions, natural and human, that have made New Mexico, Texas, or Alaska unique. In fact, I argue that the land teaches that conditions are local, that identities are forms of adaptation, and thus, that universal mythologies are always suspect.

The contemporary understanding of race as a social construct, as an inhabited perspective, illuminates the relevance of racial identity to any form of self-representation, including intellectual inquiry. As suggested in *A Portrait of the Artist as a Young Man* when James Joyce's artist opines, "This race and this country and this life have produced me . . . and I shall express myself as I am," my exegesis in this book is both an intellectual and a personal history of race and place markedly influenced by my identity as a Japanese American.[10] My personal history within a racialized identity is the starting point and end product of the history I investigate. As I recount my travels across the contemporary Idaho landscape as Eastern traveler, explorer, researcher, angler, and third-generation Japanese American, what I find there is the by-product of the refracted angles of my vision from the various subject positions that define me. My reconnecting of these positionalities to their historical roots is an attempt to disrupt their fixity and illuminate the processes by which the West and Japanese Americans were imagined and constructed, including by themselves. The form of the book, a hybrid of scholarly writing and personal narrative, is, thus, part of the argument itself. As Diane P. Freedman and Olivia Frey note of the works included in their collection, *Autobiographical Writing across the Disciplines*, "Here the personal background is not an incidental fact of the research, but that which, quite complexly, shapes the process of searching and discovering."[11] I hope, as well, to counter the absence of a diversity of voices that chronicle the American West and respond to other scholars, such as Patricia Nelson Limerick and Peter Balakian, who have lobbied for the use of language and narrative forms that will make historical inquiry more relevant to a wider audience.[12]

My argument develops then not explicitly but implicitly. The body of my text often lacks the argumentative rhetoric that dominates academic discourse: explicit signposting and objective exposition. The book is a narrative of the discovery that I claim in this introduction and chronicles the progression of my views of Idaho, as I rediscover its history by considering the role of race in the development of its natural and human realms, the line between them. I chart my entry and movement, physically and intellectually, into these Western spaces, their material, aesthetic, and intellectual realms—via river, poem, legal statute, and map.

In chapter 1, I trace the propagation of these mutually constitutive ideas about race and place by analyzing Jefferson's writings and the diaries of members of the Lewis and Clark Expedition—the first whites to explore Idaho. I conceive of Jeffersonian democracy as a grid: a set of parallel cross-hatched lines that defined not only his literal vision of its expansion across geographic space but also its spread across social space. While this design allegedly promises the individual uniform rights to mobility and opportunity, the lines that defined this space in America historically have consisted of laws and ideologies that inherently restrict the lives of nonwhites and other beings defined as foreign or "weeds." I outline how a shared vision of an agrarian all-white West became the basis for an array of government policies, including the nation's cartographic system and local marriage laws, that conflicted with the region's racial and environmental reality. While the Corps of Discovery's journey pointed to this contradiction, eventually a system of ideological and material control developed over the region's Indian and later Chinese populations that overrode contesting ideas about race and place. It established a process in which Western places were defined and controlled from the outside, and I discuss this history in the context of the region's currently notorious antifederalism.

In the second chapter, I focus on the influence of these connected ideologies of race and nature on public policy and popular culture during Idaho's early statehood. Both local and federal government policies illustrated a solidification of this control over the region's human and nonhuman residents, and I pay particular attention to how water resources connect the histories of these Westerners and Americans in general. I discuss the manifestation of these ideas in relation to the state's official seal and also to the poetry and fiction of well-known nineteenth-century American writers, particularly Walt Whitman and Mary Hallock Foote, and also the more obscure work of Idaho pioneer poets. During Idaho's early statehood Japanese migrated into Idaho in increasing numbers, and I use oral histories, memoirs, letters, and poetry to detail how Nikkei, [13] like the state's nonhuman residents, adapted to the now-established American racial and environmental realms that defined the state, especially the development of its water resources. Some Nikkei were prototypical yeoman farmers. They made important contributions to Idaho's agricultural development, providing a crucial labor force for its nascent sugar beet industry and for the development of its railroad infrastructure. However, their racial identity limited their access to the West's promise of economic and social mobility, and they were typically represented by other Idahoans, like Chinese and wolves before them, as pests who threatened the state's social and environmental welfare. This was never more apparent than during World War II.

In chapter 3, I discuss the World War II incarceration of Japanese Americans and specifically the Minidoka Relocation Center in southern Idaho, an institution described by the federal government as a "pioneer community." The policies of the federal government agency that ran the relocation centers, the War Relocation Authority, continued to reinforce the vision of an agrarian democratic West, despite the ironic contradiction Relocation represented and the obvious racialist ideology it enforced. At times, internees directly protested the federal government's pioneering mandate and offered alternate visions for their wartime home that even included the allegedly more contemporary cultural concepts of desert preservation and outdoor recreation. War Relocation Authority documents and internee literature illustrate how the government promoted agricultural production among relocated Japanese Americans and viewed its management of this ethnic group in light of both this iconographic image of the West and its prior experience managing American Indians. The WRA's records indicate that the Japanese American "problem" was commonly viewed in relation to the federal government's ongoing relationship with the country's indigenous minority. Moreover, the treatment of American Indians immediately following World War II, defined by the policies of termination and relocation, was similarly influenced by the Japanese American Relocation. In this instance, then, Japanese Americans, to borrow Gary Okihiro's classic formulation, can be seen as neither "black nor white" but red.[14] My omission of African Americans in this exploration of racial formation is due not only to the historically small number of African Americans in Idaho but also to my attempt to offer this alternative vector for understanding racial formation in relation to environmental history. My focus in this instance is most specifically on ethnic Japanese, but I hope this work invites similar projects that will recover the conjoined racial and environmental history of other locales and groups so we have a more multivalenced and multitiered view of American places.

In the final chapter, I discuss the region's Japanese American history in relation to Shoshone and Mormon history and the fixed iconography of "pioneers," "savages," "saints," and "model minority" that simplifies these individuals' roles in shaping the West. For Japanese Americans, their entire history risks being eclipsed by the internment and the dominant narrative of patriotism and citizenship some have leveraged in the postwar years as a means to regain a hold in the social fabric designed to exclude them. Meanwhile, other narratives such as the wartime experiences of Idaho's nonrelocated Nikkei community and the devastating dissolution of Japanese American communities as a result of federal wartime policy remain mostly unacknowledged. In this chapter, I discuss these issues and the acrimonious debate among Japanese Americans over a proper commemoration at Minidoka as an example of the struggle to shape a serviceable history and identity in a landscape dominated by master narratives of identity and place. In such contestations, the importance of regional influences, the inherent local conditions that explain the complex reality of Western places and peoples, becomes clear. Yet, we remain under the still powerful specter of a homogenizing mythos and categories of identity that attempt to contain and explain. We all must endure and appreciate our connections to the lands we call home. No matter what they are named.

Chapter 1

THE INNOCENCE OF OUR INTENTIONS

Thomas Jefferson, the Corps of Discovery, and the Natural Progression of Idaho

In all your intercourse with the natives treat them in the most friendly & conciliatory manner which their own conduct will admit; allay all jealousies as to the object of your journey, satisfy them as of its innocence.

THOMAS JEFFERSON, Instructions to Meriwether Lewis, June 20, 1803

I can conceive a community, today and here, in which, on a sufficient scale, the perfect personalities, without noise meet; say in some pleasant western settlement or town, where a couple hundred best men and women, of ordinary worldly status, have by luck been drawn together, with nothing extra of genius or wealth, but virtuous, chaste, industrious, cheerful, resolute, friendly and devout. I can conceive such a community organized in running order, powers judiciously delegated—farming, building, trade, courts, mails, schools, elections, all attended to; and then the rest of life, the main thing, freely branching and blossoming in each individual, and bearing golden fruit.

WALT WHITMAN, "Democratic Vistas"

The imposed view, however innocent, always obscures.

BARRY LOPEZ, *Arctic Dreams*

We had only an e-mail message—a protestation in response to my friend's query about information on flyfishing in Montana. It came from some professor at Idaho State: "Take out a map. Look at the Continental Divide west of Montana. Notice how ALL the rivers flow west into Idaho! I don't understand it. Why would you go to Montana with everyone else?" Indeed. I should have known from the moment I sat down in my seat in that climate-controlled 727 at Logan and noticed the three guys in front of me—cowboy hats, special flyfishing glasses, cases of expensive Sage rods, and thick Boston accents—my escape to wide open Big Sky Montana might lack some elbow room. With the deep snowpack just starting to melt that July and most of the big rivers unfishable, or not fishing well, it seemed as if every visiting fisherman in the state had herded onto Rock Creek. Fred and I turned to one another, "Hell with this. We're going to Idaho!"

We bought a map in a gas station outside Missoula. He was right. Running up the western side of Montana like a granite wall, the Bitterroots provide a formidable natural barrier between Montana and Idaho, in fact, the longest stretch of the Rocky Mountains found in any state. This geologic feature, the Idaho batholith, is a near-solid mass of granite that oozed out of the earth's crust some hundred million years ago when Idaho was violently shaped by the collision of continents. Out of these mountains flow the rivers he had mentioned—the Lochsa, the Clearwater, and the St. Joe. They pulled us, filled us with expectations, with the delectable anticipation of the traveler. The spaces of the imagination filled with images, ideas of the Pure West. We stopped in Missoula for more flies and for a rain jacket to replace the one I had left at work back in Boston. Inside Bob Ward's, the salesman offered some dry flies for Idaho and carped about the crowding of his home waters. "Hell, I hardly fish now until the fall."

Ranches, oddly placed suburbanlike homes, and gas stations eventually gave way to stands of white pine as we climbed into the Bitterroots through one of only three paved roads that bridge Montana and Idaho along a two-hundred-mile stretch. It was just over these mountains that Meriwether Lewis and the Corps of Discovery would measure up their own expectations of these places during a far less comfortable experience: where Lewis would realize that the Pacific was not just over these mountains, that the trail the Nez Perce followed each summer to hunt buffalo out on the plains of Montana would not, as other Indians had assured them, be an uncomplicated five-day journey. It was, instead, a harrowing and nearly disastrous push through snow and hunger. The names they gave to the places here recall that September trek in the Bitterroots—Colt Kill Creek, Lonesome Cove, and Hungery Creek.

Over Emmylou Harris crooning, "roll . . . roll a long way on," Fred read aloud passages from the journals of these previous travelers, our predecessors, the Corps of Discovery: "The road through this hilley Countrey is verry bad passing over hils & thro' Steep hollows, over falling timber &c. &c. continued on & passed Some most intolerable road on the Sides of the Steep Stoney mountains, which might be avoided by keeping up the Creek which is thickly covered with under groth & falling timber."[1] I looked out over the guardrail, a hundred, maybe two hundred feet down into pines, rock, and brush. Unlike Lewis and Clark, the first white men to ever see this part of what is now the state of Idaho, we had detailed maps and a government-built highway to take us down the Lochsa by a grove of trees commemorating Bernard DeVoto, the influential editor of their journals. We imagined only fish, the rise of a wild cutthroat to a fly floating in gin-clear water. We drove with the windows open, and the scent of pine filled the car as we imagined the feel of the Lochsa's cool water.

At the time of their mission, at the opening of the nineteenth century, Idaho was part of an unexplored, unmapped territory next door to the United States, a vast expanse of wilderness that nevertheless contained meaning for Americans who had never seen it. The passage of the Corps of Discovery into this area, now part of the present-day state of Idaho, marks the beginning of a process by which Idaho's meaning and the development of its environment became shaped by Americans and their institutions, including their definition of democracy. Today, the physical environment of Idaho signifies the influence of these ideals and can be "read" in light of these influences. These dominant ideologies that define Lewis and Clark's journey included myths of the region's inhabitants and similarly dubious ideas about race that would shape Idaho's landscape.[2]

Before reaching Traveller's Rest, their encampment below the trail to Lolo Pass into Idaho, the Corps, while heading north along the Bitterroots in what is now western Montana near the Bitterroot River, encountered a group of Indians. Just as to this day many of the places previously named by Indians now carry the names Lewis and Clark chose to define them— the Jefferson River, the Madison River, the Marias River—these Indians would forever be known by the inappropriate label of Flatheads. They were, in fact, Ootlashoots, a tribe that did not practice the flattening of their infants' foreheads. Moreover, the racial mythologies that the Corps carried from back East along with their instruments, guns, and trade goods led them to an astounding discovery about the "Flatheads." Corps member Private Joseph Whitehorse recalled in his diary that "these savages has the strangest language of any we have ever Seen. they appear to us to have an Empediment in their Speech or a brogue or bur on their tongue ... we take these Savages to be the Welsh Indians if their be any Such from the Language."[3] The possible discovery of the lost Welsh tribe, a pervasive myth that at the time dated back hundreds of years and had been used to explain the presence of such wonders as the earthen mounds in the Ohio river valley and the Aztec ruins, was part of Jefferson's charge. He had emphasized in his instructions to Meriwether Lewis the importance of collecting an array of information on all Indians encountered during the trek. In fact, Jefferson hoped that this expedition, his fourth attempt to probe beyond the republic's western borders, would uncover these lost Welsh.

But he was most concerned with collecting information about Indians for economic and political reasons. In his instructions to Lewis, Jefferson listed a series of specific lines of inquiry, "the extent & limits of their possessions; their relations with other tribes or nations; their language, traditions, monuments; . . . what knolege you can of the state of morality, religion & information among them, as it may better enable those who may endeavor to civilize & instruct them." Charged with discovering a navigable water route to the Pacific, the Northwest Passage, "whether the Columbia, Oregan, Colorado or any other river may offer the most direct & practicable water communication across this continent,"[4] Lewis and his men trekked across the continent not only as curious geographers but as conquering ethnologists as well.

Indians were, for Jefferson, another "native" species and, thus, objects of scientific inquiry fit for study, and discoveries about the natural characteristics of Indians were vital in defining a place for them in the growing republic. In *Notes on the State of Virginia*, written in the early 1780s as a response to a series of questions submitted by a French diplomat, Jefferson included information about the Indians of America in two sections. The first discussion is in the section entitled, "Query VI, Productions, Mineral, Vegetable and Animal." Jefferson had devoted the first five sections of the text to outlining the colony's land features and waterways, and in this following section he addressed the misconceptions about the region's flora and fauna, especially as described by Count Buffon, a prominent French naturalist. Jefferson tried to invalidate Buffon's observations about America's indigenous and nonindigenous animals—the putative corruptive influence of its soil upon them. He listed Buffon's contentions: "1. That the animals common both to the old and new world, are smaller in the latter. 2. That those peculiar to the new are on a smaller scale. 3. That those which have been domesticated in both, have degenerated in America: and 4. That on the whole it exhibits fewer species."[5]

After listing information on animals to counter Buffon's theories of American inferiority, including tables of animal weights and populations in the New and Old Worlds, Jefferson directed his inquiry to "the man of America" and provided a list of Buffon's observations about America's aborigines. Indians, or "savages" as Buffon defined them, were "feeble" with no "ardor for his female" and with "no activity of mind." They were naturally inferior. Jefferson listed attributes of Indians based on "what [he had] seen of man, white, red, and black, and has been written by authors, enlightened themselves, and writing amidst an enlightened people." He noted of the American native that "his vivacity and activity of mind is equal to ours in the same situations" and, moreover, that the less favorable characteristics found in Indians were erased with the influence of civilization.[6] What he proposed, of course, had to be consistent with his claim that the American environment was uniquely fit for all beings and the democratic society that would develop there. Jefferson believed not only that Indians possessed natural traits that made them suitable for inclusion in the republic but also that their bloodline could merge with whites. He told them, "Your blood will run in our veins, and will spread with us over this great island."[7] Despite Jefferson's claims, however, during his presidency federal policies were aimed more at exterminating Indians and removing them from the advance of American democracy than at including them in its evolution. Numerous treaties robbed Indians of their homelands and forced them to relocate, a process that would define the experience of most Western Indian nations over time.

Twenty years after Jefferson wrote his text outlining a course for democracy's development in America, the Corps of Discovery traveled across the continent under his presidential orders. Their discoveries both reaffirmed and deconstructed Jefferson's imagined West, which like their compasses, sextants, and timepieces, they used to guide them in their journey of discovery. A game plan for the West, its natural and human development was already on the board.

The Space of Democracy

Thomas Jefferson can be understood not only as the ideological architect of American democracy and its spread westward but as its geographic architect as well. He chaired in 1784 the government committee that planned the development of the Western Territory and appointed the first Geographer of the United States. His imagined charting of that republic was consistent with his faith in a uniform expansion of the West by individual landholding farmers, dividing the land into squares by lines oriented north-south and east-west that crossed at right angles. The uniform individual squares possessed by each landholder were a fitting manifestation of democracy's promise of equality. As Andro Linklater notes in *Measuring America*: "The balance in the square was also intrinsic to Jefferson's vision of democracy."[8] It was this basic shape, in fact, that became the basis for land surveying as the young republic began the process of mapping the nation and distributing its territory. As President, Jefferson instructed Lewis, his private secretary and longtime friend, to take precise compass readings and to chart out the edge of the frontier along the lines of longitude and latitude, the tidy ordering of space that Jefferson used to define both the geographic and social expansion of the republic. He ordered, "Beginning at the mouth of the Missouri, you will take observations of latitude & longitude at all remarkable points on the river . . . The courses of the river between these points of observation may be supplied by the compass the log-line & by time, corrected by the observations themselves. The variations of the compass too, in different places should be noticed."[9] Such a division of the land was by no means a "natural" solution and prior colonial powers in America had used alternative means of land surveying. Jefferson's system assumed a uniform and abstract space that conflicted with the variations of topography, resources, and fertility that defined places so that "without personal knowledge of the country, picking the right square in the grid became a lottery. Some squares might have no water supply, while others could consist of nothing but swamp."[10]

Thomas Jefferson had not only equipped Lewis and Clark with the most up-to-date cartographic instruments available, but he also arranged for Lewis to receive instruction in how to operate this equipment, part of his intensive pretrip tutoring in Philadelphia, home of the American Philosophical Society. Its members constituted the leading scientific minds in the young nation. As one historian notes, "The venture was not only to accomplish all that Jefferson had hoped, but also to prove to be the first and one of the most important exercises in the application of scientific practices and instrumentation attempted by the young republic."[11] However, these "practices and instrumentation" proved a hindrance when interpreting geographic information from Indians, who commonly relayed knowledge of the land verbally and upon whom the Corps of Discovery was vitally dependent on its journey. Throughout their trek, Lewis and Clark relied on native knowledge of the land to guide them, but American Indian cartography relied not on a putative universal ordering of space but on the experience of unique places. Even when they did utilize pictorial representations of the land, Indian map makers depended on systems unfamiliar to men trained in Western cartography, with its uniform spaces gridded-out in lines of latitude and longitude.[12] Indians did not orient their maps in relation to a north-south axis but more commonly to the movement of the sun; distances were often expressed in units of travel not in a universal unit of measures, such as a mile, league, or kilometer. In "Orientations from Their Side: Dimensions of Native American Cartographic Discourse," Peter Nabokov notes, "For many American Indian peoples, the land was often its own best map and demanded knowing first on its own terms, almost as if the topography had itself possessed some sort of volitional authority."[13] Contrasting ways of defining places would continue to plague Indian and white encounters during this exploration and throughout the history of the American West.

Subsequent federal legislation attempted to enforce this uniform ordering of space and to codify this method of dividing up the West, which in the late eighteenth century included what we now define as the Midwest. The actual surveying of the land was a laborious endeavor accomplished by the use of fixed lengths of chain that surveyors had to plant all across the expanding republic.[14] In his recounting of such land surveying near his childhood home along the Canada–United States border, in this instance by the Canadian government, author Wallace Stegner details the impracticality of such a system when confronted with the mud, swamps, escarpments, and even bugs that defined his home: the reality of Western places.[15] Originally, a part of Oregon Territory, which included present-day Oregon, Washington, and parts of Montana, Idaho later became part of Washington Territory, and later, in 1863, its own territory: a massive box-shaped region that included present-day Idaho and most of Montana. This earlier shape, as well as that of present-day Western states such as Colorado, North Dakota, South Dakota, and Washington, illustrates Jefferson's planned design for westward expansion. The later morphing of Idaho's borders represents this tension between the assumed orderly nature of Western cartography and the disorderly reality of Western places such as Idaho, where "straight lines are not a common feature."[16] In 1887, Congress proposed slicing off the northern mountainous region of Idaho and making it part of Washington Territory. Today, the inclusion of this region as part of Idaho still defies logic, and only one roadway connects Idaho's mountainous northern region to the populous and mostly arid southern part of the state. In fact, throughout its development, this mostly mountainous region has more often been defined in relation to parts of Washington, as part of the Inland Empire, as the region is known.[17] An even more basic flaw of the grid, one not adjusted for until 1803, was the failure to account for the curvature of the earth; seemingly equal plots of land were not, in fact, equal—especially taking into consideration the definitions that demarcated its social space.

The Lewis and Clark journey was an extension of this mapping and, thus, the beginning of the imposition of a fixed system of controls over the rapidly expanding boundaries of the republic.[18] In fact, the trek expanded the reach of these modes of knowledge, because Lewis and Clark were well outside the territorial boundaries of the United States when they crossed the Continental Divide. Soon after their journey, however, the young republic would rush in to fill these places. Sometimes the connection between them was both immediate and explicit. Only a few years after they returned to the East with the Corps of Discovery, John Colter and Peter Weiser returned to the region as cartographers and helped create some of the region's first maps. Today, a tributary of the Snake River in southeastern Idaho is known as the Weiser River.

The close association between Lewis and Clark and Jefferson contextualizes the role of the Corps in the development of the American West, including Idaho. The Corps's journey was an extension of Jefferson's imagination: his desire as President to map, define, and expand the boundaries of the United States; to extend the gaze of scientific inquiry into the West's geology, vegetation, human and animal life; and also to control its economic base and racial composition. As historian Mark Spence has noted, "As Jefferson's 'eyes,' Lewis and Clark saw the West in terms of the president's ideas on Indian relations, foreign policy, and the role of the federal government in shaping future national economic development."[19] The diaries of these men thus provide an historical grounding for how the process of development in the West was always bound to influences from outside its borders and how an imagined West led to the exploitation of the landscape and maltreatment of its human and animal inhabitants in a process couched in language that defined such acts as "natural."[20] Writers have defined this expedition, a federally funded sojourn by United States military personnel into contested regions outside its national borders in an attempt to establish trade relations and political control, as empire building, scientific discovery, and personal triumph.[21] Jefferson has long been considered the intellectual founder of the republic's democracy and, more recently, an important figure in its racial history, but only lately have scholars looked to his legacy to explain the environmental history of that democracy as it spread westward.[22]

Jefferson believed the American character and its qualities of independence and self-determination were a product of its unique landscape. As he noted in Notes on the State of Virginia, a combined natural history and political philosophy, America was meant for farming: "Those who labour in the earth are the chosen people of God, if ever he had a chosen people, whose breasts he has made his peculiar deposit for substantial and genuine virtue."[23] Jefferson's vision of America was geographically expansive, especially considering the potential payoff had Lewis and Clark discovered the Northwest Passage—a doorway into Asia. It was, however, only an extension of the Virginia he knew: fertile, temperate, easily explored and mapped out on paper—quite unlike the Bitterroot Mountains, "this horrible mountainous desert," as a soldier of the Corps of Discovery described after his trek through them.[24] Jefferson owned the nation's most extensive collection of texts about the West, some of which pointed to the impracticality of this agrarian vision, and Jefferson never traveled farther west than his native Virginia. Yet he discounted the bleaker assessments of the West's natural potential and imagined a place not much different from his beloved views from Monticello.[25] Lewis and Clark may have imagined a West fairly similar to their native Albemarle County, but experience would certainly prove to these men that the West was something else.

Jefferson believed that the political health of the young nation depended upon the existence of yeoman farmers, all small landowners, and on extension of their conquest across the barriers of space and time, pointing out that "Our governments will remain virtuous for many centuries as long as they are chiefly agricultural; and this will be as long as there shall be vacant lands in any part of America."[26] He had unsuccessfully proposed legislation in Virginia that would have established a generous land grant system to individuals, but as President an even greater opportunity to install his vision arose. Before Lewis and the Corps of Discovery left for St. Louis, Jefferson negotiated the Louisiana Purchase, an agreement that doubled the size of the young nation and would help provide the open spaces that insured democracy—a democracy envisioned as land hungry.

Despite the seemingly uniform spaces of opportunity provided for individuals within the boundaries of Jefferson's democracy, its potential was barred to many. Unlike Walt Whitman, who would later envision in his poetry a melding of peoples to create a new race, a race of Americans, in Jefferson's imagined America it was not enough for an individual to possess a desirable character, to be "virtuous, chaste, industrious, cheerful, resolute, friendly, and devout" as Whitman had imagined the new Americans in his 1863 essay "Democratic Vistas."[27] Jefferson feared American democracy would corrode with the inclusion of too heterogeneous a mix of individuals, and an essential trait in defining fitness for inclusion was race. Three years after the completion of his manuscript outlining the course of American democracy, Congress passed its first piece of legislation regarding naturalization.[28] The Naturalization Act of 1790 decreed that "any alien, being a free white person who shall have resided within the limits and under the jurisdiction of the United States for a term of two years, may be admitted to become a citizen thereof."[29]

In *Notes on the State of Virginia*, Jefferson laid out his vision for the future, as one in which African Americans enjoy emancipation, but only outside of America's borders: "they should be colonized to such place as circumstances of the time should render most proper, sending them out with arms, implements of household and of the handicraft arts, seeds, pairs of the useful domestic animals, &c. to declare them a free and independent people." Jefferson's plan for exporting African Americans was to insure the homogeneity necessary to prevent a democratic society from dissolving into factions. Jefferson also felt that African Americans would require protection from whites. In addition, he argued that their differences from whites—"the first difference which strikes us is that of colour"—made them a natural threat; and, he noted, there are "real distinctions which nature has made."[30] Although Jefferson could not empirically prove their inferiority, he suspected this was the case, and he believed further scientific inquiry into the nature of the races would prove his suspicion an observable truth. The historical reliance of American institutions upon scientific rationalism to explain, in particular, the racial inequality that has defined American life also traces back to Jefferson, as does a compunction to expel outsiders, to label them unassimilable. Later proponents of white superiority have continued to turn to Jefferson to support their beliefs, and Jefferson has been a figure of approbation in recent times due to his writings on race, especially slavery.[31] This exclusionary view of who could constitute the body politic further defined the borders of Western expansion, in racial terms, and access to private land ownership and citizenship became a crucial means of further demarcating racial lines in the West, excluding those whom Jefferson likely never imagined filling its spaces.

If Jefferson, the seminal figure of American democracy, failed to recognize the inherent contradictions in his envisioned America—a democratic republic based on the universal natural rights of only some individuals and a national economy based on international trade that could support an infinite number of small independent farmers *in perpetuum*—then is it any wonder that Americans should be blind to the "unnatural" character of this process and the signs of it around us? The ideal of the yeoman farmer became the foundational rationale for influential federal agencies in the West and how writers of the West have explained and mythologized its history. From the Homestead Act of the 1880s to the huge Bureau of Land

Management reclamation projects of the twentieth century, the federal government has doled out its largess in the name of the independent small farmer discussed by J. Hector St. John de Crèvecoeur, Henry Nash Smith, and Frederick Jackson Turner.[32]

In a state like Idaho, both mountainous and arid, an agriculturally based society was at odds with geographic reality. Even today, the rugged northern and central parts of the state remain sparsely populated and difficult to get to from most of the rest of Idaho. The southern part includes the northern edge of the Great Basin Desert. As John Logan Allen so succinctly stated in his book about Lewis and Clark, "The geography of logic and theory and desire had been tried and tested and found wanting."[33] Indians told Lewis and Clark of the inhospitableness of these regions and their sparse resources. Despite the mythologization of their trek, members of the Corps of Discovery, and several other government agents after them, did point to the unfeasibility of carpeting the West with yeoman farmers. As a result of experiencing the reality of the West, knowing its places "via the body" as Indian maps assume, they came more fully to appreciate that it was a place not only unpredictable and challenging but often unfit for human habitation, let alone agriculture.[34] Cultural practices would have to adapt, as the Corps did when they read Indian maps, first tasted salmon, and burned out the hollows of trees to make canoes.

Unfortunately, like Jefferson, who was a man of the Enlightenment who believed knowledge was best grounded in rational scientific inquiry, but who also held deterministic environmentalist views based upon a Romantic sensibility that made logic and illogic companion pieces, much of the West's current physical and racial landscape is the result of the historical intertwining of similarly contradictory ideals. Yet, these places are often defined as the result of a reasoned process, even if they are more often the product of the imposition of a system ill-suited and in contestation with what the environment suggests. Both the persistence of Jeffersonian agrarianism and the reliance on Enlightenment reasoning help mask not only the unnatural character of Western places but the contesting minority views that have provided alternatives for their development. A brief outlining of Jefferson's views of nature traces the teleology of current tensions found in the West: the unique mythical status of agricultural life and the environmental costs of Western land use practices; the conquest of unwanted animals and peoples in the name of a natural democracy and their continued persistence—their "propensity to persist, to escape exclusion, and to defy both 'naturalization' and eradication;"[35] and the unique role of the federal government as both agent of control and also guarantor of a rebellious individualism.

The Long Reach of the Imagination

After a few days of camping and fishing along the Lochsa River, meaning "rough water" in Salish, so the Forest Service sign assured us, we headed upriver and took some trophy pose photographs at the sign recounting the river's history: "The wild 'Lochsa' did not yield to the traveler or reveal its beauty to America until the highway was completed in 1962." Before heading back over the pass, we stopped at the Forest Service's visitor center. A young woman greeted us. "Look around," she offered. They had field guides to identify all forms of local species, videos, a map of the local sprawl of federal forestland up on the wall, and pamphlets and books about the Nez Perce. Those seemed to be selling well.

We looped back down into Montana and headed up I-90 to fish Kelly Creek—only a name and a blue squiggly line on the map, but already filled with visions of wilderness and wild fish. Finally, we found the route back down into Idaho that the Forest Service map offered, an "unimproved" gravel road that had me maneuvering between washouts and huge potholes that put the rental car's oil pan in frequent peril. Only later did we realize that, like Lewis and Clark, we had missed the desired route over the Bitterroots, gotten off the path. Their Indian guide had mistakenly led them off the trail that the Nez Perce followed on their annual migration to the buffalo hunting grounds of western Montana. The men crossed down the steep hills and onto the banks of the Lochsa, where they supped on a colt and named a little stream in memory of that meal. It would be another week before they would make their way out of these rugged mountains. It took us hours to go a handful of miles. We finally pulled into a little makeshift campsite, made camp in a late rain, and ate peanut butter sandwiches washed down with cold beers.

For two days, Fred and I drifted gaudy flies to bright Westslope cutthroat, one of the few remaining healthy populations of this native species left in the continental United States, in water we had to keep reminding ourselves was deep, deeper than it looked because the water was so clear. On the last morning, one of those misty Northwest mornings that leaks into the limbs, we headed up the trail away from the road and spent the day alone, content to just stand under a rock ledge and watch the rain fall. I thought of wolves, wolves having just been reintroduced to this area by the federal government to make Idaho more natural, wild again. In his journal, Joseph Whitehorse noted that, for him, the howling of wolves one night during the push through the Bitteroots was a propitious sign: it surely meant that much needed game was near their campsite.

Lewis and Clark experienced nature, in what would be the future home of "reintroduced" wolves, as a place where nature and culture had already firmly intertwined. In his book about their journey, *Our Natural History*, Daniel Botkin writes that Lewis and Clark "record(ed) their encounters with wolves in typically neutral notes about sightings, abundances, and actions of the wolves."[36] Jefferson commanded Lewis to record his journey in the objectified language of the scientist: "Your observations are to be taken with great pains & accuracy to be entered distinctly, & intelligibly for others as well as yourself."[37] This would explain the direct and unordained comments, such as "great nombers of wolves were about this place & verry gentle. Capt. Clark killed one of them with his Sphere."[38] Yet, these entries do not exclude the possibility that these men were also affected or motivated by folk tales and other subjective constructions about the region's flora and fauna, such as the common view that wolves were ravenous and violent beasts worthy of destruction. Americans had already exterminated the once wide-ranging wolf from many areas by 1805, as Thomas Jefferson noted in his outline for America, *Notes on the State of Virginia*: "The laws have also descended to the preservation and improvement of the races of useful animals . . . to the extirpation of those which are noxious, such as wolves."[39]

A wolf is usually noted in the journals when it is shot. And its image as a ravenous predator is present in the hunters' language,[40] as on the morning of August 15, 1805, when Captain Lewis noted, "This morning I arrose very early and as hungary as a wolf."[41] The Corps's recordings, especially those of Lewis, are a complex history that include elements of objective record keeping, inherited cultural bias, selective editing, and confusion stemming from the intellectual challenge of defining an often bizarre and spectacular landscape. They are a record both of facts and of fictions but not the artifact of a rational or natural progression. How else can one explain their role as agents of an institution that would in the span of less than one hundred years encourage the destruction of these native wolf populations and later attempt to restore them by the introduction of nonnative wolves, often over the loud protestations of local residents whose individual voices it supposedly represented?

The meaning Americans ascribed to elements of this environment—such as wolves—was complicated by factors well beyond the frontier. By

1805, wolves had already become products, were already being represented in terms of their worth in a market economy, one that would drive the early exploration of this area and from far beyond these mountains. In his journal, John Ordway noted that "one man who went out hunting to day killd a woolf & kept it for the tradors who Give as much for a woolf Skin as a Beever Skin."[42] The early exploration of Idaho subsequent to Lewis and Clark was driven by exploitation of its natural resources to meet the needs of an international market, one dependent upon the unreliable whims of fashion—on American and European consumers' desire for fur garments. It was the fur trade that first lured whites into Idaho, and only the discovery of other resources would change the territory's status as a relatively ignored wilderness, one the federal government, much to the chagrin of some residents, seemed little concerned with until whites discovered its mineral wealth. In fact, it was not until 1868 that the federal government even defined Idaho, the actual landmass that would eventually constitute the current state, and its eventual borders set by Congress resulted in a significant loss of areas rich in natural resources. The influential role of the federal government in the future of Idaho and its residents explains the contemporary feelings of colonization that pervade regions of the state. In a state like Idaho, where nearly sixty-four percent of the land is under the control of some federal agency, it is not surprising that a strong antifederalist movement should find a home, and many of its most radical proponents discover a ready rationale for their beliefs in the writings of Thomas Jefferson.

On June 15, 1994, the federal government announced its intention to restore wolves to regions of central Idaho and also to Yellowstone National Park. The following year, over the vociferous complaints of many Idahoans, the federal government released a group of wolves in the Selway-Bitterroot Wilderness. Not only did interested parties such as hunters and ranchers rail against this program, but so did the Idaho government. After losing in the courts, the state legislature, in a mostly symbolic act, passed a law forbidding its own fish and game agency from participating in the restoration program. In an effort to appease the state, the federal government listed this wolf population as "experimental," a designation that allowed for the destruction of wolves that attacked livestock or became otherwise threatening to human interests. In 1999, the first such wolf was killed after Nez Perce and U.S. Fish and Wildlife personnel verified its activities. The tribe has been a major player in the recovery program: drafting the original environmental impact study and monitoring the wolves. Recently, the rules that allow private landowners to shoot wolves preying on livestock were loosened, allowing landowners to kill wolves they believe are threatening their livestock. The program has been a success, and federal biologists recently claimed that the growing wolf populations may soon allow for declassification of the wolf as "endangered." The federal government has also handed over management of the program to the state, which is considering a hunting program to thin out the wolf population in northern Idaho. In 2001, the state House, in a vote of 52–2, demanded that the wolf program cease and, moreover, that all wolves be removed by "whatever means necessary."[43]

Many of the opponents of the wolf management program have based their views on the historical image of wolves as four-legged serial killers, killers that, as one reader of the state's largest newspaper noted, "enjoy humans."[44] However, the antiwolf arguments are also economic. One of the more prominent antiwolf voices is that of the Central Idaho Wolf Coalition, which notes that the restoration program, upheld by "liberal judges who do not live in Idaho," will bring extreme hardship to "mom and pop businesses."[45] The main thrust of the group's argument is that the wolves will damage the area's big game hunting, which supports an array of local businesses, and the Idaho Fish and Game Department cites the wolves as the major factor for the decline in elk herds in the region. The area's former congressional representative, Helen Chenoweth, is an especially vocal critic. Known for her virulent and often outlandish comments about the federal government, Chenoweth has defined the program as "a tool to further halt logging, mining and recreation besides placing undue restrictions on private property."[46] For proponents of wolf reintroduction, the attraction of wolves to the state's increasing number of ecotourists provides a new economic opportunity, one that has boomed in Yellowstone National Park. Either position depends upon the consumption of Idaho's natural offerings.

It is well outside of the frontier West, especially back to Washington, back to Monticello, to England, or even back to Asia that Americans must return in order to understand fully the current issues that involve Western sites, our historical manipulation of these places and all they contain. It is not just knowledge of the West, how it has changed over time, that we need to resolve conflicts over protection of the wolf or of the salmon that fed the Nez Perce for centuries. Or how we are to confront the migration of foreigners into our lands. We must uncover the ways in which our views of nature have changed, remained the same, been forced upon us, or stifled contradictory views. We must remind ourselves how some were cast out of the Garden of the West because of the restrictions upon this imagined and expansive democratic space and how these histories all connect to underlying ideals that chart a human evolution steered by a federal republic—not a natural process.

Daniel Botkin's use of "our" in *Our Natural History* is symptomatic of a similar assumption that has warped historical perspective: his natural history does not include the views and experiences of the West's multitude of human inhabitants. For instance, what of the Nez Perce? As stewards of the wolf introduction in Idaho, the Nez Perce are attempting to restore neither wilderness nor economic opportunity. They seek to restore their way of life—a culture.[47] As Horace Axtell, a Nez Perce elder, notes, the wolf represents a continuity disrupted by the process Lewis and Clark began. He describes the release of the reintroduced wolves in Idaho: "I had the opportunity to welcome [them] back to the land here. I sang our religious songs to welcome them back. Then I looked into the cage and spoke to one of the wolves in Nez Perce; he kind of tilted his head, like he was listening. . . . It was like meeting an old friend."[48] Are their views of the West, their view of democracy's expansion into its spaces, not to be included in "our" natural history, in much the same way that the Forest Service defined the Lochsa's beauty as "unrevealed" until a highway offered it to vacationing automobile travelers in the 1960s?

The Spontaneous Productions of Nature

When members of the Corps of Discovery finally did make it out of the Bitterroot Mountains and out onto the Weippe Prairie, they encountered a band of Nez Perce Indians, who offered them food, shelter, and information about a watercourse to the Pacific. They promised to be friends of the nation these men represented and accepted their gift of an American flag. While the encounter was friendly and the Nez Perce kept their promises to Lewis and Clark for many years, for the native inhabitants of northern Idaho, the world that Lewis and Clark represented would change these lands and the Nez Perce role in it. The world was shrinking.

Only a few decades after Lewis and Clark left the Nez Perce lands in north central Idaho, a small contingent of Nez Perce traveled East to meet with their old friend, William Clark, who was now the Superintendent of Indian Affairs. The exact mission of the Indians was unclear, but word soon spread that they desired the white man's religion. In 1836 then, a group of missionaries traveled to the region and established a mission.

Among them were Henry and Eliza Spalding, who set up a homestead among the Nez Perce. Unlike their colleagues, Marcus and Narcissa Whitman, who settled among the Cayuse Indians, Henry Spalding believed in a rapid civilization of the Indians, and the Bible and the plow were the keystones of that process. The missionaries built a church, a school, and a mill, and Henry Spalding not only learned the challenging Nez Perce language but wrote the first Nez Perce dictionary and translated biblical texts. He also established a farm, on which he introduced to Idaho that most quintessential and recognizable of its food products—the potato.

Henry Spalding shared Jefferson's belief in the role of agriculture and private property in civilizing the American Indian. Jefferson had described Virginia's local Indian bands as people "who lived principally on the spontaneous productions of nature."[49] Obviously, such a way of life was inconsistent with Jefferson's agrarian republic, in which, as Charles Miller notes, "the equation is that labor or occupancy, plus land, equals property."[50] The widely held belief that Indian lands were vacant because Indians did not farm them justified not only changing their cultures but claiming their traditional territories. Despite his claims that Indians should be converted into farmers, Jefferson's actual policies toward Indians were geared more toward grabbing their land, rather than to making them part of what Henry Nash Smith called the "fee-simple empire."[51] The 1804 Land Act, which decreased the minimum size of land grants and, thus, made land more accessible to settlers, authorized the government's control "over all the public lands of the United States to which Indian title has been or shall hereafter be extinguished."[52] Henry Spalding was well aware of the contrasting Weltanschauung between whites and the Nez Perce, for whom private and exclusive ownership of land was inconceivable.[53] As he wrote in a letter: "Another cause of excitement is their land—They are told by the enemies of the mission, that people in the civilized world purchase their land & water priviliges. This touches a chord that vibrates through every part of the Indian's soul—that insatiable desire for property."[54]

In a narrative parallel to that of many other Indian groups, the Nez Perce found their lands increasingly encroached upon by whites. In 1855, representatives signed an agreement with the governor of Washington that secured nearly all of their original homeland, but the discovery of gold in that region in the next decade brought an influx of gold seekers who cared little for these boundaries. Another agreement was made with a group of Nez Perce, this one reducing the Nez Perce reservation to one-tenth of its original size. Their former territory was then gridded-out and put up for sale in the tidy squares Jefferson imagined, which made the commodification of land a simple and, for some, lucrative endeavor. Despite the increasing pressure of whites upon their homeland, the Nez Perce remained remarkably faithful to their early promise to Captain Lewis. Eventually, however, tensions arose both within the tribe and with whites. Violence erupted. Some Nez Perce refused to move onto the reservation and surrender their traditions. They were ordered to move within the boundaries set by the later treaty, and federal troops were on their way to enforce these limits. A band of young men struck out against a group of whites infamous for their hatred of Indians, and so began the embattled retreat to safety by a small band of warriors and hundreds of women and children known as the Nez Perce War.

After the conflict, the Nez Perce suffered further threat to their way of life as the federal government imposed upon them the keystone of Jeffersonian democracy: private land ownership. The Dawes Act of 1887 required that the remaining reservation land, owned collectively by all members of the tribe, be divided up into privately held square parcels and that, therefore, these traditionally mobile hunter-gatherers transform themselves into yeoman farmers. Many of the government's agents, including Alice Fletcher, who directed allotment on the Nez Perce Reservation, felt that they were changing these natives for their own good.[55]

The Dawes Act, which provided Nez Perce the opportunity to own separate parcels of tribal land, to be held in trust by the government for twenty-five years, rapidly accelerated the loss of land and attendant economic hardships of the Nez Perce. The act allowed undesignated lands to be opened for white settlement, and as Elizabeth James details, the widespread practice of leasing land to white farmers and the mandatory rules of inheritance further accelerated the loss of Nez Perce land. Jefferson's "natural order" of property rights, which required that land be divided equally among the next generation, became the definition utilized during allotment. This meant that a family's original 160 acres would quickly dissolve into increasingly smaller portions over time. This plan contradicted traditional Nez Perce living patterns, where people lived in extended family groups. In addition, the mobility characteristic of Jeffersonian democracy—the freedom to move freely within its spaces—was now not available to the Nez Perce. They had once placed their villages along the drainages of streams and rivers, in relation to the land's resources and close to their traditional staple—salmon. Now they had to live in nuclear family units separated from traditional living groups. Accessing the hunting grounds, rivers, and other food sources that defined their mobile way of life now meant trespassing on someone else's land, violating someone else's rights.

Within sixty years, the land controlled by the Nez Perce shrunk by two thirds.[56] Although the relations between Lewis and Clark and the Nez Perce had been friendly, it was the Corps's trip that initiated this destructive process of change, the involvement of the United States government in Indian lives, despite what Jefferson claimed in his instructions to Lewis were the "innocence of their intentions." Nez Perce medicine man Smohalla described the crisis this way of viewing the land brought to the Nez Perce:

> My young men shall never work. Men who work cannot dream, and wisdom comes in dreams.
>
> You ask me to plow the ground. Shall I take a knife and tear my mother's breast? Then when I die she will not take me to her bosom to rest.
>
> You ask me to dig for stone. Shall I dig under her skin for bones? Then when I die I cannot enter her body to be born again.[57]

The Nez Perce and other American Indians were not residents of an untouched and underutilized virginal landscape, and the claim that they did not use the land was symptomatic of the clouded perspective by which Americans traditionally have viewed the West and the alternative views for its future. Alan G. Marshall contests the widely accepted belief that the Nez Perce did not practice agriculture. He notes that they not only used tools but also fire to increase yield and were successful enough to produce food surpluses. These agricultural practices were related to social order and included notions of ownership, suggesting that Nez Perce society was more complex than historians have traditionally claimed. This "mode of agriculture," Marshall notes, "was so unusual as to be largely invisible to Euro-Americans."[58] Nez Perce understanding of their relationship to nature was clearly in contrast to the one which would come to conquer the West, and their resource use provided an alternative to the dominant land use practices that have left a legacy of exploitation, pollution, and species extinction. Today, the wild salmon that fed Lewis and Clark, which are estimated to have numbered in the millions at the time of their journey, now teeter on the edge of extinction.[59]

Contemporary travelers on Highway 12 in Idaho, the Lewis and Clark Highway, often remark how the area looks much as the Corps of Discovery saw it; yet the steep hills along the banks of the Lochsa and Clearwater have been heavily logged and some even sprayed with DDT.[60] In the Clearwater National Forest, over 4,000 miles of road, used mostly for logging, cut through the steep ravines. Logging trucks occasionally roll by on their way to local mills, and the place is more often seen as a playground for tourists than as homeland of a people. In Cougar Canyon, a gas station/restaurant/general store/motel along Highway 12—one of those places where you stop for gas, a cool soda, or an indoor bathroom while on your way to somewhere else—signs of a truer West line the store's shelves. Here, a diverse blend of people coalesce and cross paths: truck drivers hauling loads from Montana, local loggers, stoned hot springs–seeking hippies, and Eastern flyfishermen like me. The tiny store's stock reflects the equally diverse needs of its patrons. Work gloves, flares, motor oil, rolling papers, and even fly floatant are all for sale. Just don't expect fresh vegetables. The eclectic stock of this store and its role as meeting place for such a hodgepodge of people are neither atypical nor a recent phenomenon here but rather the history of the West, even in these isolated spaces of north central Idaho. The vision of Jeffersonian democracy, the role of the yeoman farmer as palimpsest for Western development, had no way of envisioning either the nature of Idaho's development or the players involved, especially when that development included those outside Jefferson's configuration of racial possibilities of "white, red, and black." Lewis and Clark set out to bring Asia to America, but it is unlikely that at his home in Monticello, Jefferson could have pictured Asia coming to America.

More Weeds

Wanting to head down to central Idaho, Fred and I drove west on Highway 11. In the familiar mode of kidding shared by lifetime friends who were again in the woods sleeping, eating, and living only to fish, Fred began to warn me in an artificially slow voice, "If you don't shape up, I'm taking you to the Hanging Tree." I thought, "Sure, Fred, imaginative. You a Regulator. Where did you come up with that one? Pretty good." We rounded a hill, and lining the right side of the car, glittering in that late day sun was a hill of sunflowers. A hill of gold in bloom. As we drove past, I kept wishing I had stopped to shoot off some frames. Fred continued on with his threats, finally saying, "We're almost there, boy."

To commemorate its centennial in 1990, Idaho peppered the state with historical markers: large signs in wooden frames, a pale green image of the state, and symbols locating that particular historical locale in relation to the nearest highway. The signs have numbers. A few sentences summarize the history. I saw a road sign, "Historical Marker Ahead," and I pulled the now dust-colored Pontiac off the road. Our unspoken routine now was to pull flush up to the sign and read: "CHINESE HANGING: Charged with hacking a prominent local merchant to pieces, five Chinese were hanged here by vigilantes. Sept. 18, 1885." It smelled. People had been using it as a rest stop. We scrambled up the hill and looked around for the tree, but saw only an empty space. We drove away. In the photo, I'm holding my throat.[61]

In 1860, gold was discovered near here, in present-day Pierce, Idaho, by men who had traveled east from Walla Walla and illegally moved into Nez Perce treaty lands. Soon this isolated mountain region witnessed a rapid influx of fortune seekers into the Clearwater River watershed. Idaho, which until then had been considered by white settlers only a barrier to be crossed and which did not even see its first town established until 1860—a Mormon settlement that its residents had believed was in Utah—immediately began to receive new residents en masse. Towns sprouted up near the mines, towns whose very names grounded their history in the Gem State's mining past: Oro Fino, Placerville, and Orogrande. Many of those who settled these towns were destitute farmers from Oregon, disillusioned ex-Confederates, and also Chinese immigrants. The movement of people eastward into Idaho is, in fact, typical of its development, since most of those who settled the state came from other regions in the West, particularly Oregon.

By 1870, the population of Idaho, excluding American Indians, was only 17,804, of which 4,724 were Chinese, more than one quarter of the territory's total non-Indian population.[62] A decade later the proportion of Asians to whites in Idaho was higher than in any other territory or state in the country. Not only does the role of mining as the catalyst for an urban settlement of Idaho contradict the agrarian myth of Jefferson's imagined West, but the fact that half of these early miners were Chinese complicates our understanding of who was a Westerner. Asians simply did not factor into Jefferson's imagined West, and an Asian perspective is absent from our understanding of these places and their environmental history.[63]

Asians' journeys into the spaces of the United States introduced another potentially incongruous people, nonnatives, into the democracy. Jefferson's fear of immigrants, their potential corruption of American democracy and its promised spaces—that "they will infuse into it their spirit, warp, and bias its direction, and render it a heterogeneous, incoherent, distracted mass"—led him to call for a limit on immigration and the right of citizenship for foreigners.[64] Although the democracy's frontier was already understood by its citizens to be closed to some, the notion of the West's prosperity, its fecundity, was still prevalent amongst Westerners of the late nineteenth century. Those deemed without a place in that imagined realm were often defined as a threat to that fertility, as "weeds," threats to the land and to life itself.[65] As one Idaho newspaper editor expressed it, "The Chinamen are coming. Lord, deliver us from the locusts of Egypt, they devour all men before them."[66] Even undesirable components of the landscape, like the plant Lactuca serriola, which become known as Chinese lettuce, manifested this antipathy to those deemed alien to Idaho. In 1895, the University of Idaho's president delivered a speech in which he opined, "Let us wage a war of extermination upon weeds, the unprofitable weeds, in orchard, home, community, and society, in the body politic and in the national life."[67]

Driving south along the Clearwater River, we passed along the edge of the Nez Perce Reservation, most of it now contained within the irregular boundaries of Lewis County. The history of Idaho's extractive past, this progression on the land, sat coded in the riverbanks and in view of the roadway: holes burrowed into hillsides, old rusty mining machinery, and too orderly piles of gravel. The names of local places, such as China Garden Creek, tell part of this natural history as well: here Chinese miners grew vegetables near the river to sell to other local miners.[68]

Despite their influential role in territorial Idaho, the Chinese miners soon left. Their presence here had always been contested, and discriminatory legislation, such as a monthly tax on all Chinese in Idaho, and incidents such as the one recorded by the Chinese Hanging Tree kept them from becoming a more permanent presence on the landscape. But their presence as well as their views of the landscape remain. In fact, a contemporary scholar presents the provocative argument that Chinese views of place were so profound that they spurned the migrants' return to China.[69] Although the influence of this attachment to their home place is likely overstated here given the hostile environment that Idaho presented, these traditional Chinese views of place are still fixed within the rugged mountain regions of Idaho. The Chinese practice of feng shui, a series of tenets that directs the placement and design of dwellings, appears in these isolated mountains. Recent archaeological explorations of former Chinese dwellings in Idaho suggest that Chinese immigrants constructed them to conform to feng shui, an indication that well before this practice became discovered by trend-conscious contemporary Americans, it had already shaped their environment, even its most isolated places. The failure, then, of Jeffersonian democracy to accommodate a variety of Americans, especially those beyond Jefferson's imagined racial catalog, meant that the presence of these people would be both tenuous and easily erased.

Postcards

Fred and I drove south to the Sawtooth Mountains, to the Sawtooth National Recreational Area, a Congressional creation nearly the size of Rhode Island that is intended to be a place defined by "outstanding combinations of outdoor recreation opportunities, aesthetic attractions, and proximity to potential users."[70] Idaho is a pretty place—a pretty place to play, especially for Easterners. Along the way, we stopped to fill up the car in Kooskia, where the Lochsa and the Clearwater merge. Something about this place—the muscled biker, the woman in the dirty dress walking home with a pack of cigarettes from the package store, the old car slowly rusting out back, and the quiet stacks of freshly cut timber across the street—made me uneasy. We filled the car up and quickly pulled out of the parking lot and back onto the highway.

Our trip was delayed for a few hours by a mudslide that blocked off Highway 95, temporarily severing northern and southern Idaho. We got out and looked at the green Salmon River as a drunken man played catch with his girlfriend to kill the time. A woman in an SUV in front of us had a bumper sticker that read, "I Fish and I Vote." When we finally pulled into McCall, play was in full swing. The nearby water, Payette Lake, was invaded by boaters, jet skiers, and fishermen. We got a room at the Lumber Man, with a thick pine stump for a chair and paintings of cowboy scenes. Across the street, we loaded up on hamburgers, coffee, pie, and the first newspaper we had seen in days. I snapped open the paper and read the first two words of the headline: "Randy Weaver."

The story was on the release of the infamous Idaho white separatist, who two years earlier had held out in his mountain cabin after a gun battle with federal agents who came to arrest him on weapons charges.[71] Northern Idaho, with its tradition of individualism and its landscape of isolated mountains, has a history of attracting those who want to escape the confines of what they see as an increasingly intrusive world.[72] Four times during Idaho's territorial period, its residents attempted to secede, and it continues to draw those with views on the fringe, including white supremacists. Along with its image as a pristine playground, Idaho also has the dubious honor of being seen by outsiders as the nesting ground of racial hatred. Tiffany Hardy, director of the Idaho Black History Museum, noted that, "As an outsider, all I ever heard about Idaho was the Aryan Nation and potatoes."[73] This image is so recognizable that it was used as the basis for an advertising campaign for the *Christian Science Monitor*.

Randy Weaver had retreated to the isolation of the rugged mountains of northern Idaho, leaving Iowa and the ills of modern America to raise his kids and to live "off the grid." He shared the antifederalist and racist perspective of many of his new neighbors and attended a few meetings of one of Idaho's more notorious Christian Identity groups, the Aryan Nations.[74] Followers of this movement commonly believe that America is approaching an end time that will include a revolution against the American government and a race war in which whites, in the tradition of the yeoman, will battle to reclaim the land. They quote Jefferson and the Bible, and they collect Nazi paraphernalia. Some discount them as fringe lunatics, but their ideology has fueled a sometimes deadly internal terrorist threat. Timothy McVeigh reminded us of that.

Many of these individuals envision the Northwest as a white homeland, a last stand for a pure white America, which they see as threatened by both unnatural mixing of the races and immigrants flooding into America. They speak of themselves as an endangered species, needing a refuge: "We seek a territorial imperative—a national state where the remnants of our people can live their ordained culture and destiny free of all alien influences."[75] Although Idaho's population remains predominately white, with ninety-one percent of its total population self-identified as white in the 2000 census, its Hispanic population is growing dramatically and now accounts for over eight percent of the Gem State's total population.[76] Idaho's Hispanic population represents a shift from the traditional ebb and flow of Mexican migrant farm laborers, especially from Texas, to the establishment of permanent communities supported by Hispanic-owned businesses. As one local Hispanic leader recently noted, "Idaho is getting browner and browner."[77] The growing Hispanic presence in Idaho, and in other parts of West, is disquieting to some, and this includes more than Idaho's infamous extremists. Though typically on the other end of the political spectrum, more liberal groups share their concerns about protecting American soil. Recently, one of the nation's largest environmental groups, the Sierra Club, endured an acrimonious debate over whether to embrace restrictions on immigration as a way to limit population growth and its threat to the environment.

Federal officials, eager to infiltrate the Aryan Nations, pressured Weaver, who had been arrested for selling illegally altered shotguns, to act as an informant. He refused. Federal agents then moved to arrest Weaver and began surveillance of his property. Weaver's teenaged son, Samuel, and a federal agent were killed when agents accidentally encountered the young man, the family dog, and a family friend walking in the woods down the ridge from the Weaver cabin. During the ensuing standoff, the commanding FBI official in the field changed the agency's guidelines for the use of deadly force; and all the bureau's marksmen, including Len Horiuchi, a third-generation Japanese American, were given the green light to shoot at any male adult, whether or not their life or that of another individual was in imminent danger. When Weaver's wife, with their baby in her arms, opened the door two mornings later as family friend Kevin Harris fled inside, Horiuchi fatally shot her in the head.

Under the headline that had caught my eye, the paper had a big picture of Weaver.

I sat with my second cup of coffee and pie, reading and thinking of Len Horiuchi shooting at Cindy Weaver for the FBI, the abused banks of the river known as the Clearwater, a shrunken homeland for the Nez Perce in Lewis County, and the discovery of Welsh Indians before them. How could we ever think anything natural would explain this land?

Fred Siewers with Westslope cutthroat trout, Kelly Creek, Idaho, 1995.

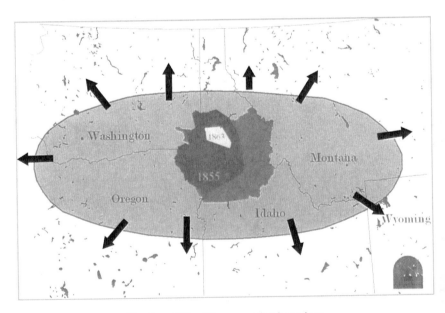

Nez Perce Tribe 1863 reservation boundary.

Chinese miners in northern Idaho, 1900.
COURTESY IDAHO STATE HISTORICAL SOCIETY.

Chapter 2

MATCHING THE HATCH

Nikkei, the Environment, and Idaho Statehood

The Westerner is less a person than a continuing adaptation.

WALLACE STEGNER, *The American West as Living Space*

The red aborigines,
Leaving natural breaths, some sounds of rains and winds, calls as of birds
    and animals in the woods, syllabled to us for names,
Okonee, Koosa, Ottawa, Monongahela, Sauk, Natchez, Chatta-
    hoochee, Kaqueta, Oronoco,
Wabash, Miami, Saginaw, Chippewa, Oshkosh, Walla-Walla,
Leaving such to the States they melt, they depart, charging the
    water and land with names.

WALT WHITMAN, *Starting from Paumanok*

Grandfather left a railroad for his message: We had to go somewhere difficult. Ride a train. Go somewhere important. In case of danger, the train was to be ready for us.

MAXINE HONG KINGSTON, *China Men*

"You'll need some Pinks." I followed him past the table of fly rods laid out like some museum display of rare artifacts to a large wooden table of drawers and cubbyholes filled with thousands of flies of fur, feather, and thread. He pointed to a series of small plastic cubbyholes. Above them was written "South Fork." I picked one up. It was small, and it was, indeed, pink. I had never seen a fly this color. It looked laughable—a fly called a Pink Albert?[1] But like anyone who flyfishes, I knew not to question this local pattern, and my visit to this Boise fly shop was about more than just buying an Idaho fishing license, being legal. It was about information, everything local. Although there are some flies that seem to work almost anywhere, trout, especially wild trout, have a habit of dining at times only on local delicacies, and the most accurate imitations of these "naturals" had better be at hand then. Spend a whole day haplessly casting to dozens of feeding fish that wholly ignore whatever is in your fly boxes and you will be forever convinced of this need to "match the hatch," as flyfishers term this acknowledgment of nature's variety and mutability, their adaptation to and mimicry of it.

So, I bought a dozen Pink Alberts in a variety of sizes, since size, too, can mean the difference between a day of stories for future telling or just a long day getting sunburnt, thirsty, and wet. I tucked them away in my box of Western flies, where they sat across from all those gaudy patterns I had used for the cutthroats of northern Idaho. I drove back to town, off "the Bench," the high plain just south of Boise proper where the railroad used to stop, past a canal, and over the Boise River. I settled back into the long wooden tables of the Idaho State Historical Society where I had spent the last few days with the recorded travels and dreams of Japanese in Idaho, what I had driven across the country to uncover. Although I was eager to get out on the water, I was content with my imaginings until the next morning, when I would have a chance to test my skills on water I had read about and pictured as a site of my own Western dreams.

For the Want of Water

That southwestern Idaho and especially its water should now draw travelers like myself to fish for sport, to kayak, and to settle in ever growing numbers would come as a shock to the members of the Corps of Discovery. As they prepared to cross the Continental Divide into what is now Idaho, Meriwether Lewis gathered geographical information from a local Indian about the area of their intended route and the region southwest of them, what is now southern Idaho. He noted in his journal the Indian's description of this region: "this he depicted with horrors and obstructions scarcely inferior to that just mentioned . . . that in passing this country the feet of our horses would be so much wounded with the stones many of them would give out. the next part of the rout was about ten days through a dry and parched sandy desert in which no food at this season for either man or horse, and in which we must suffer if not perish for the want of water." Although this area was devoid of accessible drinking water, it was not without water. The impressive Snake River cuts through this apparent wasteland, but it was described to Lewis in 1805 as "a large river that was navigable but afforded neither Salmon nor timber." The man who related this information, a Northern Shoshone, known to Plains tribes as "Snakes," claimed to have relations beyond this inhospitable area and described "a country tolerable fertile and partially covered with timber on another large river which ran in the same directions as the former."[2]

Southern Idaho is primarily arid. The Great Basin Desert reaches its northern end in southern Idaho and curves westward into eastern Oregon and Washington. Boise, the state capital located in southwestern Idaho, is one of the fastest growing cities in the West, yet it enjoys an annual mean rainfall of only twelve inches.[3] During the first week I visited the area, the mercury pressed over 100 degrees nearly every day. The "dry and parched sandy desert" described to Meriwether Lewis is the Snake River Plain, where the mountains that constitute most of porkchop-shaped Idaho's northern and central regions spill out into the lava fields of southern Idaho.[4] The plain was formed by a hot spot in the earth's mantle that crept eastward from Oregon, melting the surrounding rock. Geologists believe the impact of a large meteorite near eastern Oregon created this hot spot seventeen million years ago. Just as today these barriers mark a distinct division between northern Idaho and the rest of the state, Indian societies developed two distinct cultures in these geographic regions. In the Great Basin region of Idaho, Shoshone and Bannock lived off the variety of game animals and plants available here and supplemented their diet with salmon from the Snake River. In southwestern Idaho, Northern Paiutes subsisted on a similar diet, and both groups were characterized by small nomadic bands. The Shoshone identified themselves so closely with their means of sustenance that they commonly named their bands after their major food source.[5]

The Snake River arcs across the plain once inhabited by these people like a u-shaped vein of fat in the filet of the chop. With several impressive waterfalls along its course and the deepest canyon in North America, Hells Canyon, it was navigable in 1805, but only for stretches. Its watershed was also blessed with huge annual runs of salmon and steelhead, in numbers William Clark described as "incredible to Say."[6] This impressive supply of fish, however, could not insure against the grim scenario portrayed to the Corps of Discovery by local Indians. It was dry scrub land and long remained for whites only a place to avoid or to pass through on their way elsewhere. Only precious metals, dreamers, and constant water would change that.

Travelers

I got up early on Sunday and stopped for a paper with baseball scores at the Circle K, that curious blend of modern American convenience and Old West symbolism. It was at the corner of Vista and Nez Perce, the latter name denoting the tradition of honoring the displaced original inhabitants of Idaho and the former suggesting the equally pervasive tradition of treating the land as an aesthetic experience: something to frame and contain. Inside the coffee shop where I had been getting my morning fix was a little state tourist office with maps and brochures. I picked up one for Mountain Home; it beckoned me to "Come play in our big backyard." I obliged.

Driving out of the Boise basin, the billboards advertising cheaper motel rooms and fast food gave way to dry scrub grass and open plain. To my right, I could see the mountains of northern Nevada and to my left the foothills of the Sawtooth Mountains—ten, twenty, maybe thirty miles away. I took advantage of those Western speed limits that acknowledge the need to get to something you can see from that distance and pushed the car up to 80. I passed the sign for exit 59B: Memory Road. And although it was 1998, I still did not want to break down out here at night. Here you can watch the rain come for hours; nothing sneaks up on you, but at the same time, you are exposed—without cover. I felt that I could blow away.

I pulled off at the Mountain Home exit, where a sign directed me to Mountain Home Air Force Base, a major local institution since World War II, and I turned left in the opposite direction, north, toward Anderson Ranch. The sunroof was down, the windows open to clear my head of the air-conditioned air, and Steve Earle sang, as he had since I left Massachusetts on I-91, about the open miles stretching out before me "down the road." The song seemed to fit much better here than in crammed-in Connecticut: all those drivers, the narrow bad roads, and gray asphalt in the rain. A few miles north of the exit and its Chevron, Jack in the Box, Subway, and Best Western, I drove by another one of those markers put up all over the state to locate history by the highway. I slowed down. It read: Rattlesnake Gulch.

Two horses stood nudging each other across a fence. A sprinkler hissed. What was now just the edge of a ranch was once the original site of Mountain Home, before the railroad came through south of here and made this spot obsolete. It was the same fate Boise risked when the Oregon Short Line railroad bypassed it and stopped five miles south in Kuna. I sped up into the hills. Sage filled the air and my pulse quickened as I got closer to the river. Cars with the latest bike racks and boats in tow, SUVs with Montana and Oregon plates, massive RVs, and pickup trucks streamed past on their way home from Sun Valley. One big pickup trundled past with a personalized grill guard "Bushwhacker 2." A sign to my right read, "This highway kept clean by the 34th Bomber Squadron."

From the window, I saw another sign again informing me that I was nearing history, crossing the site of Goodale's Cutoff, a northern side route of the Oregon Trail. Between 1840 and 1860, tens of thousands of earlier Americans passed through Idaho here, if for far different reasons. During those years, 53,000 people made the journey to Oregon through Idaho along the Oregon Trail.[7] For them Idaho was a place to hasten through until, just as in the Clearwater region, something valuable was found that could make them dream, and later this dry land could be made new.

Planting Faith in the Desert

When men discovered gold and silver in Idaho's southern region, it quickly became a site of intensive mining. In the 1880s, an assorted lot of dreamers and schemers spilled into the Wood River region northeast of Mountain Home seeking their fortunes from the land. Arthur Foote was a young engineer from back East whose wife, Mary Hallock Foote, was a widely published illustrator and author hailed as "an authentic voice of the West."[8] Mary had already accompanied her husband on various excursions into Mexico and to the high mountain mines of Colorado. Although such locales were quite foreign to a woman of her set, as the title of her memoirs, A Victorian Gentlewoman in the Far West, suggests, none was more hostile than Idaho. She wrote upon arriving in her new home, "But—darkest Idaho! Thousands of acres of desert empty of history. The Snake River had an evil name—the Boise, the source of our great scheme, emptied into it and was lost in it."[9]

The "great scheme" to which Mary Hallock Foote referred was her husband's dream of building a massive irrigation canal in the Boise River Canyon, a project he began in 1883. Although the entire territory of Idaho was sparsely populated and its agricultural production small, Foote was determined to build an agricultural miracle here where "there was not a tree in sight—miles and miles of pallid sagebrush."[10] In his messianic zeal to complete his project, an eventual ten-year struggle that ended in failure and imperiled the Footes' marriage, he seemed an equal to Thomas Jefferson. Mary Foote recalled the vision: "Multiply that inconstant water a hundredfold, store it in those reservoirs the man talked of building up in the crotches of the hills, cover the valley with farms, and even to the mind of the misbeliever, here was a work worth spending a lifetime for, even the one life that is man's in this world."[11] Her account of their Idaho years not only chronicles the personal and environmental struggles that the Footes faced in attempting to implement this vision but also the role played by outside forces in Washington, New York, and even London in their project.[12] Once again, the East was driving Idaho's progress.

Due to the scale of Arthur Foote's irrigation project, he was dependent upon outside partners for the large sum of capital it required, and his wife's memoirs recount the comings and goings not only of family and friends but of these men, too. Mary eventually blamed the project's failure upon these financiers, who lacked a similarly expansive vision. "All schemes must learn," she wrote, "but the fundamental causes of our failure were the lack of teamwork between New York and London, and the meddlesome impatience of little-minded men."[13] Finally resigned to failure, the Footes left their isolated canyon home east of Boise, and the hundreds of trees they had planted slowly died for want of water.[14] But where the Footes and their partners left off, others would follow, and Idaho would indeed bloom. As Mary Hallock Foote noted in her memoir, "It was faith we planted and that did not die."[15]

The Idaho imagined by the Footes was on hold until the territory attained statehood in 1890 and received both the technical expertise and large-scale capital needed to develop its expansive regions, what a pioneer poet described as "mile upon mile of sun-scorched earth; / mile upon mile of desert plain; / a treeless waste, scarce trod by man; / A wilderness unblessed with rain."[16] The water projects that Foote's company had begun were eventually taken over by the Bureau of Reclamation, which completed the oddly named New York and Idaho Canal that brought water to the Boise area. The very naming of the project emphasized the long reach of the Eastern centers of commerce and finance into Idaho's development, as well as that of the federal government.

Despite the observations of the Corps of Discovery and later expeditions, the West remained a dreamland for farming, and federal policies often promoted such development, regardless of logic, cost, or environmental impact. The Corps's John Ordway described the potential of one such region: "This country may with propriety well be called the Deserts of North America for I do not conceive any part of it can ever be Setled as it is deficient of or in water & . . . of timber & too steep to be tilled."[17] The federal government ignored those charged with the mission of exploring and studying the West as official fact finders, as agents of scientific inquiry. John Wesley Powell, the geologist who studied the feasibility of Western expansion in these regions of the West, concluded that the reach of Jeffersonian agrarian expansion had met its limit in these arid lands. His firsthand knowledge of Western places led him to propose a plan for the development of the West that emphasized limiting property holdings and organizing political institutions around water systems. Farmers would band together to form cooperatives that would control water resources at the local level, and property boundaries would be based on the distribution of natural resources. Powell based his suggestions not only on his experiences in the field but on how other Westerners, such as Mormons and Mexicans, had adapted to it.[18]

As the power that explored, mapped, and owned the West, the federal government was in a uniquely influential position to steer its development. The warnings of early naysayers, including those most knowledgeable about the area's natural limitations, however, were easily drowned out by the marketing call of railroads and governments that conspired to fill the West. As historian William Robbins notes, "The boosters ignored, resented, and shunted aside the careful investigations of John Wesley Powell and others whose scientific findings simply did not fit the prevailing ethos."[19] The putatively rational, yet often irrational, policies of government agencies typify the agricultural colonization of Western spaces, a process Frieda Knobloch notes was defined by the "imposition of state power and institutional knowledge production, deployed by ranks of official experts and even military agendas on western territory and objects."[20]

Policies such as the Homestead Act, the Desert Land Act, and eventually the Reclamation Act brought settlers cheap land and water but also greater federal control over their lives in the "deserts of North America." Sixty percent of the land irrigated under the Carey Act of 1894, which ceded large tracts of public land to states that then sold them to private interests to develop water projects, was in Idaho.[21] More direct federal involvement and control came with the birth of the Bureau of Reclamation in 1902. Massive federal water projects such as the Boise Reclamation Project and the Minidoka Reclamation Project provided water to southern Idaho and forever changed its terrain and history. In these conquests of the natural environment and its limitations, participants were seen as the progeny of Jefferson's vision, as one irrigation booster noted, "true, loyal American yeomen who would plant that glorious emblem of brotherly love, the stars and stripes, so deep and firm in that irrigated soil."[22]

A turn-of-the-century poster promoting the recently irrigated area of Blackfoot in southeastern Idaho shows a man and a woman standing on a green grassy hillside, looking out over a valley filled with bundles of hay and neat squares of green that stretch off into the horizon's golden sky. The scene is revealed by the man's hand pushing back a leafy tree limb. The poster looks like no place in Idaho but proclaims, "Golden Opportunities—Blackfoot, Idaho." In areas of southwestern Idaho, such as Nampa, where in 1891 local residents hired an Australian rainmaker who guaranteed half an inch of rain for a $500 fee, similar visions would finally appear only when the completed Boise Valley Project began carrying water into the region. The project, however, also brought them into a complicated and often fractious relationship with the federal government. Many farmers immediately complained of the government's repayment schedule for the project and of the administrator's inefficiency.[23]

Arthur Foote had worked for the federal government and during his time in Idaho was part of the United States Geological Survey's Irrigation Survey, the project headed by Major John Wesley Powell that investigated the feasibility of Western irrigation projects. Although numerous private endeavors like Foote's had succeeded in bringing water to southwestern Idaho, only the large-scale projects of the federal government could fully water Idaho and bring the state out of the darkness Mary Hallock Foote described, so that today the very word Idaho brings to mind another word: potato.

Arthur Foote had planned reservoirs as part of his irrigation project, but he could not have foreseen the scale of the project that began in 1911 in the canyon land north of Boise. Here, near Arrow Rock, where he had camped with his family at a large split rock, rose the deepest dam in the world at that time. The dam's name derived from the large rock, where his wife alleged, "Indians on their hunting or war parties would shoot arrows to discourage the intentions of any evil spirit watching them from that crack."[24] The Boise River was first diverted around the site of the dam, and between 1911 and 1915 federal workers built a massive structure 348 feet tall that would supply water to 170,000 acres of irrigated farmland.[25] The massive wall of cement and the millions of gallons of water it contained would insure the thirsty dream of Jeffersonian development for once barren southwest Idaho. A local paper described the changes the land had undergone as "this transformation of a weary stretch of sagebrush desert into an abode of thrifty and contented citizens."[26]

Members of Lewis and Clark's expedition and their Shoshone informants could never have imagined out in the middle of that "parched sandy desert" a city the size of Boise, which between 1990 and 2000 grew by over forty-six percent. With a population in 2004 of 190,117,[27] it is the largest city in the state. In fact, nearly all of the state's major population centers lie in the Great Basin. In American popular storytelling, Boise, or any other example of our settling of the West's arid regions, stands as a symbol of triumph and success. Historian Mark Fiege, in his book-length discussion of Idaho's agricultural landscape, notes that "in Idaho, farmers, engineers, journalists, poets, and others propounded a tale in which people renewed themselves by turning wilderness into a beneficient, productive, beautiful land. Through irrigation, they transformed a desert waste into a fresh, modern, industrial-agricultural landscape, an environment in which they reaped more and sowed less, and where water flowing through ditches was laughter to their ears."[28]

Water was so vital to the state's development that Idaho's Constitution, written in 1889, has an article concerning water rights and usage, and Idaho's is the only state constitution to devote a separate article to water rights. Article Fifteen addresses water rights issues such as state regulation, the term of water rights, and the right to divert natural waterways. Section 3 of Article Fifteen makes explicit the legislators' deference to individual water rights: "using the water for domestic purposes shall have the preference over those claiming for any other purpose."[29] The article places agriculture next in the hierarchy of water uses. John Wesley Powell's urgings to organize the state around drainage systems and, thus, possibly avoid conflicts over this precious resource went ignored.

By the time of the constitutional convention, Idaho courts had already established the concept of prior appropriation as the controlling water rights doctrine in Idaho. This meant that ownership of water was conferred upon the party who utilized it. Use it or lose it. Courts rejected alternative definitions of ownership, such as Powell's plan to confer water rights in the land. Section 3 of Article 15 also indicates that agricultural interests are deemed preeminent. Together, the legislature and courts installed a legal framework that would both support the agricultural development of the state over other interests and also lead to continual disputes over water resources. It is not surprising that the majority of the convention's delegates were, in fact, farmers.[30] In 1890, in a case concerning water rights, the Idaho Chief Justice explained that this doctrine was an adaptation to Idaho's unique landscape. In his opinion, he described how Idaho's pioneers developed this definition to meet the unique challenges of the land. The judge noted that "the demand for water they found greater than the supply, as is the unfortunate fact still all over this arid region. Instead of attempting to divide it among all, thus making it unprofitable to any, or instead of applying the common-law riparian doctrine, to which they had been accustomed, they disregarded the traditions of the past, and established as the only rule suitable to their situation that of prior appropriation."[31]

The framers of the state constitution also acknowledged the historical tensions within Idaho between its individual residents and government agencies, and they placed serious restrictions upon state power.[32] Increasing federal presence in Idaho, however, not only would bring water, wealth, and thousands of newcomers to Idaho but would also promote the kind of relationship that its residents had often resented. Nevertheless, the rapid change that outside influence brought could be celebrated by most of its residents. Between 1890 and 1900 alone, Idaho's population doubled, from 88,548 to 161,772.[33] In the thirty years following statehood, irrigated acreage increased tenfold. Potatoes headed eastward from its fields, and Arthur Foote's imagined Idaho now became a place on earth:

> Where once the Indian, wild and free
> Rode forth at dawn beneath the skies,
> To join the chase in savage glee,
> Cities and villages arise;
>
> While nature, 'neath the soft caress,
> Where all was wilderness before,
> Beams o'er the land in gratitude,
> And gladly yields her bounteous store . . .
>
> And from the East the iron horse
> Bursts upon thee in his might
> Of Progress he the messenger;
> A flashing meteor of light.
> Arouse thee Idaho! Shake off
> Thy slumbers! Scatter hence the shade!
> Awaken to the glittering dawn
> Of thy great future, n'er to fade![34]

Like Walt Whitman a decade earlier, this poet of turn-of-the-century Idaho, George Wheeler, imagined Idaho's original residents as figures who once rode free in wild Western spaces, but who had now vanished.[35] Although the nomadic lifestyle of Idaho's native people had ended, Shoshone, Bannock, and Paiute—like the Nez Perce in the north—were still in Idaho. Whites, however, tore them out of and off the land, like the sagebrush and ironweed, to clear the path for Progress and its "soft caress." In 1869, the federal government removed all Shoshone from the Boise Valley and relocated them to Fort Hall Reservation, south of Blackfoot.

In 1890, Emma Edwards Green began work on the official state seal of

Idaho. When the seal was adopted on March 14, 1891, the fundamental mythology of George Wheeler's poem became the official visual representation of the state. The Great Seal of the State contains two figures, a white man and woman on either side of a shield, which is a window into a landscape where a man leads a horse and plow through a green field by a blue winding river that flows from the snow-topped mountains past a homestead. It is a view Jefferson would have appreciated—a western Monticello. At the foot of the shield are a bushel of wheat and cornucopias spilling bright fruits. Emma Edwards Green described her iconography: "The shield between the man and woman is emblematic of the protection they unite in giving the state." The man is a miner: a lone figure in khaki pants, a shirt rolled up to bulging biceps, and a rakish red scarf around his neck. He has a pick slung over his right shoulder and leans against a shovel. Green commented, "As mining was the chief industry, and the mining man the largest financial factor of the state at that time, I made the figure of the man the most prominent in the design."[36]

The female figure on the left looks away from the viewer. Unlike the man, she has no active role in Progress. She does, however, possess a multitude of selves. According to Green, she signifies "justice, as noted by the scales; liberty, as denoted by the liberty cap on the end of the spear, and equality with man as denoted by her position at his side." She is the Libertad of Whitman's hopeful poems of the young democracy's westward expansion. What unified all the meanings of Green's woman was her garb: it was Idaho, the land itself. Green explained, "as Idaho was a virgin state, I robed my goddess in white and made the liberty cap on the end of the spear the same color."[37] If Idaho were a woman—chaste, open, and just—her suitors, however, still had to be chosen for her and some would always be rejected. Some Idaho residents were consigned to the other side of that shield and spear: never to touch the white robe, Idaho.

Why Hop Sing No Can Marry

In her memoir, Mary Foote twice noted another member of their household in Idaho, a Chinese cook, referred to only as "our perfect little Chinaman" and as "a little Chinese dandy (and a dandy cook)."[38] As in northern Idaho, Chinese moved into the new mining regions of the Wood River, but by the time the Footes arrived in Idaho, the Chinese view into its future had been closed. Although they accounted for roughly a third of Idaho's total non-Indian population in 1870,[39] their numbers quickly declined as legislators at both the state and federal level promulgated a phalanx of discriminatory pieces of legislation, including the federal Chinese Exclusion Act of 1882. One of the first acts of the state legislature was to pass an unconstitutional law aimed at Chinese. The legislation barred Chinese from holding mining property and was a compromise to appease the state's Democrats, who advocated a total exclusion of Chinese from the state. The state's constitution already barred Chinese from holding public office, acting as jurors, and voting.[40] These measures were a continuation of the history of anti-Chinese measures in effect during Idaho's territorial period, such as the monthly head tax applicable to all Chinese. The provisions of this earlier legislation allowed authorities to seize all property upon failure to pay the fee and to sell the property at auction almost immediately.[41]

In addition to these discriminatory pieces of legislation, anti-Chinese sentiment in the West often led to mass expulsions and violence. Local whites in Idaho beat and murdered Chinese. The Chinese Hanging Tree that I visited with my friend in northern Idaho is but one site of the violent episodes of Chinese history in Idaho. Given the sentiments of many local authorities, many similar acts were likely never recorded, never named by a sign along the highway. In fact, authorities were often the very agents of denial, as when police officials in Boise forced Chinatown, "the group of filthy shacks," out of the downtown in 1901.[42]

Even if the Footes' cook were a "dandy," fine clothes and all the charm in the world mattered little if this or any other "Chinaman" sought to woo a white woman or her companion piece, the land. They had, as the popular phrase suggests, only a Chinaman's chance. Nativist views about sexually predatory and impure "Chinamen" and the attendant need to protect white women made any intimate contact among them unlikely and, in the eyes of some, dangerous. A California man summed up this view, which dominated much of the Western landscape and which echoed Jefferson's fear of white racial degradation. He claimed, "Were the Chinese to amalgamate at all with our people, it would be the lowest, most vile and degraded of our race, and the result of that amalgamation would be a hybrid of the most despicable, a mongrel of the most detestable that has ever afflicted the earth."[43] Lawmakers in Idaho made sure that no hybrid race arose on Idaho's body. The territorial legal code barred "marriages of white persons with negroes, mulattoes, Indians or Chinese,"[44] and state law later barred marriages between whites and "negroes or mulattoes."[45] By 1890, approximately 2,000 Chinese remained in Idaho; that number fell to 1,500 by the turn of the century and continued to decline for decades. By 1910, there were fewer than 1,000 Chinese in Idaho.[46] The immigrant Chinese population in Idaho was predominately male, and this also prevented them from establishing a more permanent presence. Most of the Chinese women who did venture to Idaho in the late 1800s were prostitutes servicing the men of Idaho's mining regions.[47] Many of the Chinatowns where Idaho's Chinese lived, ran restaurants, and grew vegetables are gone. On the west side of Boise is an area cut off from the revitalization projects—all the new shiny glass windows and clean wide sidewalks—that characterize downtown Boise today. It is a separately defined space, Garden City. Its main drag's curious name, Chinden, represents the once large Chinese presence here and the gardens these travelers tended.[48] In 1976, a Boise woman recalled, "we used to get our vegetables from the Chinese . . . Yes, Garden City. And then at Christmas time they would give us little bowls with balls in them you know. And I have one of those little bowls here somewhere."[49]

I remember, as a kid, watching a *Bonanza* episode on TV. Hop Sing, the Cartwright's servant, had fallen in love and went to town to marry his white sweetheart, who had suddenly appeared for this episode.[50] The courtship was left to be imagined by the viewer. At the courthouse, however, the judge revealed that he could not marry the couple in the state of California. Hop Sing, looking puzzled and forlorn, asked, "But this is America. Why Hop Sing no can marry?" Hop Sing could not marry his white lover in California then, nor in the Gem State, for much of its history.[51]

Many of the discriminatory acts of legislation created during Idaho's early statehood specifically targeted Chinese immigrants. However, the overall rationale behind such legislation, that virgin Idaho needed to be protected, proved applicable to later Asian immigrants. New rules and new definitions were created when the time came to counter a fresh threat, new weeds on the land. Later, when Japanese moved to the state, lawmakers passed an amendment to the state's antimiscegenation law in 1921. This provision was now extended to include "mongolians."[52]

Native Species

As I rolled up Highway 20, the land grew more desolate. It was covered in hardscrabble lava cuts, and the air was cooler. In places, the hills bled a salmon color in the morning light. A sign indicated that I was now in the Boise National Forest. Though I was looking for the turnoff down to the South Fork of the Boise, I couldn't help but drive fast. The West, after all, is about speed and open spaces. Coming down a hill, I spotted the sign, turned onto the gravel road, and drove over a cattle guard and toward the canyon. I stopped by an old wooden home left for weeds and rain to overtake and shot off some frames. The cattle stared, chewing in silence beside some Western dream gone wrong.

At the top of the canyon was a sign: PROCEED WITH CAUTION. The road wound down to the dam, hugging the edge of the basalt canyon wall on the right and falling away to the river on the left. Over the edge was a freefall of a few hundred feet. There was no guardrail. The road seemed to define what lawyers mean by "assumption of risk." As I downshifted into second and drove with uncharacteristic caution down to the river, a local with a trailer in tow pulled up on my bumper. The out-of-state license tag and pro football team logo on the back of my car marked me as another tourist sent to inconvenience him.

Once down in the canyon, I drove slowly, gawking at the clear water strewn with boulders, gravel, and a million likely holding places for trout. Where to start? Pictures of those big wild rainbows in the fly shop were in my head. I finally pulled over in a turnoff to my left and raced into my waders, boots, and vest. It was 9:30 in the morning, later than I had planned, but no one was here. A river to myself. Since it was still cool, I decided to fish wet flies, to try some of those universal patterns I always carry, and to wait until the warm sun of afternoon cued the Pink Alberts. An unknown leak in my waders let me know just how cold the water was and probably why no one was here. I broke out my water thermometer: 53 degrees. The morning proved futile.

I worked my way up the near bank, and by noon flies and people began to hatch off the water. The trout turned on. Cars raced down the gravel road and shot flumes of dust behind them. "Wild trout under pressure," was how the guidebook had described the South Fork.[53] Drift boats began to appear along with a flotilla of those new one-man paddleboats that make their human passenger look like some bizarre amphibious creature with plastic fin feet and a pontoon midriff. People streamed past, flailed away at the middle of the pool, and headed just as quickly downriver. No one raised a fish.

I could see a pod of feeding rainbows, but they were hard to reach in the deep fast water that kept me close to the bank. One had a back the size of my upper arm. But with each watercraft, they went down, stopped feeding, and I sat on the bank cursing the intrusions. I noticed, under the bushes ahead, a group of fish rising only a few feet off the near bank in the shallows, and soon I was casting to the largest fish I had seen all summer. I shot out thirty feet of orange fly line and laid my Pink Albert down right into one's feeding lane. It took. After a few minutes, I brought it to the bank: a fat cutthroat nearly twenty inches long.

A man outfitted with one of those pontoon boats and a tan cowboy hat drifted into my hole and hit some casts to the opposite bank, where that bruiser had been rising. "Howdy!" he offered in that open Western way that immediately forgave his presence—that and his obvious familiarity with this water. Although he caught nothing in the hole, he floated down below me and began picking off fish feeding tight to the bank. By the time he was out of sight, I had seen him land three fish.

I decided to risk getting washed downstream and struggled across the river to fish the other bank. My right foot was numb. As I scrambled up scree on the bank, I noticed ants in the bushes. Upstream, I could see a large fish rising under a tree, and I tied on a tiny black ant pattern. I slowly worked my way into the river below the tree, so that I could cast under it. I made a cast and tried to spot my fly, but it was impossible to pick up. Yet, when the water exploded, I knew where it was. My reel screamed as the rainbow raced downriver, leaping, and taking out line. I smiled all the way back to Boise.

When I showed up at the fly shop the next morning, Clayne asked, "So, how did you do?" When I recounted, as nonchalantly as I could, my outing, he replied, "I have a feeling you're a pretty good fisherman." I nodded. "Yeah, we Pennsylvania boys know a little something about fishing." He seemed especially impressed with the cutthroat, as they are rare in the river. Cutthroat are the native nonanadromous trout species of Idaho, and four major subspecies still exist in Idaho. It was this fish, in particular the Westslope cutthroat, that Lewis and Clark ate in northern Idaho and before that in Montana. Lewis noted these fish in his journal, writing that "the trout are the same which I first met with at the falls of the Missouri, they are larger than the speckled trout of our mountains and equally as well flavored."[54] Today, this cutthroat's scientific name remains *Oncorhynchus clarki lewisi*.[55] Although they rise readily to a fly, as I discovered in the same Clearwater River drainage of the Corps's trek, cutthroat trout have been supplanted in many Idaho waters by rainbow trout. Beginning in the late 1800s, government agencies stocked this primarily Pacific slope fish in the cutthroat's native range to appeal to the desires of anglers who preferred the acrobatics and tenacious fight of the brightly slashed fish. As a result of this continued wildlife management practice, along with the inevitable damage to riparian environments caused by Idaho's resource development, Idaho cutthroat are threatened. When forced to compete with the more aggressive rainbows, cutthroat either are eradicated or interbreed with rainbows, producing a hybrid commonly called a cutbow. In 1990, this native species, the cutthroat, became the official state fish of Idaho.

Those "wild rainbows" I caught on the South Fork were not wild, not natural, not original. Their presence in the South Fork of the Boise River is due only to human intervention.[56] Now, the very presence of a cutthroat trout in this water, its native range, seems aberrant. In fact, the South Fork of the Boise is, despite the "wild" quality of its fish, a very unnatural river. The consistent flow of cool water year-round in this desert canyon is provided by the Bureau of Reclamation through the release of water from Anderson Ranch Dam. Originally scheduled to open in 1946, Anderson Ranch Dam's construction was delayed by the start of World War II and not completed until 1950. It was built to supplement the growing needs of Boise Valley agriculture, and the impact on fish habitat was just a fortuitous side benefit. As my weathered guidebook noted, "This is a tail race fishery that offers better trout rearing and living conditions than if the dam wasn't there."[57]

I continued going back to Clayne's store to buy more flies, to read fishing magazines, and, most of all, to share stories. He told me I needed to head down to the Owyhee River in the southeast corner of Oregon: big browns. He slid forward some pictures of him and Mike Fong, a well-known fishing writer. I had read his articles and seen him on TV. I wondered, how do I get that job? A trophy photo: Mike holds a giant brown trout that they pulled a nine-inch trout out of before releasing.

When he asked, I told Clayne what I was doing out there, how I was researching the experiences of Japanese in Idaho. He had stories for that, too. He used to work delivering milk out to some of the farming camps of Japanese, and he recounted their honesty and also their angling prowess: "They were the best. Up there at Silver Creek. Using 3 lb. test with a single salmon egg. They would stand there like cranes. The best fisherman I ever met was Ed Fujii."

Pestilent Little Yellow Men

I checked the Idaho map and looked for the Owyhee, but only its upper reaches were there and in a corner of the state without any paved roads. The river proper was in Oregon, on the other side of the Owyhee Mountains. It was the river flowing through a "country tolerable fertile and partially covered with timber" that Lewis had been told of by that Northern Shoshone 190 years earlier. The river's name is another marker of migration from the Pacific into Idaho. North West Company's legendary trapper, Donald Mackenzie, explored this section of Idaho in 1819, accompanied by a group of Hawaiian laborers. The name Hawaii became transformed by the British into Owyhee. Mackenzie sent three of these men into an unexplored region of this territory, and they were never seen again. No sign of them was ever found. From this incident, the river they went up to explore and the geographic features around it became forever known by that breathy word Owyhee.[58] Labor from the Pacific would continue to be an important foundation of Idaho's development, and these early Hawaiians were later followed by the large influx of Chinese during Idaho's early mining booms, including one in the Owyhee district in the 1860s. Once the Chinese began leaving Idaho, new immigrants from Asia replaced them: the Japanese.

Records of the time, including those kept by Japanese associations in the United States, account for no Japanese in Idaho in 1890.[59] But Japanese, in fact, had begun to move into Idaho as early as the 1880s.[60] Labor contractors recruited Japanese men from West Coast cities such as Seattle and San Francisco, from the sugar plantations of Hawaii, and even from Japan to work on Idaho's railroads. As early as 1892, 1,000 Japanese were at work on the Oregon Short Line, the rail line that cuts across southern Idaho, roughly paralleling the Snake River's course.[61] Since the Iron Horse was the messenger of Progress, in order for it to reach Idaho, railroads needed to be built. Chinese had been the major railroad workforce in the West, but with passage of the Exclusion Act in 1882, their numbers soon dwindled, and railroads turned to Japanese workers in unprecedented numbers to build the railroads of Idaho in the 1890s. The Union Pacific imported these men to grade the right-of-ways, dig the tunnels, and build the bridges for Idaho's future.

For the next ten years, Japanese constituted the largest group at work on the rail lines of the state.[62] The progress of Idaho was upon their backs. As one of these men's daughters later noted, "Tamura, Miyasako, and Kora, who later made their homes here in Boise valley, were on a crew that moved lava rock for the railroad to Murphy. It took two of these small-statured men to lift a heavy rock onto the back of a third man, who had cushioned his back with a gunny sack and stood stooping by the flatcar. The first two renewed their hold and heaved the boulder from the man's back to the flatcar. These rocks still face the bank to reinforce bridges along the Boise River."[63] As work on the Oregon Short Line progressed and more Japanese came to work on it—eventually some 3,500 men—at major rail stops such as Nampa, Caldwell, Boise, and Pocatello, Japanese communities took root.[64] After the turn of the century, an increasing number of Japanese women entered the United States, many of them married women, and this promoted the establishment of a permanent Japanese American presence here.

Even before this, the growing Japanese population in Idaho, along with fears of white laborers for their livelihood, incited the state's media and white residents to action. The Idaho legislature passed a measure that barred municipalities and private businesses from employing "any alien who has failed, neglected or refused, prior to the time such employment is given, to become naturalized or to declare his intention to become a citizen of the United States."[65] The state's major newspaper reported in 1892 that "these pestilent little yellow men [had] almost wholly supplanted white section hands." In the early 1890s, white citizens of Idaho began running Japanese out of their local towns and into the sagebrush plains. In late July of 1892, a series of towns used an alleged smallpox epidemic as the rationale for running Japanese out of several towns and discouraging any more from "flocking into this part of the state." The first incident was in Mountain Home, where one hundred years later I, a third-generation Japanese American, would be invited to "Come Play in [Their] Big Back Yard." That this sort of expulsion would spread was not surprising, given that this same newspaper account noted, "The action of the Mountain Home people will not excite condemnation, as it may influence the Japs to keep without the state."[66]

A few weeks later white Idahoans forced Japanese out of Nampa, Caldwell, Payette, and Boise. Although newspaper reports acknowledged that medical authorities discovered only "one genuine case of smallpox" amongst the Japanese population, they used language that suggested these people were a pestilence upon the land whites had claimed as their own. The newspaper writer noted, "The feeling in this town and vicinity is deep and people are determined to protect their wives and little ones from the dreaded scourge." So great was the fear of the infectious "Japs" that, like Christian Patriots in Idaho's Panhandle today, some citizens then were "talking of going to the mountains until all danger is past."[67] Even if the authorities had acted only on a temporary basis, in the need to address an immediate public health issue, local residents saw this as an opportunity to make sure that Asians never entered the promised world of Idaho's state shield. An article in the state's major paper noted that "a majority of the citizens are determined that they shall not return. A gentleman from that town [Nampa] said last evening that the Chinese, too, would be told before sunrise today that they must speedily leave, never to return."[68]

The Japanese, however, did stay. They were vital to the development of the railroad, the only feasible transportation infrastructure that could tie Idaho to the outside world it was so cut off from geographically. Given Idaho's late start as a state, it had to connect quickly to outside markets for its growing resource-based economy to prosper. As the *Idaho Daily Statesman* noted in 1897, railroad companies increasingly relied upon Japanese labor: "Short Line Section men are very generally Japanese now and their quitting work would cause the company much inconvenience."[69] Company officials considered them ideal workers, as evidenced by one official's comments before Congress: "they require less watching, they are peaceable and tractable . . . their camps are free from disturbance . . . and they are most adaptable."[70]

They were also cheap. On average, Japanese railroad workers in Idaho earned only $1.00 per day in 1892, and they were at times paid as much as $2.00 per day less than white workers.[71] Pay increases came neither often nor easily. Given the increased labor conflict in the United States during this period, especially in Idaho, it is not surprising that Japanese workers occasionally went on strike. The prize won, however, was sometimes startlingly small. In early August of 1897, Japanese workers went on strike in protest of a 10-cent pay cut, from $1.25 per day to $1.15 per day. A compromise was soon reached by which they accepted a 5-cent pay cut. After the strike ended, a company official pointed out that the company was, after all, providing the workers now with both free wood and water.[72] In a later incident, Japanese section hands struck in the summer of 1905, only so they could rest.[73]

At roughly the same time, Idaho's sugar beet industry began, and it, too, relied on Japanese labor. Throughout the West, companies had looked to Japanese workers to do the taxing work of tending and harvesting their fields, and companies recruited Japanese to work in the growing beet fields of Idaho.[74] In 1906, in Nampa, the Oregon Short Line's central station in southwest Idaho, a sugar beet factory that required a 289-foot well, a 95,000-gallon water tank, and an overall investment of over $1,000,000 was built.[75] Although it was located in the sagebrush desert, Nampa, from its establishment in 1885, was advertised by the Oregon Short Line as a kind of new Eden:

IRRIGATED LANDS

★ ★ ★ ★ ★ ★ ★ ★ ★ ★

SECURE A HOME

IN IDAHO . . . .

The Choicest Garden Spot of the

Rocky Mountains

In fact, Nampa often was referred to as New Jerusalem, though its name apparently came from that of a local Shoshone chief. Clearly, such claims were, at the time, stretches of the imagination. Once the railroad set down in Nampa and the water came to it from the various irrigation projects in southwest Idaho, however, it experienced a boom. As a recent history of Nampa notes, "with these two enterprises, Nampa was 'christened.'"[76]

Some current histories do acknowledge the vital role of Japanese in this process of giving places in Idaho a name. However, the cost of their effort is sometimes obfuscated by the tendency to tell a tale of Progress and to collapse the lives traditionally outside this tale into a generality. In his comprehensive two-volume official *History of Idaho*, published in 1994, historian Leonard Arrington writes, "as Buddhists and Shintoists, the Japanese had learned to accept what happens, to show gratitude for what they had, and to know that everything would come out right."[77] Yet newspaper accounts of the time, such as those about striking Japanese railroad workers, suggest more than just passive fatalism. In the *Idaho Daily Statesman* of September 2, 1903, an article, "Japanese Discharged," recounts the release of A. Asano and H. Haruta, two Japanese who were "alleged to have assaulted Section Foreman Dahlgren." That these workers would apparently lash out at their overseer certainly questions the image of Japanese men who would merely "show gratitude for what they had."

Such statements also gloss over the deprivation and the abuse these men faced. The article about Asano and Haruta explains that the local authorities released them because "it was soon brought out that the confession secured . . . from the prisoners, while in jail, was obtained by undue influence."[78] Without their accounts, we can only imagine just what "undue influence" was. Accounts from other Japanese and markers in the landscape tell us that these men may often have found little in Idaho for which to show gratitude. Just as nature had little reason to "beam o'er the land in gratitude" once Progress had claimed Idaho, Nikkei in the young state often had to endure Progress's march.

Digging through the folders of interviews, photos, and other files at the

State Historical Society, I came across two small pieces of paper torn out of a tablet. They had no label to identify who wrote on them. They were maps. The first showed a highway curving down across the top edge of the paper, with what looked like trees represented underneath. A railroad line ran along the bottom, parallel to the edge of the paper, and an old road snaked between the highway and the railroad line, past a little box marked "GRAVE." On the second page was a drawing of the grave. It had, as the notations on the paper indicated, a small iron fence around it. It read:

KANKUI OHAYE
NATIVE OF JAPAN
DIED MAY 14 1891
AGED
42 YEARS

The location of the grave was near a place called King Hill. There was no town or street name. I wondered if it was in Nampa and who visited there. I remembered the words of another Idahoan who recounted their lives: "And they worked through the winter and it was really hard for some of them, because they didn't have enough, they didn't know anything about nutrition. And some of the earlier ones, they really ruined their health by eating dough balls. Flour and water, they didn't have good food. And some of the young men died. They're buried in a cemetery here in Nampa. Almost lost and lone people."[79]

Memory Road

In scraggly handwriting on the sheet of paper, above the name on the marker, was written "3 missing letters." Not even the name of the man remained. Absences.

I made a photocopy. It sits pinned on a bulletin board above me as I write this, for it haunts me. It haunts me as do my own absences, what memory must recover.

I sometimes recount the images: my aunt hurriedly burning all things Japanese, a yard sale, and a scroll of family history my father remembered his mother showing him as a child.

After my father died, while cleaning out his office and sorting through the years of his medical career, I came across articles I had never seen. After his own rail trip along the Oregon Short Line, accompanied by an armed guard, my father recounted his awe at the skyscrapers of Philadelphia. There was a photo of him and three other young Nisei,[80] on what I imagine were the library steps of Temple University.

A postcard fell out of a folder—another Hayashi. It was his statue in some town in Japan. He sat cross-legged and proud. I had never seen the name. No one knew who he was. There is now no one to ask.

When I was a kid, my best friend and I, the one I traveled with in northern Idaho that summer, spent hours picking through the ripped-open ground of new home sites in our neighborhood searching for fossils. Today, he is a geologist. And, I wonder, how much different this is: sorting though the land and seeking some imprint of the past, a story, something I can hold in my hand to say, "This happened."

Steelheads

It was Wednesday morning. The too cheery news anchor on the TV informed me it was a day when "we might see that mercury hit 100 again!" It was nearly the end of August, and the total precipitation for the month read 00.00 on the TV screen. Up the Boise Canyon, near the old site of the Foote's Stone House in the Canon, a brush fire started by a road crew burned perilously close to the new expensive homes that look out over Boise. Smoke drifted down into the city. That week newspaper and TV reports excitedly reported the news that someone had paid $1,000,000 for a plot of land up there.

I drove through town on my way to Nampa and passed by one of the new buildings rising up downtown. A banner read, "Future Home of the Steelheads." I could only snicker at the thought of a minor league hockey player from Moose Jaw landing in Boise and stepping out onto this moonscape. "Pretty dry here, eh?" The only skates I saw were rollerblades on a tanned woman who zipped through downtown with sunglasses and a Walkman, hopping curbs, and flashing a barbed-wire pattern tattoo on her back.

Steelhead are the native anadromous species of the rainbow trout, and they once swam throughout much of the Snake River drainage, their movement limited only by natural barriers like Shoshone Falls. Lewis and Clark noted them several times in their journals as they passed through the Columbia River drainage on their way to the ocean in search of that elusive Northwest Passage. Like their freshwater cousins, steelhead are a prized quarry among anglers for they possess the same fighting habits of freshwater rainbows, but in a long taut body adapted to the open Pacific. When hooked, a steelhead, which can reach well over twenty pounds, will seek the shortest distance between itself and the Pacific. Many an angler has had the thrill of racing down a Northwest river trying to catch up with this fish. The official highway map of Idaho notes that they "symbolize all that is wild in Idaho." Again, loss is commemorated, the costs of the dominant vision's "soft caress where all was wilderness."

Steelhead populations, like those of the cutthroat, in Idaho and throughout the West are reeling from the body blows of development. In recent years, their populations have crashed. They are now protected by the Endangered Species Act, and it is illegal to keep, or to "harvest," a wild steelhead in Idaho. Only hatchery steelhead, identified by their clipped adipose fin, may be kept. As recently as the early 1960s, the number of wild steelhead passing through the uppermost stretches of Idaho's rivers was estimated at over 100,000 fish. During much of the 1990s, the number was less than 10,000, although the numbers have recently rebounded.[81] The precarious state of this species, the epitome of all that is "wild in Idaho," is mostly the result of the very process that brought such astounding development to this isolated area: the large dams that have tamed its major rivers and brought cheap power to its homes and businesses and potatoes to my grocery store. Not only do these dams provide a daunting unnatural barrier to spawning fish heading upriver to their birth waters, but they act as a thresher for the smolt heading downriver. They also diminish overall water quality. The first dam built on the Snake was near Boise and was to provide power to the Owyhee silver and gold mines. Its location is now a historical site. But for the steelhead, the series of dams and associated reservoirs that men have imposed upon these waters are not, as the Idaho Power brochure I got back at that coffee shop claims, a history to tout. This may be, as the brochure claims, "Fun Country!" for boaters, jet skiers, and others, but not for steelhead.[82]

Monarch

It was hot, hot, hot. I scanned the radio dial for any decent music to drown out the dull hum of the rental car's air conditioning: religious stations, pop radio, and classic rock. "Thank god for NPR," I eventually exclaimed. For connections to back East.

I was driving west on I-84 to Nampa, to meet with Mary Fujii Henshall, a local Nisei who has spent years collecting her family's history and speaking about local Nikkei history to civic groups, classrooms, Kiwanis, and travelers like myself—a restless graduate student with a need to discover the earth. Everyone had said, "You should talk to Mary." I had read about her father, Henry Fujii, in the articles I collected in Boise. Her brother, Ed, was that talented fisherman whom I heard about from Clayne. I thought about the fishing he must have seen before all the big dams were completed, before Idaho became discovered by the angling world, and how digging uncovers the connections between us.

The map she mailed me noted a shopping center with a Safeway, that chain of grocery stores common in the West. I saw it and knew I was not lost. She had warned me that people get lost driving out her way. The city was billowing outward toward Boise. The farther west I drove, away from the old center of town, the newer were the small bunches of stores, restaurants, and gas stations that commonly define today's American landscape. During the 1990s, Nampa grew by over eighty percent, and it is now the state's second largest city. A sign on my right, demarcating another one of those pockets of drab convenience, read Owyhee Plaza.

I did, as she had warned, end up driving by her house, but soon realized when I saw the open dry fields—the first I had seen in Nampa—that I had passed her driveway. I turned around and pulled into the gravel drive. Her house was set back in a thick stand of trees. A bulldozer rumbled on the slope above and kicked up dust. By the time I closed the car's door, she was standing at her front steps in a bright shirt and orange beads, an even brighter grin. "Well, hello, Robert!" She led me into her home and invited me to sit on the big green couch. There were articles and photos out in anticipation of my visit and cool lemonade. I looked around the living room: framed photographs of loved ones, plants, a sleeping Persian cat, and lots of rocks. It was surprisingly cool with no air conditioning.

She hurried around the corner and just as quickly came around the other side, a small cage in her hand. It held a butterfly. It was a monarch with a tiny white tag on its wing. The state butterfly of Idaho had found a friend here.

Mary raises them. This one was to be released that day. She told me how they were threatened now because of destruction of their host plant, the milkweed, on which the female lays her eggs and on which the larvae feed before their eventual emergence into the sky.

"People just think it's a weed, and they cut it down."

I realized then how this weed had vanished from my own childhood home in Pennsylvania when all the new houses went up. I used to run through fields of blackberries, mustard, and milkweed. I can't remember the last time I saw one. But the monarchs, like Westerners, including those similarly classified as weeds, as outsiders, have adapted before. In fact, as I later learned, the land shelters the monarch. The sap of the milkweed contains a chemical that birds find unpalatable; when a bird tries to eat this butterfly, it soon changes its mind.

I told Mary how, when I lived in Oregon, I looked out the window one day to see the sky filled with them. I ran outside and just stood there by a plum tree, turning and turning in the black and orange confetti.

We talked about the changes the land of the West had seen, so that now the history it holds was threatened with erasure. Her father once filled boxes with arrowheads found in his fields. The owls had left the fence posts up the road, and the polliwogs no longer filled the irrigation ditches.

"That's what happens to the monarch, you know. When you have a mall, and it's all paved over, and you have a freeway or something. . . . They're not going to be home."

I thought of this symbiotic pairing: a Japanese American woman and a butterfly. It reminded me of the standard conflations of the past, the romanticized fetishisms of the Western gaze into the East, of "Un bel di," the aria from Puccini's famous opera *Madama Butterfly*. In Puccini's work, a white American naval officer conquers his own butterfly—a Japanese woman, Japan herself. Americans have moved little beyond these views of Asian female identity, as sexualized and submissive. And, though Asian American scholars and writers have sharply critiqued this history of American Orientalism,[83] little attention has been paid to Asians' views of the American environment, how they have offered visions of it that complicate dominant narratives of the land they share with other Americans.[84]

To Touch the Earth

If Puccini's opera *Madama Butterfly* was but another stereotypical portrayal of Japanese women and Japan, Puccini had at least one thing right: American men and their expansive visions would play an important role in the lives of the Japanese. Since 1639, Japan had remained isolated from Western influence. Admiral Perry's "opening" of its main harbor in 1853, however, served as the catalyst for major changes in Japan. It brought about the Meiji Restoration that unified Japan and began its rapid modernization and industrialization at the turn of the century. Jeffersonian democracy was, after all, a land-hungry vision that provided a rationale for American colonialism, both in the Americas and in the Pacific. In fact, during the Lewis and Clark Centennial Exposition and Oriental Fair in 1904, the Corps's long ignored journey was recollected and celebrated as the precur-

sor to the colonial expansion into Asia that defined America after the
Spanish-American War.[85] Even Walt Whitman, the poet of democracy, had
not been averse to American expansion across the seas. He celebrated it:

> I chant the world on my Western sea,
> I chant copious the islands beyond, thick as stars in the sky,
> I chant the new empire grander than any before, as in a vision it
>   comes to me,
> I chant America the mistress, I chant a greater supremacy,
> I chant projected a thousand blooming cities yet in time on those
>   groups of sea-islands,
> My sail-ships and steam-ships threading the archipelagoes,
> My stars and stripes fluttering in the wind.[86]

Whitman wrote these words, an address to Libertad, on the occasion of a
visit by a Japanese diplomatic delegation to the United States in 1860. In
the poem, he described the Japanese and Japan from an Orientalist perspective similar to Puccini's. He portrayed the Japanese delegation as feminine, passive, and erotic.

> The Originatress comes,
> The nest of languages, the bequeather of poems, the race of eld,
> Florid with blood, pensive, rapt with musings, hot with passion,
> Sultry with perfume, with ample and flowing garments,
> With sunburnt visage, with intense soul and glittering eyes . . .[87]

Whitman respected the contributions of these "bare-headed, impassive
envoys"; but they represented a race, like the Indians before them, upon
whom the sun had set. Their future was now at the feet of America: "They
shall now also march obediently eastward for your sake / Libertad."[88]

And come they did. When the Meiji government instituted new taxes to
support its modernization—programs to centralize Japanese life in education, economics, religion, and military affairs—Japanese farmers found it
increasingly difficult to shoulder the new burden. Scores lost their farmlands. During just the 1880s, over 300,000 Japanese lost their land.[89] Once
the Japanese government eased restrictions on emigration, Issei men traveled eastward in search of opportunity.[90] The first wave of migration was
to Hawaii, where most of them worked on the sugar plantations, many as
contract laborers. It is where my grandfather began our American story,
one that would eventually lead him to die a prisoner under its open sky in a
place in Idaho called Minidoka.

Between 1885 and 1924, 180,000 Japanese traveled to the continental United States, settling primarily along the West Coast.[91] Many of these pioneers shared a vision similar to the Jeffersonian dream of independent farmers spread across these open spaces. Having been displaced by the economic conditions at home, they sought to establish themselves in the soil of places like southwest Idaho. Henry Fujii, Mary's father, came to Idaho in 1907. He recalled his dream years later: "I want [to] become farmer in America."[92] These pioneers from the Pacific, however, would soon find that their visions—though consistent in many ways with those of Jefferson, Whitman, and Arthur Foote—would not easily find a foothold in the virgin land of the West. The mass immigration of large numbers of Japanese women to the United States at the turn of the century created the opportunity to establish communities in California, Washington, Idaho, and wherever the Issei traveled into America. Yet, along with this settlement of the West by Japanese grew nativist fears about its imperiled purity. In an article dated June 7, 1900, in the *Elmore Bulletin*, entitled "The Japs Are Coming," the writer denounced the influx of Japanese into Idaho because, they "are utterly destitute of all the characteristics that go to make up civilized man in the Anglo-Saxon or American sense. . . . They are, moreover, like the Chinese, absolutely unassimilable."[93]

Despite the popularity of these views among white Americans, in some instances, these "Japs" displayed the cultural markers that allegedly defined Americans before they even landed on its shore. They already were marked by qualities that constituted a "civilized man in the American sense." The recognition of this by official gatekeepers could even allow them entry into the West and its putatively democratic spaces. When he arrived at the port of Seattle in 1906, Henry Fujii, then Hajimu Fujii, was met by his hometown friend, who acted as translator for Henry as he passed through immigration services. The immigration official asked Fujii what was in his bag. When his friend Hashitani related that he had mostly books, including a Bible, the official immediately waved Fujii through, never searching his bag.[94] Fujii's identity as a Christian highlights the problematic assumptions of historians who attempt to explain the Nikkei experience in Idaho, in the West, based upon a collective, homogeneous, and inflexible Japanese identity. The West was already in the East. In 1907, the Reverend Orio Inouye of Seattle came to Boise to solicit the help of state officials in establishing a colony of 500 families near Nampa—a Christian colony.[95]

Reverend Inouye's attempt to lobby local legislators was necessitated by a state law that barred Asian immigrants from land ownership, legislation originally promulgated during the territorial period to deny mining claims to Chinese.[96] Individuals like Henry Fujii, who sought to establish themselves as farmers, were forced to lease land from others, and under these conditions they began their work of transforming the state into the garden others had long imagined. They were crucial contributors to the state's first major agricultural industry—sugar beets—and not just as pickers. By 1913, they grew over one third of the state's entire sugar beet crop.[97] After leasing small plots of land and raising cash crops, such as lettuce and radishes, for truck farming, Henry Fujii purchased forty acres of land in 1918 by using the one loophole that these land laws allowed. Since his children were by birth "natural" citizens of Idaho, American by birthright, he purchased the land in their names and eventually enjoyed a career as a successful and innovative farmer.

Henry Fujii sold produce throughout southwestern Idaho, and he shipped his fresh produce across the sage flats along the Oregon Short Line that he had briefly worked on when he arrived in the Northwest. Yet, the agricultural success of men like Henry Fujii and their families in "these deserts of North America" was seen by many as a threat. Across the West, beginning in California, a new wave of discriminatory legislation swept away the loopholes in existing land laws. In 1915, the first such measure directly targeting the Japanese was introduced in the Idaho legislature, but it failed to pass. Representative Thompson of Minidoka County, speaking in support of a later version of such a bill, argued, "When we take property from the Japanese we are only taking back our birth right. They have no right to inheritance in this country . . . they are unassimilable. If they are not, why do we have marriage laws?"[98] To Thompson, past discrimination provided the rationale for further denial of rights. It was only natural. Each subsequent legislative session voted on a form of the bill until it finally passed in 1923. However, the lobbying of sugar beet companies and Japanese associations, groups which worked in conjunction with Japanese officials to protect the rights of Issei in the area, insured Japanese the opportunity to continue to lease land for five-year periods.[99] It was, at the time, the only state in the West to allow Japanese aliens to lease land.

In 1921, Mr. Fujii purchased another forty acres, the land upon which his daughter still lives. That same year, he testified at a meeting at the Boise First Congregational Church on January 23. He was president of the

Japanese Association of Idaho, and at this meeting he expressed his strong connections to his adopted land. "Mr. Fujii, a Japanese farmer living near Nampa, spoke briefly of his love for America and his desire to have his children raised as Americans."[100] The meeting had been called to discuss the latest proposed alien land law, and a guest speaker, Colonel John P. Irish of California, was invited to speak about the status of this issue in his home state. Colonel Irish noted the outrageous claims by Californians that Japanese would take over their state. Irish remarked that the Japanese generally farmed land that "no white man would touch," and that "when the history of agriculture in California is written that chapter in it that will honestly tell the work of Japanese genius and toil in the reclamation to fertility of bad lands will read like a romance."[101] Yet if, as Colonel Irish claimed, this story of Issei in the West were told, it could not "officially" be a romance. It was still a story of love from afar, a love unrequited, since they could not claim the land, the white robe of Idaho, or any of her sister states.

At nearly the same time that members of the Boise community met to discuss the state's alien land law, the federal government was cementing the foundation of such discriminatory measures, the alien status of nonnative Asians. Takao Ozawa was a Japanese immigrant who had been denied citizenship, and his case eventually reached the United States Supreme Court in 1921. Ozawa's seemed the ideal test case, given his embrace of American life and his lack of Japanese cultural markers. He met the required residency and language requirements of the Naturalization Act of 1906, the amended version of the nation's original 1790 naturalization legislation. He spoke English at home and had raised his children as Christians. Observers agreed that his character was beyond reproach. Ozawa saw himself as a model American, claiming, "My honesty and industriousness are well known among my Japanese and American acquaintances and friends; and I am always trying my best to conduct myself according to the Golden Rule."[102] The Quota Immigration Act of 1921, which limited the number of immigrants from each country to three percent of the number of foreign-born persons of that nation counted in the 1910 census, had effectively diminished future Japanese immigration to a trickle. However, some argued that the body of the American polity was still threatened. Eventually, the Supreme Court ruled against Ozawa and for the United States. The Court determined that the group of persons eligible for naturalization, "free white persons," did not include Asians.[103] According to the Court's holding, prior judicial and also scientific inquiry had established a "racial and not an individual test . . . fortified as it is by reason and authority" that excluded Asians from this classification. The Court further noted the need to prevent "a confused overlapping of races and a gradual merging of one into the other, without any practical separation."[104] Again, the reasoning of scientific inquiry had defined the makeup of America. It was taxonomy. For more than thirty years, Japanese immigrants would remain unnatural residents of America.

More Rock Hounds

Despite passage of Idaho's Alien Land Law, Henry Fujii continued to work the land owned by his children in accordance with the natural rights conferred upon them as native inhabitants of Idaho. He grew lettuce, potatoes, corn, hay, and onions. In 1936, he established the Japanese Onion Growers Association, for which he served as president for over thirty years. Mr. Fujii was a pioneer of large-scale onion farming in Idaho. He recalled in a 1971 interview, "I had, the first year, I had five acres onions. And farmers round here, nobody seen any five acres onions, so Mr. Lewis, living over here, Lewis Avenue. Mr. Richard. Charlie Suckers. All neighbors come round here and see how I take care of five acres. And next two, three years, they all have thirty, forty acres onions. . . . But that's the way we started onion growing around this section."[105] In 2001, Idaho's total production of onions ranked third in the country.[106] Fujii even found use for the waste of his onion fields. As insulation, he lined the attic of his home, in which I sat that hot dry August morning looking out over the Owyhees, with the onion skins left over from harvest. After he retired, Henry Fujii recalled his first impression of Idaho: "We thought it's a good farming country. That's [what] we wanted."[107]

I left his home, after talking with his daughter for nearly six hours about his life and the crossings of my own family on this land, how it has shaped me. I paused to look at the white storage building and the old house the Fujiis built when they first bought this property. Mary and I walked out in the heat by the old Japanese garden at its entrance. Only some stacked lava rocks now hint at her father's work. Kids had broken into both buildings in the past and stolen things, even door hinges. Mary makes sure to lock the house.

I thought of a poem her mother wrote that Mary read to me, a Japanese senryu:

Arrowheads
Indians lived and dreamed here.

The land is full of stories if we look: stories of how people and species learn to adapt. How the dreams, both natural and unnatural, meet and shape the land, and how sometimes that is all we have left. How even play has a toll we must pay. How some of us have learned—by pain and pleasure, by memory and vision, and by experience and force of law—to match the hatch.

Before I left, Mary showed me the rocks: petrified wood, rare minerals, semi-precious stones, and geodes her father collected when he became a rockhound upon retirement.

"See how pretty they are when you cut them open?"

She placed a clear slab of mineral the size of a small book on top of a playing card, "Look into it," she beckoned. Somehow, the card appeared embedded halfway in the rock, just like the light in the desert, another trick of the eye.

She was still standing on her driveway as I waved and drove down to the fields, where a sign marked the new housing development that would now claim this space of Idaho, these forty acres: Fujii Farms.

Under the smoky Owyhee Mountains, the orange bulldozer labored, swept away the earth to lay the pattern of streets, cables, and new foundations. This place is christened again.

The Great Seal of the state of Idaho.
COURTESY IDAHO STATE HISTORICAL SOCIETY.

The Irrigating Ditch by Mary Hallock Foote.

Henry and Fumiko Fujii's sixtieth wedding anniversary, 1971.

Chapter 3

O PIONEERS

The Democratic Spaces of Minidoka

Democratic social space would, ideally, be a universal and everywhere similar medium in which rights and opportunities are identical, a space in which the right and even the ability to move from place to place is assured . . . the absence of limits, openness to immigration and expatriation, internal mobility: these would seem to be essential features.

PHILIP FISHER, "Democratic Social Space: Whitman, Melville, and the Promise of American Transparency"

Oh, give me land, lots of land
Under starry skies above
Don't fence me in.

COLE PORTER, "Don't Fence Me In"

O resistless restless race!
O beloved race in all! O my breast aches with tender love for all!
I mourn and yet exult, I am rapt with love for all,
Pioneers, O Pioneers!

WALT WHITMAN, "Pioneers! O Pioneers!"

Just outside of Twin Falls, I passed by a field that exploded in splotches of yellow along its edges. The fencerows and roadside were lined by tall flowers, the common sunflower. Off in the distance was a gap in the earth, where the Snake River winds through this dry plateau. Twin Falls derives its name from the nearby waterfalls that have since disappeared with the introduction of irrigation and hydropower to the region. Locals wryly refer to them as "Double Drip."[1] Even the yellow-headed sunflowers, indigenous to Idaho, hinted at the manipulation of this landscape, having first spread across the state with the introduction of agriculture and now found most commonly in the waste spaces of farms.[2] At one time, investors had hoped to make the area a vacation spot, where travelers would come to view the spectacular Shoshone Falls, a few miles upriver. The falls, once called the Niagara of the West, are still there but are often completely dry due to the massive amount of water drawn out of the Snake for irrigation.

The city's current notoriety comes from its college basketball team, one of the best junior college programs in the nation, and from the 1974 attempt by Evel Knievel to launch himself across the Snake River just outside of town. On the other side of the river, the side Knievel never reached, I passed by the obligatory truck stop and motel that define most exits off the major interstate slicing through southern Idaho. A few miles up the road were lush rolling hills and horses gamboling behind white fences; an iron gateway had a huge sign, El Rancho Casta Plente. Somehow the sign did not fit well with the Idaho I had imagined, especially the history I drove here to find: the World War II concentration camp just north of here, where nearly 10,000 Nikkei, mainly from the coastal Pacific Northwest, lived out amidst the sagebrush and rattlesnakes. I took a left and headed west, drove a few miles and saw the telltale structure, a squat, boxlike barrack across from the small county airport. But there were no signs, nothing telling me this was it, and I reached over the seat and looked at the map. I had made a wrong turn back at the highway; I turned the car around, and after fifteen minutes I came across a sign, another one of those large wooden frames with a map and brief synopsis of the site that the state has placed all over Idaho:

> HUNT
> EXCLUDED FROM THEIR WEST COAST
> HOMES BY MILITARY AUTHORITIES, MORE
> THAN 9000 JAPANESE AMERICANS
> OCCUPIED HUNT RELOCATION CAMP 4 MILES
> NORTH OF HERE BETWEEN 1942 & 1945

I lay down on the quiet rural highway and took some pictures of the sign. It was peppered with bullet holes, dozens of them.

The Closing Frontier

Masuo Yasui had made it. Having emigrated to the United States in 1903 with little but his fanciful dreams of success, by 1941, he owned several hundred acres of farmland in Oregon, near Hood River, operated a successful general store, and had helped organize the area's first agricultural association, the Mid-Columbia Vegetable Growers Association. With assets of more than half-a-million dollars, he enjoyed many of the perquisites of the American middle class. He owned a comfortable home in Hood River and his children were in college. One son, Minoru, was a lawyer, and when he graduated from the University of Oregon School of Law in 1939 at the age of twenty-three, he was the first lawyer of Japanese descent in Oregon's history.[3] Near the terminal point of Lewis and Clark's journey, Yasui's life seemed a fitting example of the Western frontier's plenipotentiary promise to the individual, to Americans.

The reality of Masuo Yasui's life, however, contrasted greatly with the frontier success story drawn from these limited facts. Yasui's Japanese ancestry had continually limited his access to the putative fruits of American democracy. What appeared as perhaps an unimpinged ascent was really a constant struggle against the limitations of a racist social landscape that defined Western democracy as white-only from its inception and which only grew worse for Japanese as perceptions of them became more menacing. Yasui's primary asset, his land, was not even his. Barred from owning property due to Oregon's Alien Land Law, Yasui had registered his land holdings under the names of his children, who were American by birthright. The Japanese attack on Pearl Harbor, however, would forever change the lives of the Yasuis and thousands of other Nikkei, erasing even the "natural" rights that their children enjoyed, as well as their presence on the land itself.

Driving along the Columbia River Gorge on I-84, you will find no signs, no historical markers to remind you of the once influential presence of Japanese immigrants such as Masuo Yasui, how they forever altered this landscape. Although orchards still line the river and surrounding area, and Hood River pears and apples enjoy near mythic status among epicures, it is the uniquely powerful and consistent winds—conditions ideal for windsurfing—that now attract people to the area. Late model BMWs, old VW microbuses, and the latest Japanese imports line the road, all with boardsail racks and carrying individuals who seek the unique thrill of flying across water. This not only suggests the way in which our use of the Western landscape has often shifted dramatically from production to recreation, uses often at odds with each other, but also how the contributions of men like Yasui have been omitted from a national mythos, the settlement of the open West. Major texts about Western American history or about the Western landscape either wholly ignore the contributions of Japanese immigrants and their children or discuss these people only from the limited perspective of their victimization.

Although no comprehensive study of the Western landscape in relation to Nikkei exists, as Western historian Patricia Limerick notes, "no Asian or Asian-American equivalents to *Virgin Land*, *The Machine in the Garden*, *Exploration and Empire* and *Wilderness and the American Mind*" have been written; individual narratives exist, and they often present a view strikingly similar to that of other American pioneers, despite the exclusion Asians experienced.[4] Masuo Yasui recalled his reasons for coming to the United States, "I heard that the United States was a huge country—and that it was a country where one could act as he wished."[5] Like their white European counterparts, these pioneers primarily sought economic opportunity.

Men like Masuo Yasui and Henry Fujii also attempted to establish themselves within the larger white community, although their lives were clearly demarcated by racial boundaries. The integration they did enjoy was often solely in economic terms; social boundaries were harder to cross. Japanese immigrants often created their own unique ethnic communities of retail stores, bath houses, and temples, products of both their voluntary ethnic solidarity and enforced segregation. Limerick notes, "the Japanese discovered a landscape of restriction—in prohibitions on alien land ownership, in housing segregation, and in episodes of harassment when they crossed certain boundaries of space and behavior."[6] Despite Masuo Yasui's prominent role in Hood River, his family remained apart from that community. The family had little social contact with their white neighbors, and the children played among themselves, often camping out along the Columbia River and fishing its then salmon-choked waters.

Just downriver, at the mouth of the Columbia, was the winter camp of Lewis and Clark, who had lived among the local Indians during the rainy winter of 1806 before they began their long journey home. The cooperation with natives necessitated by their trek at times forced Lewis and Clark and their multiracial group of military men, civilian guides, and interpreters to glance beyond their culture's narrow view of race. In some instances, their actions suggested new possibilities for racial relations in the growing democracy, possibilities that faded upon their reentry into it. When the Corps of Discovery pondered where to make camp that winter, all of its members voted, including both Sacajawea, the teenage Shoshone "wife" of Toussaint Charbonneau, and also Clark's slave, York. However, when they returned to the East after the successful completion of their remarkable journey, York never received any compensation for his part in the quest, and Clark repeatedly denied his requests to be freed. [7]

The restrictions placed upon members of the Japanese American community after Pearl Harbor, culminating in the eventual incarceration of their West Coast population, were merely extensions of the historical exclusion of minorities from America's Golden West. Despite evidence from both the FBI and the Naval Intelligence Service that Nikkei posed no threat to national security, on February 19, 1942, President Franklin Roosevelt signed Executive Order 9066. This act empowered military officials "to prescribe military areas . . . from which any or all persons may be excluded, and with respect to which, the right of any person to enter, remain in, or leave shall be subject to whatever restrictions the Secretary of War or the appropriate Military Commander may impose in his discretion."[8] That order, and others that followed, never specifically mentioned Nikkei, but were directly targeted at them and their mobility. The order basically ceded to the military control over defining these sensitive regions and to whom these restrictions would apply, placing great power in the hands of the area's commanding officer, General John Dewitt. Dewitt first issued orders designating the entire West Coast of the United States and the southern part of Arizona a military zone, Military Area 1. The remaining sections of these states were later deemed, by the general's orders, Military Area 2.

The predominance of "military necessity" in the governing of this geographic region set into motion the eventual stripping away of individuals' constitutional rights, but only ethnic Japanese citizens suffered the loss of their allegedly "natural" rights. The next month all people of Japanese ancestry, as well as Italian and German aliens, who resided on the West Coast were required to adhere to a nightly curfew. They had to be home between the hours of 8 P.M. and 6 A.M. Travel outside of a five-mile radius of one's home was forbidden. Public Proclamation Number 4, issued on March 27, 1942, mandated that all affected residents of Military Area 1 remain in that region after midnight March 29. Nikkei were now a threat to the land itself: to irrigation canals, seaports, and hydroelectric dams. Rumors circulated about fifth column activities: how "Japs" were planning to poison their produce or the water supplies of the West. Local politicians and the media agreed that the "Japanese problem" needed containment. "Herd 'em up, pack 'em off and give them the inside room in the Badlands," wrote Henry McLenmore, a columnist for the influential Hearst newspaper conglomerate, which took a virulently anti-Japanese position.[9]

Masuo Yasui's attorney son, Minoru, a member of the Army Reserve, was living in Chicago when Japanese planes struck Pearl Harbor. He immediately resigned his position there at the Japanese consulate and left Chicago to report for active duty. At the train station, however, he was prevented from purchasing a ticket and had to visit the Union Pacific's legal office before he was authorized to ride the train. Min returned to Oregon, where he attempted to report for duty at Fort Vancouver but was denied.

The FBI had arrested his father, along with hundreds of other prominent Issei in the first few days following the attack, and he was now held at Fort Missoula in Montana. Distressed by the apparent unconstitutionality of the federal orders affecting West Coast Nikkei, which he viewed as "an effrontery to the name of democracy," Min decided to challenge the first order deriving from the discriminatory 9066, the curfew order.[10] He intentionally had himself arrested to force a trial that would test the legality of these government directives. Before his trial date, the federal government issued evacuation orders, and all Portland area Nikkei were forced to report to a temporary "assembly center," where they would await their fate, eventual removal to a "relocation center" in Idaho.

This assembly center was on the grounds of the North Portland International Livestock Exposition, and its horse stalls became the new homes for these residents of the greater Portland area, who had not been charged with any crime or violation. Authorities soon moved Min to the Multnomah County Jail to await his trial on June 12, 1942. After his day in court, he returned to Portland Assembly Center, and in September he was sent to Minidoka. The following month he returned to Portland to hear the verdict in his case. He lost. The presiding judge ruled that Min had, in effect, renounced his citizenship because of his work at the Japanese consulate, and he sentenced him to one year in jail and a $5,000 fine. Min Yasui immediately appealed his case to the Ninth Circuit Court of Appeals which, under pressure from federal authorities, refused to rule on it, sending it instead directly to the United States Supreme Court. Meanwhile, Min spent his days writing letters and poems while living in solitary confinement in a windowless six-by-eight foot cell. He did not bathe for weeks. Although he was confined under such inhumane conditions and had not received the backing of prominent groups like the American Civil Liberties Union or the Japanese American Citizens League, Min remained steadfast in his legal struggle.[11] In response to an Easter greeting he received in 1943, Min wrote, "At a time like this, when the world is at war, and when I am physically confined within a tiny solitary cell, I can still thank God that my mind, my spirit and my soul is free."[12] Finally, on June 21, 1943, the court handed down its decision. It reinstated Min's citizenship, but claimed that, contrary to the original judge's opinion, the federal government did have the right to restrict the lives of citizens during wartime. Only one judge dissented.[13] Police escorted Min Yasui, once again an American citizen, to the fenced boundaries of Minidoka Relocation Center.

Although Idaho's Nikkei community and the neighboring Snake River, Oregon, Nikkei community avoided relocation since they were outside of Military Area 1, federal authorities issued restrictions on their movements. The hysterical claims of local politicians and media and preexisting nativism made the Issei and Nisei of the West Coast a single entity, a monolithic racial beast that was best hidden away in the interior West by the long reach of the federal government. West Coast Japanese had actually volunteered to resettle in Idaho before evacuation became mandatory, but this migration soon met with resistance, especially from Idaho's governor, Chase Clark, who was adamant in his refusal to allow Japanese from the West Coast to settle in the Gem State. When Nikkei arranged to purchase land to establish such communities, on several occasions Clark intervened to bar the purchases, despite the fact that the federal government officially encouraged such "voluntary" resettlement. He envisioned an invasion: "My only thought now is to keep Idaho for Idahoans, and not to sell it to the Japanese. There is nothing un-American about my taking that position. If we permit them to come in here and buy the land, there would be one hundred thousand here before the summer starts."[14] To Clark, all Nikkei, regardless of citizenship status, were "Japanese," and thus the rights they enjoyed were of no consequence. He justified his position by claiming that "recognizing their constitutional rights and being good to them is flowery language."[15] During this period of "voluntary evacuation" 305 Nikkei settled in Idaho. Despite the restrictions of Public Proclamation Number 4, some Nikkei were still allowed passage out of Military Area 1. Over 4,000 left to resettle in other regions, most in areas of California within the region designated Military Area 2, from which they, too, would later be evacuated.[16] They had escaped nothing.

The federal government shared a similar view to the one expressed by Idaho's xenophobic governor. As the ironic title of Mine Okubo's memoir, Citizen 13660, indicates, the government reduced Nikkei to a nonparticularized subject, a gesture in contrast with the vaulted status of the individual in Jeffersonian democracy and the popular cultural mythology of the American West. The policies and actions of the War Relocation Authority, the federal agency created to manage the relocation, illustrate this historical tendency to treat Nikkei as a homogeneous foreign body that must be managed and contained. Ted Matsuda, a Seattle resident at the outbreak of the war, who was interned at Minidoka, recalls in his diary that his family became family 17625.[17] In my father's WRA files, I found that we were family 6447, and that he was assigned the cataloglike designation, 6447-A.

The wartime relocation of Nikkei, like the earlier forced removal of Indian tribes, is an obvious example of the misuse of this wide-sweeping power; yet, the federal government also directed the lives of its more traditional Western pioneers. As the steward of this space and its largest land owner, the federal government, since the days of Lewis and Clark, has explored, defined, and restricted access and use of much of this land. Current debates about such disparate issues as the recent 2000 census and range management are only the latest eruptions of the historical tension between the federal government and individual citizens of the West. A fear of this centralized power, and not just shared feelings of racial superiority, has acted as a significant philosophical touchstone for many of our democracy's most violent internal enemies: the Oklahoma City Bomber, WAR, the Brotherhood, and their northern Idaho brethren, the Aryan Nations.

Although the lives of individual Americans have at times moved outside of the reach of the republic, especially in the more untamed regions of the West, the federal government has always retained the right to enforce its will. Japanese Americans, like American Indians, know this too well. The American government's unique ability to enforce that power has recently come to light with research that has uncovered the extent of the Census Bureau's cooperation with the War Department during the relocation. Although the then bureau director, Kenneth Prewitt, claimed that the bureau "did not technically violate the law at the time," it provided detailed information on America's Nikkei population that authorities used to pinpoint them for relocation.[18] Within three days after the Pearl Harbor attack, the bureau issued reports that provided tabulations of the Japanese American population down to the city block.

The Minidoka Relocation Center, also commonly referred to as Hunt, was on federal property, on ceded territory that was part of the massive Minidoka Reclamation Project, an offshoot of the agricultural vision that shaped Idaho. In fact, three of the relocation centers were situated on federal reclamation land: Minidoka, Tule Lake, and Heart Mountain. Most of the camp's administration came from the Department of Agriculture, including its first director, Milton S. Eisenhower, who was, at the time of his appointment to the War Relocation Authority, the land use coordinator for the Department of Agriculture. The director during most of the WRA's existence, Dillon Myer, was the prior assistant chief of the Soil Conservation Service and immediately before his appointment, the chief administrator of the Agriculture and Adjustment Administration. The transfer of personnel from the Department of Agriculture to form the WRA signified a transfer of an institutional philosophy, one that had previously defined Nikkei in terms of their potential to realize the traditional plan of an agricultural West.

Pioneers in the Grid

I followed the sign's directions up a narrow and winding road that crawled over hilly and broken country filled with sagebrush. "What will it look like?" I wondered. As I ascended a short hillock, I saw trees and a canal filled with swiftly moving green water that threatened the banks. A pickup zoomed past. I saw some people standing around the canal. Fishermen? No, just kids out playing with their dog. I scanned around me looking for something, not sure what, but something that would mark this place. But all I could see were farms off in the distance to my left. When I crossed over a short bridge, a small parking lot, red sign, and peculiar lava rock tower told me I had found it. The wind had picked up. It threatened rain.

Out here on an open lava plain, between the Sawtooth Mountains and the Snake River, the government built Minidoka on a 68,000-acre tract of land that was part of the Gooding Reclamation District.[19] Like other parts of southern Idaho, this region's development depended upon large-scale water projects. Average annual rainfall is only ten inches in south central Idaho, and the soil is porous and volcanic. By 1907 the North Side Canal began providing water from the Snake River, and white settlement in the region quickly increased with the growth of agricultural production. But in the early 1940s, the local economy was still suffering from the Depression. Local contractor Morrison-Knudsen received the government contract to build the camp and began construction on June 5, 1942. The $3.5 million project provided well-paying short-term jobs for the local residents and a temporary boost to the local economy. When the first group of evacuees from the West Coast arrived by train in August 1942, the camp's construction was still far from complete and, thus, even the minimal living standards set by the government were not met for several months. Between 250 and 300 individuals were to share only eight showers and baths. When the first evacuees arrived, however, even these were not working. It would be several months before the center had functioning toilets. At Minidoka flush toilets were installed during the last days of January, 1943; it was as cold as ten below zero that month. Residents soon built dividers between toilets to provide themselves some measure of the privacy they had lost as numbered people. Nisei poet Mitsuye Yamada recounts the impact of this depravation:

> Our collective wastebin
> where the air sticks
> in my craw
> burns my eyes
> I have this place to hide
> the excreta and
> the blood which
> do not flush down
> nor seep away.
>
> They pile up
> fill the earth.
>
> I am drowning.[20]

Minidoka's original residents came from two main "evacuation centers," Puyallup, a former fairground, which held people from the greater Seattle area; and Portland, which included Portland area Japanese Americans. Just as the columnist Henry McLenmore had hoped, these individuals and families were herded onto trains and sent into desolate spaces inland. They rode in cars, with the shades drawn at night, down from Oregon on the rails of the Oregon Short Line, the same line built by Nikkei immigrants at the turn of the century. As Lonny Kaneko's poem "Family Album" suggests, their first encounter with the Idaho landscape was often disorienting:

> The locomotive steams over names like Puyallup,
> Boise, Twin Falls, and Burley; it heads
> where men throw nails and two-by-fours
> into desert air. They fall into long lines.
>
> Soldiers empty the car of names
> like Naganawa, Namba, Hiroshige
> and prod faces named George, Linc, or Naomi
> into rooms furnished with sawdust and sage.
>
> The sign says MINIDOKA
> Nobody knows what it means.[21]

The center's name was already part of the local landscape, as it had been used earlier by the Oregon Short Line to name a town along the railroad, one based supposedly on an Indian word. Former relocatee Martha Inouye Oye recalls that her new home's name had an unintended irony: "I don't know what it means. However, to the Japanese it sounds similar to their phrase, 'Mina do ka?' which translates, 'How is everyone?' Evacuees all thought that was a big joke . . . 'How is Everyone Relocation Center.'"[22] The majority of Minidoka's residents were, like Martha Inouye Oye, urban dwellers from the temperate coastal cities of Portland and Seattle, where the seasons of the year often seem to consist of only two—fog and rain— and where travelers learn how many shades of green are possible when they experience the lush flora that covers the earth there. To those unaccustomed to the desert—its muted tones, gnarled plants, and empty openness—the land was alienating. In *Nisei Daughter*, Monica Sone describes her first glimpse of Idaho: "When the dawn finally broke through in sharp white slits all around the window, I threw open the shade and gulped at the sunlight. The scenery had changed drastically overnight. The staring hot sun had parched the earth's skin into gray-brown wrinkles out of which jagged boulders erupted like warts. Wisps of moldy-looking, gray-green sagebrush dotted the land."[23] Work crews had bulldozed and cleared the surrounding groundcover from the building site at Minidoka, and the now disrupted and denuded ground was especially vulnerable to the strong desert winds. Dust storms are one of the most common recollections from many of the relocation centers, and at Minidoka, these events were noteworthy for their intensity and frequency. In Sone's memoir of her internment, she recounts her arrival at the camp: "On our first day in camp, we were given a rousing welcome by a dust storm. It caught up with us while we were still wandering about looking for our room. We felt as if we were standing in a gigantic sand-mixing machine as the sixty-mile gale lifted the loose earth up into the sky, obliterating everything."[24] The spartan housing units, with their tar paper and two-by-four walls, proved an inadequate defense against the dust. Internees battled dust both outside on the camp grounds and inside their crudely built living quarters. In another poem, Mitsuye Yamada writes,

> But the Idaho dust
> persistent and seeping
> found us crouched
> under the covers.[25]

The camp consisted of three discrete groups of buildings: the administration buildings and housing, segregated from the rest of the camp, and
two groups of internee housing, all of it arching across an area over three
miles long and approximately one mile wide. Most barracks were divided
into six separate rooms; each room was to house an entire family. Twelve
of these barracks normally constituted a block; and each block had, in
general, its own mess hall, latrine, laundry, and recreation hall. Minidoka's evacuee housing consisted of thirty-six such blocks spread out over
the dry Snake River Plain. The sprawl of the camp, its open spaces, caused
one of its WRA employees, Elmer Smith, to consider the psychological effect of this expansiveness and to offer a possible view from the perspective
of those imprisoned within it. Smith later recounted his early impression,
"At first one is impressed with the wide expanse of the project. One feels
as if elbow-room was present. . . . The wide space . . . gives one a feeling of
not being 'behind barbed wire.' One could also assume, as I did, that the
psychology of the residents and the administration would be influenced."[26] Unlike Smith, who equated Minidoka's sprawling layout with
a sense of freedom, the daily lives of internees only reinforced their lack
of it, and its spaces undoubtedly suggested something else. The design of
the camp, with blocks and other camp structures laid out in a gridlike
pattern and with centralized common facilities, forced internees into a
regimented flow in which individuals often had to wait for all their basic
needs. As Mitsuye Yamada recalls:

> Lines formed for food
> lines for showers
> lines for the john
> lines for shots.[27]

Seichi Hayashida, another former Minidoka internee, recounted, "I remember lining up and, breakfast, lunch, and supper we had to wait in
line." His wife further noted, "Every now and then they'd get ice cream. I
think there'd be a mile or a block long line to get it."[28] The stultifying
sameness—"all residential blocks looked alike"[29]—and the regimentation
of daily life were the darker side of the uniform democratic social space defined by Philip Fisher: "the universal and everywhere similar medium" he
describes as the spatial representation of Jeffersonian democracy.[30] These
women and men did not reside and freely move within a region of equally
shared rights but were forcibly moved around the West and incarcerated
within and expelled from it. For those outside the lines that demarcated ac-

cess to American democracy's potential, the West had become a prison. The generic layout of the camps reinforced the legal and political status of its denizens, an uncertain existence under a universal plan of social control. As historian Richard Drinnon has noted, the relocation was a dark manifestation of the federal government's institutional philosophy of centralized rational planning, one invested both in science and in racism.[31]

As manmade components of the landscape, the camps affected the internees in other significant ways. The hurriedly fabricated structures signified impermanence, a transitory condition that matched the indeterminate and uncertain status of their residents. How long would they be here? Would the Nisei, born in this country and its natural citizens, lose further rights of citizenship? Where would they eventually go? Unlike the communities of Westerners who had preceded them, Minidoka's barracks were not built to house people seeking work—farm hands, miners, loggers, or railroad workers—who would leave when the land was exhausted. Nor were these homesteads of mobile men and women taking their chances to settle on the land. This compound was the physical symbol of Executive Order 9066, institutional architecture that signified federal control over these individuals' movements and futures.

The majority of these "relocation centers"—the official government term—were in sparsely settled regions of the American West, and their role in the history of Nikkei in the United States is, perhaps, the most telling contradiction to the myth of democratic space and the inherent freedom signified by the Western landscape. Despite this obvious contradiction, or perhaps because of it, the federal government appropriated the language of this mythology when describing these concentration camps. The War Relocation Authority's first director, Milton Eisenhower, mandated that the definition of a "relocation center" was "a pioneer community, with basic housing and protective services provided by the Federal Government, for occupancy by evacuees for the duration of the war."[32] The Nikkei were told that they were traveling inland to establish new "pioneer communities." Okubo, in *Citizen 13360*, recounts one of the government's pre-evacuation instructions: "Be prepared for the Relocation Centers. Bring work clothes suited to pioneer life."[33] In internal documents, the War Relocation Authority administrators at Minidoka often referred to their prisoners as "colonists." These pioneers or colonists, however, were not travelers into the West seeking to establish self-sufficient communities and prosperity on reclaimed land.

The prominent role that Japanese immigrants had played as agricultural producers and innovators in the West, however, was not forgotten by the War Relocation Authority, and this was made clear by the institution's original plans for relocation.[34] Thomas D. Campbell, an agricultural engineer credited with providing formative influence upon the agency, outlined his vision of the relocation in a letter to President Roosevelt. Campbell wrote, "There are many and various projects between the Mississippi Valley and the Rocky Mountains . . . which have been abandoned or are in receivership, in poor financial condition, or partially used. . . . The various governors, who are opposing the movement, can be shown that, in addition to being a military necessity, it can become an asset. Land in Southern California has its high value today, to a great extent, as a result of the ability and industry of the Japanese."[35]

Some discussions of the internment suggest that the eventual decision to relocate the Nikkei and to solve the "Japanese problem" was influenced solely, or primarily, by California agricultural interests. But the chain of events involved many players, including General John Dewitt and other military officials, the WRA, and groups from outside the Military Areas from which Nikkei were banned. General Dewitt actually lobbied for a larger evacuation that would include German and Italian aliens. Some Californians also worried about the possible decline of the state's agricultural industry if Nikkei were relocated. Labor shortages were already exacerbated by competition with war industries, and some of these agricultural interests also disliked the thought of importing Mexican or black laborers to meet their needs.

On February 2, 1942, California's governor, officials from the departments of Justice and Agriculture, and General Dewitt met. Here the first plan for evacuation within California arose. As historian Roger Daniels has recounted, "What the 'California plan' eventually proposed was that all Japanese be removed from the coastal areas in which most of them lived and placed in camps in the interior valleys of the state, one hundred to one hundred and fifty miles from the seaboard. From these camps labor gangs of men, women, and children could emerge by day to work the crops, but be kept under constraint at nightfall."[36]

Eisenhower envisioned a relocation program that would mirror the work camps of the Civilian Conservation Corps. Nikkei would reside in work camps and way stations throughout the West from which they would provide agricultural labor. However, many Westerners, including Governor Clark of Idaho, strongly opposed the importation of Nikkei into their region and felt the relocatees needed to be more tightly controlled if they were to be sent into their states. In the area near Minidoka, local sentiment was against such a plan. In February, a farmers' congress at Twin Falls voted 371–41 against the use of evacuee labor.[37]

In April of 1942, WRA officials met with Western governors and other officials to develop a more workable plan for the relocation. Although Eisenhower's plan was rejected, the labor potential of this mass migration was still a formative notion within the authority. WRA's own written history, published in 1946, acknowledges, in particular, the influential lobbying of sugar beet interests: "By March 29 . . . the labor demands from these interests upon the War Relocation Authority had already reached the point where they could not be ignored or even temporarily set aside."[38] The government authorities began to utilize the internee work force almost immediately. Even before these people had been "relocated" to places such as Minidoka, they began working fields in areas near the assembly centers. To allow internees entry into these work spaces while still controlling them as local populations insisted, the military simply extended the geographical reach of the restricted areas that Roosevelt's order created but did not explicitly define. The first group of such workers came from the Portland Assembly Center and began work in the sugar beet fields of eastern Oregon on May 21, only a few weeks after the center had opened. Roughly 10,000 individuals worked in the fields by the end of the year—a whopping ten percent of the total evacuee population. Many worked in the sugar beet fields of Idaho.[39]

When some of these workers finally ended up relocated to Idaho, they found the government continued to insist upon agricultural productivity, both inside and outside of the camps. Originally, Eisenhower envisioned the centers as self-sufficient communities, and the WRA continued to insist that the camps strive for this. Eisenhower's replacement, the man who held the job from 1942 until 1946, Dillon Myer, mandated a production quota for Minidoka, and he threatened to decrease the center's food allocation to push for increased production from the camp's farm. In May, he was quoted in the center newspaper, the aptly named Minidoka Irrigator, "If your production falls substantially below this figure, we will be unable to provide a ration of the quality and quantity now planned."[40] The administration budgeted forty-five cents a day to feed each evacuee, and federal officials were pressured by the public to provide only a subsistence diet, not to coddle the "Japs."

On April 24, 1943, WRA employee Vernon Kennedy sent Myer a letter reporting on his trip to the West Coast to gauge public sentiment about the relocation program. He reported that "the people of the Pacific Coast feel that the evacuees should be producing for the war effort and should not be consuming essential food products and other supplies without making a contribution. They feel that they should be placed mainly in the field of agriculture."[41] Minidoka residents quickly complained that the food ration was insufficient to meet basic needs, especially those of active developing children. The WRA listened and began supplying afternoon snacks for children. Complaints about the camp food, however, continued.

In April 1943, the *Northside News* published a letter by former local resident Reverend Walter E. Harman. The reverend complained about Japanese being allowed outside of the camp, and he listed reasons for his argument. They included: "Probabilities are that most of them are better housed, and better fed than when in their western coast homes. To say that these Japanese have been denied the privileges of a citizen is not saying anything very compelling. . . . We are denied the privilige of buying all the meat we want—or shoes—or sugar, or coffee etc."[42] Sensitive to public opinion, the WRA mandated that "At no time would evacuee's food have higher specifications than or exceed in quantity what the civilian population may obtain in the open market."[43] Moreover, they also required that the average daily cost of feeding an evacuee not exceed the cost of feeding a member of the Army. Meatless meals were common, and when meat did appear on the camp menu, it usually consisted of mutton, a food foreign to many relocatees. At times, the food was spoiled. On September 23, 1942, a rash of ptomaine poisoning hit Block 34.[44]

After the Spanish Consul came to examine camp conditions in August 1943, Issei residents at Minidoka drafted a ten-page report in which they disputed the government's food allocation figures and complained about the recent reduction of the milk ration.[45] Meanwhile, local residents outside the camps continued to complain about their own suffering and the relative comfort enjoyed by Minidoka's residents.

At Minidoka, the residents quickly began transforming the areas surrounding their new homes into productive farmland, just as other Nikkei, like Masuo Yasui, had cleared the tree stump-covered region of Hood River, Oregon, to transform it into an agricultural jewel. They cleared, irrigated, plowed, and fertilized the seemingly infertile areas around the camp. Although Minidoka residents arrived too late in the year to plant crops, they established a farm the following spring and turned this region into the productive agricultural land the Bureau of Reclamation and later federal agencies mandated. In the fall of 1943, the farm's first full year of production, the camp's farmers harvested over 1,100 tons of crops from their 250-acre farm.[46] Enough potatoes were harvested to last a year, and a cellar was built to store them. Minidoka's residents were successful despite the fact that few were farmers by trade. As one former Minidoka resident, C. T. Takahashi, recalled, they had to teach themselves: "And then the desert out there, we fortunately got water up on the irrigation and everybody wanted to [stop] doing nothing so they all started farming. And I started farming in front of my place and I had to get books to farm. I didn't know nothing."[47]

During the second year of the farm's operation, the acreage under cultivation increased to nearly 850 acres, and workers harvested over 3,800,000 pounds of crops.[48] Eventually, the camp farm was successful enough to export food to other camps, but it never met the production goals set by the WRA. As indicated by Mr. Takahashi's recollection, internees also created private gardens outside their barracks—victory gardens. Not only did the residents plant crops, but they also built a hog farm, poultry plant, tofu plant, and a cannery and pickling plant, where as a caption in the Minidoka Interlude, a kind of yearbook publication from 1943, notes, "nappa and cabbage (had) been pickled to suit the residents' taste." Agricultural production in the camp was presented by the WRA as a means by which the residents could help not only themselves but the larger war effort. In the Minidoka Interlude, the camp's chief of agriculture at the time, William E. Rawlings, claimed, "Food for victory."

The historical mandate to make these desert lands productive was now part of a national war effort, and people who had been considered threats to that effort were now asked to contribute to it. Included in this same publication are photographs of children's victory gardens, where little kids stand in an open plot within the camp, hoes in hand, or stand in front of a barrack with smiles and slices of their homegrown watermelon. Although such practices may have been motivated by a desire to aid the war effort, they also supplemented the meager diet provided by the WRA with fresh produce and specialty crops not otherwise found on the dining hall tables. But many Minidoka residents refused to work on the farm and resented the WRA's push for agricultural productivity. The administration constantly faced labor shortages because of this resistance and its own policies.

Working the Land

Internees also provided critically needed labor for farms outside the camp and were credited with saving many harvests from ruin. As noted earlier, their role as a potential labor force persuaded Western government officials to admit them into their states. The demands of the war effort catalyzed a dramatic increase in production goals; local sugar beet growers were encouraged to more than double the acreage under cultivation the previous year.[49] The use of evacuee labor began almost immediately, and it, too, was presented as an opportunity for Japanese Americans to contribute to the war effort. Despite the early misgivings of many area farmers, by May 1942, all of south central Idaho was opened to evacuee labor. Sugar beet companies, as they had in the early days of the industry, turned to them to meet their labor needs. In September 1942, several sugar beet companies from the intermountain West met with WRA officials in San Francisco and agreed upon a work contract for a large-scale seasonal work program. In Boise and Idaho Falls, the WRA opened up additional offices to manage the program.[50] Representatives of local sugar beet companies visited Minidoka to recruit workers and advertised regularly in the camp newspaper. In its annual report, the Amalgamated Sugar Company acknowledged the role of the WRA and its charges. The report noted that roughly two thousand Minidoka residents, an "army of harvesters," had worked that year in the fields of Idaho, "the food production front," in the production of this "essential weapon of war . . . quick energy food." The company further urged these workers to aid them next year: "The challenge is now laid down to all able-bodied Japanese who love to breathe free air and earn their own living."[51]

The WRA's official policy of encouraging such work created an odd situation. Wages inside the camps were set by the WRA: professional workers, such as physicians or dentists, received $19.00 a month, and laborers were paid $12.00 a month. Outside of the camps, however, market forces fixed wages at higher levels than those mandated by the WRA. Therefore, although the WRA insisted on agricultural productivity in the camps, it competed against itself by promoting the use of evacuee labor in the more lucrative outside economy. The WRA policy also allowed these individuals to escape temporarily the confines of the center and to live outside in work camps. Although white residents' fears of the evacuees had, at first, barred the implementation of the plan WRA officials originally proposed, the

widescale use of evacuee farm labor became a major component of Minidoka's operation.

Although many Idaho farmers were eventually eager to employ camp laborers, the anti-Japanese sentiment that had prevented the implementation of the original WRA plan persisted and may have, in instances, been
exacerbated by the presence of these West Coast Nikkei. The WRA carefully gauged public sentiment by studying local press accounts and tried to
encourage local writers to promote acceptance of the relocation policies.
Minidoka Reports Officer John Bigelow had numerous contacts with one
local news writer, Bernard Mainwaring of the *Idaho Free Press*. In a letter
dated January 19, 1944, Bigelow thanked the writer for being one of the
"level headed public spokesmen."[52] A few weeks later, Mainwaring replied
to Bigelow's letter, and he noted the relative tolerance of local farmers:
"The farmers around here take quite a decent attitude toward the Japanese, I think." He did, however, note that the influx of Nikkei into the area
was not a condition locals wanted to see continue indefinitely. Mainwaring wrote, "But they do object and strenuously to making South Idaho a
dumping place for the Japanese from the coast, who in the normal course
of events would return there after the war. They rather resent the attitude
of the coast people in trying to dump what is their own problem onto the
interior and they will resent any help in such a scheme that may be given by
federal officials."[53]

The WRA staff at Minidoka had already investigated the public sentiment toward evacuees in the farming communities of southwestern Idaho,
and the center's Community Analysis Section had issued a report that January. These field reports focused specifically upon the resettlement of
evacuees in the area, but their conclusions indicated an often widespread
animosity toward the entire evacuee population. Even in areas where there
was public acknowledgment that their labor had saved large amounts of
crops from ruin, as in Caldwell, they were unwelcome. The report noted:
"Cafes, taverns, barber shops and recreational establishments do not welcome evacuee trade and many display 'No Japs' signs."[54] The anti-Japanese sentiment of Idahoans also extended into the areas immediately surrounding Minidoka and included the labor camps.

Minidoka's Community Analysis Section issued a similar, if more thor-
ough, investigation of farm–evacuee labor relations in Idaho later that
year. Analyst Elmer Smith visited the local labor camps to investigate "a
number of rumors current in the center as well as certain well known negative incidents between Japanese-Americans and Caucasians that have oc-

curred in neighboring communities."[55] Unlike those of the two analysts who preceded him, Smith's reports relied on extensive interviewing of the evacuees, and they differed greatly from the purely factual reports generated by his predecessors, who focused on statistical information. He noted in his final report, in fact, that "the following presentation is a subjective one from the point of view of the present analyst and is recorded for the purpose of attempting to show how he looked at certain situations . . . and some of his personal experiences which might have bearing upon his recorded reactions." Among the "personal experiences" that may have shaped Smith's reportage, he listed his study of the relocation in Utah, his work with Nisei students at the University of Utah, where he was a professor, and his participation in interracial organizations in Utah. His final report includes often scathing assessments of the WRA-appointed staff. Smith noted that controversial reports, such as his report about local labor relations, were the ones most quickly disregarded by the WRA, who considered him, "a 'thorn' in the side of some of the administrators."[56]

Smith's report indicated that widespread discontent existed among evacuee laborers, many from relocation centers outside Idaho, such as Manzanar and Poston. Some of these workers were as young as thirteen years old. A common complaint was the racial intimidation suffered by them and not effectively discouraged by law officials. Evacuees recalled being run off the street by cars and being denied access to businesses and transportation. In one case near Burley, five teenagers were made to crawl on their hands and knees in the city park. Many towns had, in fact, implemented curfews as early as 1942 to restrict the movements of evacuee farm laborers. When a group of teenage laborers from the camp near Burley complained to the camp director that they had been shot at while standing on a bridge overlooking the Snake, the director was told, upon investigation by local authorities, that some local boys had merely been shooting at magpies. Only in Blackfoot did conditions seem acceptable. Smith noted that evacuees reported conditions at the Burley Farm Labor Camp were worst. This was due to not only the threatening acts of local residents but also housing conditions; as Smith wrote, "The workers are housed in the stables, and the living conditions are very congested, with little or no privacy. One Nisei voiced his reaction by saying, 'This is like we had in the assembly center—only worse!'"[57] Another common complaint was the pay evacuees received. Many believed that they were to be paid a flat hourly rate, but instead piecework by the acre set the pay scale. Many workers claimed that they could only make between $1.50 and $2.50 per day, after deductions for room and board, and that was only if the weather was good.

In November 1943, such conditions created a potentially violent confrontation at one labor camp. Following several days of poor weather, during which anxious farmers began bidding against each other for available manpower, one group of laborers refused to work unless their employer raised his wage scale. These nine men were paid ten cents for each sack of potatoes they picked, but they argued that the prevailing wage was now fifteen cents per sack. WRA officials from Minidoka arrived at the scene and negotiated a twelve-cent per sack wage with the farmer, Mr. Kunkle. The work crew, however, rejected the higher wage and refused to resume their work on Kunkle's field. Kunkle, in turn, refused to pay them for the prior day's work, and a group of local residents gathered at his farm, threatening the laborers. Many of these local men complained to WRA officials on the scene about the agency's lenient policies, which allowed workers to return to the camps when it pleased them. They also warned that if these men did not leave, they would be hanged that night. A truck from Minidoka was then sent for, and the men rode to the safety of the camp's confines. In his report to Harry Stafford, Employment Officer Joseph Beeson related the chain of events and noted that the recent conditions had "caused a minority group of the workers involved to assume a belligerent and boisterous attitude that is not conducive to good relations."[58]

That same fall, in the *Hunt Hi-Lites*, the newsletter for the camp high school, student Mas Okada expressed the WRA-sanctioned view of picking potatoes in a poem entitled, "Answer the Call!"

> We will be picking
> That Idaho gem
> While some be topping
>   the sugar beet stem,
> But whether be spuds
> Or sugar beets,
> Our goal will be
> To repeat.
>
> Another VICTORY for UNCLE
> Sam[59]

The *Minidoka Irrigator* had also boldly claimed in its first editorial on September 10, 1942, that "Our goal is the creation of an oasis. Our great adventure is a 'repetition of the frontier struggle of pioneers against the land, its elements.'"⁶⁰ Despite Okada's patriotic prosody and the camp newspaper's pioneering spirit, the aims of the WRA were clearly not universally embraced. Not only did workers protest their treatment in the fields outside Minidoka, but they rejected the WRA's call to contribute unselfishly to the camp's self-sufficiency, regardless of conditions. Farm work in this part of Idaho was often hot, difficult, and uncomfortable. In the summer of 1943, WRA Director Dillon Myer mandated that farm workers complete a full eight-hour day in the fields. Minidoka officials began to provide transportation to and from the fields because workers had been leaving the fields early so that they could have sufficient time to walk back to their barracks and wash up in time for meals. The already disgruntled field workers did not appreciate this increase of their workday. They had already complained about work conditions in the fields, and on July 14, the field crews decided not to work. Only a few workers showed up the following day. Regulations allowed for the termination of employees who were absent for three consecutive workdays, and on the third day of the boycott most workers returned to the fields.⁶¹ However, this was not the end of worker protest on the Minidoka farm.

On August 5, a meeting of the camp's agricultural division was held to investigate the ongoing worker discontent and the recent walkout of several women field workers. Farm foreman Mr. Kamaya laid out for the administration some of the problems inherent in the WRA's policies. He noted that changes in supervisory personnel caused resentment from the workers. The low wages created no incentive for the field workers to work the full eight-hour shift. He claimed: "If you could pay them like on the outside, they would do the work. If you would pay fifty cents an hour instead of five cents, one-third of these people could run this farm. You don't think of it that way." Kamaya pointed out that the absurdly low wages were not the only issue at hand. The work conditions at the camp farm were poor, even cruel. The farm was spread out over 200 acres and, at that time, far from any dining or lavatory facilities. Workers were completely exposed to the strong Idaho sun. In the summer, the air temperatures in this part of Idaho often soar above one hundred degrees. The Minidoka administration seemed not to have considered the effect of these conditions upon the work crews. Later in his testimony, Kamaya stated, "I want to get the job done. The people say that the sun is too hot and that the dust makes it terrible to work. There is a lot of difference in working inside and out in the hot sun. There is also the water thing. Can't we have drinking water?" Assistant Project Director Davidson responded, "We have to remember that this farm is part of the project. We are trying to conform to certain regulations. You have been a good driver, Mr. Kamaya."[62]

The dialog then moved to the irrigation of the farm and who was responsible for overseeing it, as well as to a clarification of the mandated work hours and corresponding payroll issues. An administration official noted that, with the $16.00 a month wage scale, the farm crews were actually receiving 8.3 cents an hour, not merely five cents an hour. The administrators then addressed the problem of insuring that workers be paid in accordance with the number of hours they actually worked, since the transporting of workers to and from the mess halls cut into the actual time spent in the fields. A WRA official from Washington pointedly asked Director Stafford if, while in Washington on business, he had used public transportation. Stafford replied, "No. I found that I had to walk most of the time back there. I understand that this is the normal situation outside. But the argument here again is that the people on the outside are doing jobs and getting normal wages. The regulations prescribe eight hours of work." Stafford's comments suggested that he felt the workers were somehow cheating the government, and they did little to help themselves. They were unfit pioneers. He stated, "I think it can be said, with few exceptions and you are one of them [referring to Mr. Kamaya] that Japanese people are willing to cooperate but are not willing to accept a tremendous load of responsibility. . . . We have a lot of people here who haven't chosen to give us any help whatsoever on the farm. . . . We have a lot of people here who are temperamental. . . . They are going to talk five cents an hour. They are going to be disgruntled. They aren't going to look at the bright side of anything."[63] Finally, he returned to the issue of providing drinking water for the workers, one of their chief concerns, and he was told by Davidson that fountains and water bags were available. Davidson noted, however, that the fountains had "gone on the bum." Foreman Kamaya noted that they did not have time to transport water, and it got spilled in the process. Stafford eventually proposed that large kegs, covered with burlap, be placed in the fields. Mr. Powers, the WRA official from Washington, assured Stafford that such equipment would be available but asked whether the camp had a sanitaria, because he felt sanitation might be a problem. "No, we don't," Stafford replied, and he recommended that fifteen kegs be requested and moved the discussion on to the issue of clarifying the work hours.[64] During Minidoka's operation, epidemics of both typhoid and dysentery struck its residents, the latter the result of exposure to contaminated food or water.[65]

Although Minidoka's administrators had overlooked the water needs of its field workers, it was very attentive to the general issue of water usage on the center. The resource demands were huge. Overnight, the eighth-largest city in the state arose on the desert plains, and its population reached 9,397 by March 1, 1943.[66] The camp required between 1,650,000 and 1,900,000 gallons of water a day.[67] A significant amount of water would be required to irrigate the camp farm. The WRA also noted in a letter to the North Side Canal Company that water from its canal, to which the WRA hoped to gain access, would be used to keep down dust, fight fires, and water "grass, shrubs and flowers" that the agency planned to plant by the residential housing blocks.[68] The Minidoka administration considered an extensive system of landscape improvements that included windbreaks and plantings of ornamental flowers. The plan, however, included plant and tree species, such as hemlock and iris, that were not only nonnative, but obviously incompatible with the arid climate.[69] Eventually, the landscaping done by the WRA was solely functional, such as the planting of rye grass to combat the dust.

Since the camp was on a tract of land under the authority of the Bureau of Reclamation, the two agencies had to come to an agreement authorizing WRA's use of the land and the water from the Milner-Gooding Canal running along the camp's northern edge. Representatives of the two agencies signed a Memorandum of Understanding on April 20, 1942.[70] The WRA's use of the local canals was a sensitive issue in the local community, and later in the month 200 farmers signed a resolution opposing any of the district's water "being used on 18,000 acres of land to which the army proposes to evacuate the Japs."[71] The agricultural economy of the area relied upon this water supply, which irrigated some 350,000 acres. The alleged fifth column threat of Japanese America meant that this vital resource was also a potential target and local residents had expressed their fears of sabotage by Nikkei farm workers. The Twin Falls Chamber of Commerce chairman had warned in February that "Sympathy for Japanese will make it easier to sabotage the Magic Valley Irrigation system."[72] As in other areas, both in the West and across the country, Nikkei were restricted from local irrigation dams and other installations deemed essential to the war effort. The discretionary power provided by Executive Order 9066 created for Japanese in America a checkerboard of open and closed spaces that highlighted their historic position as outsiders. The WRA's negotiations in relation to Idaho's precious water resources illustrated again the influential role the federal government played in defining who could be a true Westerner.

In early 1943, the North Side Canal Company negotiated with WRA officials to fix the terms of the WRA's access to its canal. One of the company's
major concerns was damage to the canal by evacuees, although not as a result of intentional sabotage. They feared that evacuees might use the canal
for recreation. Harry Stafford wrote the North Side Canal Company on
March 18, 1943, and claimed that the WRA planned to build two swimming pools near the canal that would be supervised. He noted, "As a third
precaution against the danger of any person being lost in the canal and
to avoid the necessity for draining the canal, we propose that a timber
screen or grating be installed in the canal at a point below the camp."[73]
The agreement between the WRA and the North Side Canal Company did,
indeed, stipulate that the WRA would "exercise every diligence to keep
evacuees out of the canals . . . and away from said canals."[74] It listed the
agreed upon uses noted previously by the WRA, which did not include
agriculture, because those needs were to be met by the Milner-Gooding
Canal. The agreement also stipulated that any construction on the canal
and resulting labor costs incurred in this work would be the responsibility
of the WRA. The WRA did, in fact, have plans for the region's canals, and
these plans were a manifestation of the Bureau of Reclamation's institutional mission.

In a letter to the chairman of the Community Council, Harry Stafford revealed the details of the agreement that the WRA had made with its sister
agency. Never was the connection between the Bureau of Reclamation's vision of a "reclaimed" West and the WRA's vision of agricultural pioneer
communities more explicit. Stafford revealed that the WRA had agreed to
use evacuees to implement the Bureau's master plan for the desert plains
of Idaho. He noted the agreement's terms: "that the Bureau of Reclamation will lay out a work progress designed to provide improvements of permanent value to the land. It is further specified that that program will include work to reduce leakage in the Milner-Gooding Canal, construction
of lateral distribution systems to supply all irrigable lands within the
Snake River Slope Area, and such drainage works as are deemed desirable
in connection with irrigation of those lands."[75] By April 1944, when Director Stafford wrote to Yoshito Fujii, the first major project of this plan was
nearing completion: the construction of a lateral distribution line that
would irrigate some 3,200 acres adjacent to the camp. Stafford noted that
the next project would be aimed at preventing leakage from the Milner-
Gooding Canal and, as with the prior project, evacuee labor would provide

the bulk of the manpower. Stafford appealed for the cooperation of this community leader by noting that this project would allow evacuees an opportunity to leave their mark here on the land. He noted in his letter, "Completion of this job according to plan would provide evacuee residents of this center with the knowledge of satisfaction resulting from a material contribution towards a permanent and lasting improvement of the Snake River Slope area."[76]

Director Stafford's appeal to Mr. Fujii assumed, however, that the evacuees shared his vision of these places, and that, despite poor working conditions, their awareness of having contributed to the reclamation of this land would be adequate motivation. The agreement between the WRA and the Bureau of Reclamation to use internee labor for this work was not only presumptuous but also probably illegal. The Bureau's enabling legislation, the Reclamation Act of 1902, stated: "in all construction work eight hours shall constitute a day's work, and no Mongolian labor shall be employed thereon."[77] As noted previously, the term "mongolian" had historically been included in or amended to legislation to specifically exclude Japanese, and this language was not removed from the Act until 1956.[78] The WRA seemed concerned with insuring an eight-hour workday for laborers, but they were less faithful to the language that defined the labor fit for Reclamation projects. Not only did they use internee labor here but also on the Owyhee Project in southwest Idaho.[79] For many evacuees, however, the canals were not pieces of a grand design for progress, but something else.

The canals did become recreational sites, just as the North Side Canal Company feared. Despite their expressed promises to the North Side Canal Company, the WRA would not build swimming pools and ignored the continued pleas of Minidoka's residents to do so. The Issei men who drafted the report to the Spanish Consul, including Yoshito Fujii, complained that the WRA had reneged on promises to provide recreational facilities and that these were especially important to a "normal pursuit of social life" in such "a congested community where thousands have to live in a limited space." Many of the camp's recreational centers were utilized for other purposes, and children often congregated in the laundry and lavatory facilities to play. The report specifically mentioned the WRA's promise to construct a pool and how the North Side Canal Company's fears were now being realized. The residents, especially children, had taken to the canals. Some were dying. These leaders directly blamed the WRA's omission for these accidents. Their report charged, "Last summer two boys lost their lives while swimming in the nearby canal. This tragedy would not have happened had there been a swimming pool with adequate safeguards."[80]

Children not only swam in the canal, but also used them as play sites, and this resulted in the kind of damage to the canals that the WRA's policies had sought to prevent. On June 26, 1943, the project engineer, Daniel Sheehan, wrote to the central block manager, Mr. Hara, to complain again about the damage that children were doing to the canal. Sheehan noted that "Rocks, boards, and trash have been thrown into the canal to dam it up or to make bridges." He implored Hara to inform the other block managers about the situation and to help insure the canal's smooth operation. He further remarked, "This matter has been called to the attention of the Internal Security and Schools and their cooperation has been requested."[81] Apparently, some of these WRA staff did just that. In a Community Analysis Section Report the following month, analyst John de Young reported on a display by second graders at the Huntville School. His report included the following poem, "Canal," by Noriko Ichikawa.

> We are not to swim in the canal
> Because it is dangerous
> But I don't know about fishin
> We are not to play in the irrigation ditch but some
> people play in it. We must stop little children,
> from playing in the ditch. This is our duty.[82]

Eventually, the residents made a beach along the canal, manned by a crew of lifeguards. And, if Noriko Ichikawa did not know about fishing, others did. A copy of the *Area B Recreation News*, dated March 9, 1944, advertised an upcoming fishing derby to be held at the canal.[83] Although not the most desirous of fishing locales, the irrigation canals at Minidoka were now being used by the residents in ways the WRA had not imagined, even if its policies helped create an environment of such inventiveness. As C. T. Takahashi recalled in an interview many years later, sometimes, if one had the right job on the project, even the outside area's blue ribbon trout rivers could be enjoyed. In 1984, he recalled, "Was good fishing up there in Sun Valley. And I used to go up to Sun Valley and get the wounded soldiers on Saturdays and Sunday and drive them down to the river to go fishing . . . Oh, yes. Oh Silver Creek had great big trout."[84]

North of Shoshone

Silver Creek still has those great big trout. Unlike many of the West's fisheries, it has not irrevocably declined, and its challenging waters and big fish are known worldwide. Once only locals fished it, including other Nikkei workers, as Clayne Baker had related to me back in Boise, when he recalled them patiently fishing hooks baited with a single salmon egg. The creek's still waters and thick vegetation, fed by cool spring waters, hold heavy wild fish that today witness a yearly invasion of anglers armed with the latest flyfishing tackle. The use of salmon eggs is banned. It is the kind of place I avoid—no elbowroom. Some rivers now feel like an urban deli counter at lunchtime, "Take a number, please." That is the last thing I want to see when I go out West: a river full of Easterners piling out of a Grand Cherokee with thousand dollar rods and ten-cent casts. Acclaim can often spell ruin for what we cherish, even when we try to be mindful, innocent. Recently, a nonnative parasite that deforms and often kills trout has spread across the West, seriously depleting some fish populations. This affliction is known by its common effect on trout behavior, whirling disease. It eventually came to Idaho, and the fishes' strongest advocates may have been the agents of their peril. The parasite is commonly spread to new waters by piggybacking on waders, wading boots, or other paraphernalia of anglers.

In Shoshone, a town named after the displaced Indians, is a gas station that has sprouted, in the few years I have been coming here, from a little rural station into a shining service station–mini mart, complete with automatic sliding glass doors. You can buy all the snack food you can handle and a big cup of whatever suits you to wash it down. The Sawtooth Mountains and Sun Valley are straight ahead up the highway, and to the right is a river that winds out into the desert, slicing into the basalt ridges of the plain and washing into the lava chutes hidden from the highway. The Little Wood's water joins up with the Big Wood west of here and eventually spills out into the Snake River. Upriver it receives the cool spring water of Silver Creek but is often completely dry upstream from there during the irrigation season. I had read about the Little Wood: lesser known, often unfished, with rattlesnakes and giant brown trout. I had dreamed it.

From the highway, I could only see it in a few places. Often it seemed inconceivable that there was any water out in this dry country, covered in sage and dark volcanic rock, the brown foothills of the Sawtooths in the distance. I tried a few pulloffs until I found one that I could drive down far enough to get close to the river. I rolled up to a bridge and ran out to the water. It was small, slightly off color, and running strong. Upriver was a stand of cottonwoods lining the bank, and starlings dive-bombed the surface. In a few minutes, I was holding the new rod in my hand: nine feet long, graphite, with a clean cork handle. A few months ago I had bought it, for just this trip, to handle big Western rivers like the South Fork of the Boise. No fish was going to be out of reach. The bank here was lined by high thick wheatgrass up to my waist, and I moved to the edge, where I could lift the rod above the grass and cast out into the river. The line snaked out of the guides and across the air into the swift water. Before I could focus, I missed a fish that lifted out of the rocks only fifteen feet below me on the bank. It would not make the same mistake again.

I moved upriver, and by then the sky was darkening. I had seen weather off to the south when I drove in, but suddenly the wind picked up. I tied on a nymph, an imitation of an insect's larval stage, added some split shots to my leader, and was able to catch a nice fat rainbow after a few casts between a seam of rocks in the middle of the river. But the line bulged from the force of the wind. I could not feel my fly drifting in the current, let alone a fish slightly mouthing it. I moved back downriver. The wind blew harder. It knocked me forward, back. It was futile. I cursed, bit off my leader, reeled up my line, and headed back along a gravelly path to the car, where my wet wading boots sat leaking onto the trunk floor as I drove south. It had begun to rain.

Don't Fence Me In

The next day, at the site of the former Minidoka Relocation Center, I pulled up to the small parking lot near the main entrance. The odd-looking lava rock structure by the road was the former guard post. Its roof had long since collapsed. Behind it was a lava rock chimney and low rock wall that stood out in the flat landscape of open space. In this building family members, friends, and other visitors waited to visit people who lived imprisoned on this dry lava plain.

Cans, tissue, and cigarette butts of more recent travelers lined the yellow brown wheatgrass as I walked around the site. Along the top of the wall I found two plaques. They were placed here as part of the centennial commemoration in 1990, during which a public history was placed on this Idaho plain. One plaque included a map, nearly identical to the one in the *Minidoka Interlude* and to other published drawings I had seen of the camp: it had the usual canal, housing blocks, and service roads. It was not until a year later, when I opened a file of the WRA records at the National Archives, that the common omission in every drawing I had seen of Minidoka became apparent. They never included the fence.

No element of the relocation centers more forcefully symbolized the evacuation and loss of mobility that Japanese Americans experienced during World War II than the fences and watchtowers. In the oral histories, poetry, memoirs, and paintings of internees, these landscape elements are ubiquitous. Minidoka's Community Analysis Section reported in April 1943 that "In the sketches and drawings of resident artists, the watchtowers and barbed wire fence stand out."[85] For those West Coast residents of Japanese ancestry who suffered internment, the force of the federal government's will upon the land was embodied in the barbed wire fences on the very landscape understood to represent mobility and freedom. As one poet of the relocation wrote:

> There is no fence
> High up in the sky.
> The evening crows
> Fly up and disappear
> Into the endless horizon.[86]

Patricia Limerick has noted that barbed wire, the main component of these fences, was itself a symbol of the American West, one that acquired new meaning during the relocation. Originally, a means to demarcate the boundaries of individual land holdings and to contain livestock, it now herded people whose every action was controlled by a vast institution that manifested itself in soldiers and barbed wire. When Minidoka's first residents arrived in August 1942, the camp had no fence. Evacuees forcefully expressed their desire to have no fence, but on October 31 the *Minidoka Irrigator* announced that a barbed wire fence would soon be built. The newspaper had reported earlier that month that Military Police would build watchtowers to serve as fire lookouts. But on the day it announced the construction of the fence, the paper also noted that the watchtowers would serve as observation points for military guards to watch not only for fire but for humans, too. At this time, restricted areas in the center were guarded by military personnel and not fenced off. One later WRA report suggested that this arrangement actually promoted harmonious relations between military security and the evacuees due to the interaction occurring at these sites.

Construction workers did not start to build Minidoka's fence until November 6. For the next six days they continued work, and each day residents of Minidoka displayed their protest of it by tearing out fence posts and cutting wires. Military Police warned the camp residents that such vandalism was subject to the levy of fines or even imprisonment, a curious threat given the circumstances. On November 12, the center contractor, fed up by the work delays, electrified the fence. WRA authorities, however, intervened, and the electrification of the fence ceased in a matter of hours, without any serious injury. Despite the WRA's quick intervention, this incident incensed evacuees. The Community Analysis Section's account of the events noted "the news of this new development spread like a prairie fire and wild rumors circulated throughout the camp."[87] Residents, through their representatives from the housing blocks, formally protested the construction and requested a cessation of the work. The Minidoka Irrigator remained neutral; however, the editorial freedom of the paper was compromised by the WRA's control of it. From its inception, the staff of the camp paper published under the watchful eye of the camp administrators, who, by right of the paper's charter, could suspend publication and distribution at will.[88] The Community Analysis Section's report of April 1943 noted: "Once the fence was completed, the paper was asked by the local administration authorities not to print anymore stories about the fence. There were no letters to the editors or editorial protests registered in the newspaper."[89]

Within the federal government, there was debate over the fence. Minidoka WRA officials, Military Police, and the Army Corps of Engineers were in dispute over the placement of the fence perimeter. The Army eventually prevailed, and it oversaw the completion of the fence in December. The fence was composed of barbed wire strands spread out five feet high along the entire perimeter of the camp. At the southern end of the camp, the fence provided a barrier to the North Side Canal, but in other areas, it also barred access to designated play areas, farmlands, and dump sites. The WRA promised residents that it would move sections of the fence the following spring. Residents did not wait. They dismantled the fence to gain access to garbage dumps, roads, and other areas, or as the Minidoka Analysis Section report on the fences noted, "to provide egress to certain points."[90] During the winter, some pulled away sections of the fence bisecting a pond along the canal that they used for skating. They spoke of building an ice rink.

In the spring, a more large-scale alteration of the fence commenced. Workers ripped out two and one-half miles of fence in April to provide access to the area north of the center at the site of the planned farmlands.

The administration noted, "It is reported that never on the project was a job attacked so willingly." Not only did this destruction of the new fence constitute a tremendous waste of resources and labor, but the WRA's own staff questioned the entire project, describing the fence as "useless" and without "any practical value." North of the camp was open sage desert and an imposing lava field. Anyone attempting escape from Minidoka faced an isolated terrain and nowhere to seek refuge. Residents could easily damage the fence, but it only demarcated "one stretch of drab sage brush from another."[91]

The administration's lack of concern for security was exemplified by their attention to the watchtowers, which remained unoccupied. While other centers had very tight security, which included strict control of their compound's perimeter, Minidoka's security was relatively loose. The opening in the fence remained, and the administration allowed residents, during daylight hours, to walk in the surrounding sage flats or to use the area by the canal for recreation. The camp's fence and watchtowers, however, remained despised symbols of imprisonment, as one resident wrote, "I don't like it because you feel like prisoners of War—more like a concentration camp than War Relocation Center when I haven't done anything wrong. I want my children to respect America and love America but with barbed-wire around such a task can never be accomplished. . . . I feel like I am caged in like an animal."[92] The administration's acknowledgment of the fence's symbolism suggests that it may also have realized the effect of allowing residents outside its perimeter, to move in open space, to not feel "behind barbed wire," as Elmer Smith described it. In a poem entitled "Search and Rescue," Mitsuye Yamada recounts this sense of liberation and one of the unpredicted consequences of the WRA's policy at Minidoka:

> We join the party
> for the feel of freedom.
> What are we looking for
> among gnarled knuckles
> in sagebrush forest?
>
> An old man
> out of his head
> wandered off they said.[93]

Residents did on occasion become lost and, in one instance, an elderly man died from exposure in the area outside of the center. He was found over two days later.[94] Not only did the evacuees use the surrounding sage-

brush flats for hiking, but they also harvested the local vegetation for both
practical and aesthetic purposes. When coal supplies were low, Minidoka's residents burned the sagebrush for heat. They also gathered it, and
other local woods such as greasewood, to make canes, furniture, and even
sculpture. These artists even cultivated special plots of sagebrush for their
projects. Mitsuye Yamada recounts this other means of reworking Minidoka's landscape in a poem from her wartime collection, "Block 4, Barrack 4, 'Apt. C.'"

> The barbed fence
> protected us
> from wildly twisted
> sagebrush.
> Some were taken
> by old men with gnarled
> hands.
> These sinewed branches
> were rubbed and polished
> shiny with sweat and body oil.[95]

In Yamada's poem, the threatening sagebrush becomes transformed by
the work of these men into a tool, a means of enduring. The gathering of
natural wood forms, called *kobu*, is a common Japanese practice that internees transplanted to the deserts of the West. The shapes are worked by
hand to soften and polish the wood and then are used as decorative pieces
or paperweights, or simply held in one's hands to soothe.

Desert Bloom

Historian Patricia Limerick has chronicled the varied responses of American travelers to the West's arid regions and how these progressed from
initial rejection to aesthetic appreciation.[96] The reactions of the residents
of this World War II concentration camp in the West suggest a blending of
all these responses. Like earlier travelers from the East, most of these new
pioneers were from homelands in temperate and lush regions. They had
never experienced such a landscape, and they often viewed it as foreign,
vacant. When Ted Matsuda recounted his train ride from Seattle to Minidoka, his account of the evacuees' responses to the dry regions of the interior West was like that of many first-time travelers to the arid American
West, such as Mary Hallock Foote. He recalled, "Everyone seemed happy
but, as we traveled up the Columbia, the green gradually faded into drab

yellow of the sun baked hills, our mood darkened. We saw through the window what we may expect in Idaho—desert like sagebrush plain." When they arrived at Hunt the following day, their reaction to their new home was indeed deflating. Matsuda recalled: "The sight of the camp right in the middle of sage brushes was sickening. Some women looked upon our new home with tears. Men faced their new situation with somber faces."[97] Unlike their Eastern predecessors, internees were not merely traveling through these regions on their way elsewhere, but were forcibly placed here to live. Their ability to transform the landscape was then not solely a manifestation of the uniquely attractive American myth of individual endurance, for these people were stewards of the federal government. Nor did their experience confirm the adoption of American ideas of landscape improvement, although they indeed transformed these areas, as they had the dry regions of southern California. Like Mary Hallock Foote, some of them came to appreciate the unique beauty of these places but did not insist upon the need to change them dramatically.

For many camp residents, especially the Issei, their internment provided them with the first opportunity to enjoy significant leisure time. Some devoted themselves to traditional artistic practices that involved the manipulation of landscape elements, such as *ikebana*, *bonsai*, and *bon-kei*.[98] In some instances, these artists chronicled the isolation, foreignness, and menace of their new surroundings, but often they created new meanings, displayed new uses for these desolate spaces and their unique elements. In the 1952 book *Beauty behind Barbed Wire*, Allen Eaton chronicles this remarkable artistic production at the relocation centers. His book includes pictures from Minidoka of sagebrush sculpture and arrangements and a photograph of several canes made by a physician at Minidoka who was also a landscape photographer. Eaton notes that evacuees often decorated their barracks with found objects—unaltered stones or pieces of sagebrush that represented animate forms or that were simply unusual. The book also includes a photograph of K. Yuasa, a professional traditional flower arranger, who stands next to a sagebrush arrangement. Eaton comments, "A book could, and probably should be written on the subject of 'Sagebrush and the Japanese,' for surely they were the first to see beauty in this commonest, and to many of us the least aesthetic of the desert plants of the western states."[99] All over Minidoka and at other camps, a variety of similar practices thrived. Exhibits of these works were held in the center, and one was also held at the Twin Falls Public Library from June 24–26, 1943.

Today, few remnants of these exhibits exist, but the land itself tells of this wartime history. At Minidoka, landscape artists and gardeners created communal gardens, including traditional Japanese gardens.[100] Many residents planted shrubs, trees, flowers, and vegetables in the residential areas of the compound. Some of these plantings, including stands of willows, still exist. Seichi Hayashida noted when he returned to Minidoka, "you see those trees . . . some of the people that were here planted those trees."[101] His wife, Chiyeko, recalled, "It was a gentleman that lived in our block that had was called the [?] gardens in Seattle, and he really made the blossoms bloom."[102] Not just professionally trained gardeners and landscape architects, however, were involved in the greening of Minidoka. As noted previously, individual residents also commonly planted victory gardens outside their barracks, and these gardens appear in photos in the *Minidoka Interlude*, where a group of people stand in front of a black tar paper–covered dwelling with a tangle of sunflowers behind them. One internee remarked of another relocation center, "the whole camp was transformed. . . . Who but Nihonjins would leave a place like that in beauty."[103]

The residents of the local community outside the camp also participated in this transformation. Despite the Minidoka administration's original plans to landscape the compound, little was done. After irrigation channels were extended into the residential blocks, the WRA did plant grasses, but these were practical measures meant to "aid materially in controlling dust and mud."[104] Minidoka administrators were concerned about expenditures that might be deemed as extravagant by the public and watchful members of Congress. Landscaping work on the project was therefore problematic. On February 6, 1943, Minidoka Director Harry Stafford received a cable from WRA headquarters inquiring about a report that the center planned to purchase $30,000 worth of shrubbery for landscaping. The cable from Leland Barrows asked, "Please supply full explanation and justification of purchase. We must answer inquiry of a nuxx member of Congress."[105] Later that year, the Minidoka administration submitted its landscaping plans to headquarters in Washington. In a letter to Robert Davidson, the center's agricultural chief, Stafford noted, "The impression we are attempting to make upon the general public is that expenses for non-essential items will be held to the minimum. Emphasis will be placed upon food production."[106]

Stafford's letter also indicated that he planned to rely upon outside contributions, and the camp administration asked for local donations of landscaping materials from the surrounding community. In March 1943, the

Minidoka Irrigator noted the first such donation of materials from Twin Falls residents and commented that "the residents are making the fullest use of cuttings, roots, bulbs, and seed which are given to them."[107] With these donations and whatever materials and equipment were supplied by the WRA, Minidoka's residents began the process of reshaping their temporary homeland. How much some came to appreciate the native landscape is indicated by an article from the *Minidoka Irrigator* in July 1944. The article noted that residents of Blocks 13, 15, and 17, bordering the northern edge of the center, were at work on a park just north of these housing units. The workmen were building a *torii*, a traditional Japanese entranceway to what would be neither a play area nor a garden. The park was designed as a wildlife preserve, intended specifically to protect native plant species. Decades before desert preservation became a recognized goal of American environmentalism, a man working on the park noted, "This is not right. We must practice more care in the future or wild life will disappear altogether."[108]

The New Indian Problem

The War Relocation Authority closely monitored these various aesthetic and recreational activities practiced by internees in the relocation centers, including at Minidoka. Administrators generated reports that cataloged the wide range of these activities, their participants, and their content. In the later years of the relocation, one community analyst at Tule Lake likened the strong interest in traditional Japanese cultural practices to the Ghost Dance: the prophetic revivalist movement that some American Indians embraced late in the nineteenth century as their traditional way of life increasingly waned under the pressures of the federal government and white settlement.[109] The past treatment of American Indians created an institutional memory within the federal government that informed their policies during this later relocation. The actions and comments of these administrators indicated how powerfully seminal ideas about race and place continued to shape the American landscape.

One of the War Relocation Authority's most basic problems was what to do with Japanese Americans once they had been placed in the concentration camps. The federal government had rounded up nearly the entire population of an ethnic group and placed these individuals in isolated regions, segregated from American society. The obvious parallels to the reservation system troubled administrators and motivated them to formulate policies in contrast to those affecting American Indians. As WRA Director Dillon

S. Myer stated in testimony before the United States Senate in January 1943, "I sincerely believe, gentlemen, that if we don't handle this problem in a way to get these people absorbed as best we can while the war is going on, we may have something akin to Indian reservations after the war."[110]

The WRA quickly began to promote resettlement of the internee population—to clear out the centers as quickly as possible. The first to leave in large numbers were college students who moved on to continue their education at the colleges and universities that accepted Nisei college students, most of which were in the Midwest and East. Next, were the young and able-bodied who could contribute their labor to the war effort. This meant that the centers increasingly became filled with the very young and the very old, and, therefore, center operations became harder to run. At Minidoka, increasing worker discontent led to more labor strikes, including one among hospital workers. The strike was eventually quashed by the administration, which sent the strike leaders to a separate prison facility on the Navajo reservation, Leupp, that the WRA used to hold problem internees. The agriculture division chief in Minidoka noted in May 1943 that the loss of workers had forced him to rely more and more on women and high school students for labor, and he requested that the regulations limiting students' work hours be changed.[111] Farm productivity dropped.

At Minidoka, the administration pushed resettlement especially hard, and the labor demands of local agricultural interests provided a ready outlet for the center population. As many as 3,000 Minidokans settled in the state, although most eventually moved back to the West Coast once it became open to resettlement.[112] Some of Minidoka's residents decided to farm in Idaho, because the climate and growing conditions were similar to the agricultural regions of eastern Washington and Oregon where they had farmed before the war. Agricultural work was strongly promoted by the WRA, and the administration at Minidoka showed internees resettlement propaganda movies such as "Crystallized Sunshine—The Story of South Dakota," "Wartime Farming in the Corn Belt," and "Pig Projects Make Profits."

Despite the WRA's call for internees to join on the "farm front," not all of their plans for agricultural resettlement were acceptable. In August 1944, a group of Rowher residents submitted a proposal for "Cooperative Colonization" to WRA officials. They understood that the government feared "another 'Indian Reservation'" and proposed that the government allocate funds to establish a large agricultural community for the several thousand individuals remaining in the camps. They quoted a *Fortune* magazine article that predicted, "Whatever the final residue, 25,000 or 45,000, it is certain that the 'protective custody' of 1943 cannot end otherwise than in a kind of Indian reservation, to plague the conscience of America for many years to come." Their plan was one Jefferson would have recognized: a self-governed agricultural community of small family farms. All enterprises were planned as cooperatives, even the healthcare system. They closed their proposal by noting, "How we live, regardless of our color, is determined entirely by the individual's ability and means. This indeed, is what Democracy is fighting for."[113] Despite its reliance on such traditional pioneering aspirations, ones the WRA relied upon, their plan to open a "new frontier" clashed with another important tenet of the resettlement program—to disperse the body of Japanese America.

In a letter included in the handbook given to all resettling internees, WRA Director Myer offered individuals encouraging words and noted that this trying time was also "a period when all of us, regardless of our ancestry, can get closer to the real meaning of American life than we ever have in the past."[114] To Myer, this process of Americanization meant ridding Japanese Americans of anything that marked them as Japanese, including community. In the beginning of the resettlement period, the WRA discouraged internees from settling in groups; the goal was to integrate them within the larger community. Although the WRA later realized that groups aided the process of reintegration into society, it still carefully controlled the process and encouraged its charges to move away from the ethnic enclaves it felt had held them apart from America.

The agency's history of the relocation notes that the goal of resettlement was "as broad a distribution of the Japanese as possible and was . . . successful in securing their dispersal throughout a great many sections of the country."[115] Since the WRA and sister agencies set the conditions for resettlement and determined the areas open to Japanese Americans, the government could closely control the new geographic makeup of the postwar Japanese American community. In fact, when it felt too many had resettled in the intermountain West and mid-Plains, it simply closed those areas off to future resettlement in 1943 and steered internees to other locales.[116] Of course, many internees had few options, especially the elderly who often lacked financial resources and were not employable, a condition for obtaining clearance to leave the centers. It is not surprising then that a significant number of internees remained in the centers into 1945 or worried about their new lives on the outside. In April 1945, a woman drowned herself in the canal, distraught over her health and the burden she would place upon her family who were preparing for resettlement.[117]

To prevent the establishment of reservations, the WRA took a hard stance and set camp closing dates by which all remaining residents would have to leave or be evicted. The WRA announced in July 1945 that Minidoka would close on November 1, 1945. Within the last month of its operation, over one thousand individuals departed, but still a few were eventually moved by force when the center closed early on October 23. In his diary, Arthur Kleinkopf, Minidoka's superintendent of education, wrote of the final day: "As we passed through the gates the last time, I thought again as I had before of Henry Wadsworth Longfellow's poem, Evangeline, and the scattering of the Acadians. I wondered how long these camp buildings would stand. As long as they do, they remain a monument to a grand scale experiment in dealing with minority group problems. As to whether the experiment was successful, only time may tell and even time may fail to answer."[118]

Some WRA officials were already certain of their success in managing people, in what their written history noted was the task of "human conservation." One community analyst boldly claimed that the relocation was "a magnificent tour de force, as different and superior in technique and administrative management from the transfer of Indians as the oxcart differs from the latest bomber."[119] Despite this administrator's claim and the apparent success of the WRA in avoiding the creation of new reservations, the treatment of these two groups by the federal government was similar and motivated by common racist beliefs, as Elmer Smith pointed out in his description of a lunchtime conversation with the center's director. He quoted Stafford as saying, "Now the way I look at things is this: I figure these people are sick. A lot has happened to them. They've got a persecution complex. They're not well mentally. You can't treat them like well people. You've got to feel that, or you shouldn't be working on this project. You've got to have an understanding for their condition. And sometimes it looks to me as if they're a lot like some Nez Perce Indians I know. Just pare a little of this culture off that they've got, get down a little farther to the primitive, and there you've got them."[120]

After the war, the WRA's Director, Dillon Myer, would receive the Medal for Merit by the President for his service and later take along with him many of his WRA staff to a new position—commissioner of the Bureau of

Indian Affairs. He would head the BIA from 1950 until 1953, during which time he would promote the federal policy of termination, one designed to dissolve the historical dependency of Indian tribes on the federal government and push them into the mainstream of American society by dissolving tribal political power, ending federal social services to Indians, and relocating them away from their reservation homelands.[121] The policy would prove disastrous for the tribes it affected, some of which had it thrust upon them despite their expressed wishes to the contrary. As Richard Drinnon notes in his scathing critique of Myer, *Keeper of Concentration Camps*: "Just as his *termination* of Native Americans meant their *relocation* in ghettos, so his *relocation* of Japanese Americans across the country meant the *termination* of their communities (Little Tokyos) on the West Coast and the breakup of their subculture. In both instances he and his staffs energetically grubbed up the roots of their charges and gave them one-way tickets away from their places of shared recollections."[122]

Rocks

I walked around there: what was left of the camp where my grandfather died, a prisoner of my country. Grasshoppers ticked off dry brush, and the recent heat wave in Idaho that summer had pushed the heat out onto these open fields. It was over one hundred degrees. Dry grass and lit-ter covered the parking lot. In the distance, farmers were growing sugar beets under the skeletal frames holding up power lines. They hummed. I sweated. I looked for something—some memento, some keepsake. I couldn't explain why, but I needed some piece of that place to hold onto, something tangible to symbolize the event that looms behind me as a specter to remind me of how history has shaped me.

I had bought a book of photographs that year of the camps as they exist today. There were black and white shots of artifacts lying on a blank background: a badge, a child's toy, a broken bowl laid out in a sterile studio. Was it something like that I sought? For the pictures haunted me, and I trolled the rubbled foundations hidden from the road in the deep grass. I came across bed springs, empty oil cans, hinges strewn about the cornflowers. None of it would do. Finally, I found an old scrap pile of cans and other unwanteds. A woman's shoe. A can of "Pure White" cooking oil. A crushed and rusted bird cage. I grabbed a few cans and put them in the trunk of the dusty car. But this felt somehow a violation. This was a car crash in American history, my family's, not a rummage bin or yard sale. I put them back. And then I saw a rock the size of a small walnut, black and white. When I'm stuck somewhere in traffic now, I'll sometimes reach down and roll its smoothness, the sun of Idaho, in my hand.

I headed back to Twin Falls, south toward Eden, the town whose lights glittered out in the distance from the fences of Minidoka fifty years ago. I pulled back out onto Highway 25 where the shot-up Hunt sign was. Next to it was another sign—PREHISTORIC MAN—informing all travelers that near here an archaeological excavation showed humans had lived here "for more than ten thousand years." It was sign number 276. The sign's final words read, "Through all these changes, man succeeded in adapting and remained here." As I drove by the El Rancho Casta Plente again, the sun was brilliant purple, orange, and red and seemed intent on spreading itself out as long as it could into the dying day. It stretched out to Idaho. The kind of sky you can only see out West.

Girls skating at Minidoka, January 1943.

Harry L. Stafford (right) and Mr. Kamaya on Minidoka farm, July 1944.

COURTESY NATIONAL ARCHIVES.

Funeral service at Minidoka Relocation Center, August 1943.

COURTESY NATIONAL ARCHIVES.

Chapter 4

HAUNTED BY WATERS

Shoshone, Mormon, and Japanese American Relations to Place

A Nisei who has a point of view on behaving is apt to find he has acquired many more friends than a Caucasian if he makes the initial step. He is interesting. He has traveled.

> Mr. Barber, chairman of the Relocation Committee, during meeting with Minidoka residents, September 8, 1943

Eventually, all things merge into one, and a river runs through it. The river was cut by the world's great flood and runs over rocks from the basement of time. On some of the rocks are timeless raindrops. Under the rocks are the words, and some of the words are theirs.

> Norman Maclean, *A River Runs through It*

The air is rich with sage and the first hint of powdery dust from the trail. You treasure the beauty that surrounds you in such abundance—treasure it for being so close to hand, uncrowded, isolated, wild and free to wanderers like so few places left on earth.

> Harald Wyndham, "Spring in Pocatello"

As I moved along the interstate at eighty-five miles per hour, the Snake River Plain glided by my window, a view of Idaho that, I imagined, a majority of today's travelers share, because like the early pioneers who passed along this same corridor, they head elsewhere. Or maybe they make the short excursion north to trendy Sun Valley, the nation's first destination ski resort, built by the Union Pacific Railroad in the 1930s.[1] When people back East tell me they have been to Idaho, that invariably means the small band of towns off Highway 75 where Old West and New West collide. One summer I drove up there to fish the Big Wood, a pretty freestone river with wild rainbows that cuts through this valley and offers clear views of the surrounding Sawtooth Mountains. Hemingway fished here. Parked on the tarmac at the small airport in Hailey, along the edge of one of the country's largest wilderness areas, were Cessnas and Lear jets. Faux western storefronts offered antiques, Indian wares, and Thai food; and off the highway were new homes that are among the most expensive in Idaho.[2]

As I came around a bend in the river while fishing, I was startled to see someone's well-manicured backyard, as if the suburbia of my native north Pittsburgh had landed here in Idaho: a gazebo, thick green lawn, and expensive shrubs. Later, as I walked along the edge of this yard to move by some other fishermen on my way back downriver, a drunken man with no shirt and a drink in hand yelled loudly and unintelligibly at me from his second-floor window. Having moved off the highwater mark of the river, I had now trespassed, and the shouts and barbed wire surrounding the other side of his property ensured that I knew this.

Although the original intent of relocation was to contain the body of Japanese America, the threat of its spread across the land, the end result was the opposite. A massive diaspora began with the resettlement of Nisei college students, such as my father, to colleges and universities in the East and Midwest. Their incarceration by the federal government ironically instituted for Japanese Americans the kind of mobility that Jefferson's America promised, yet in the opposite direction and in contradiction to the autonomy it symbolized. Thousands would follow these college students out of the West. Of the total population of 120,313 internees who at one time were under the control of the WRA, 54,127 resettled out of the West.[3] For many Nikkei, even when the West was eventually opened to resettlement, it could no longer be home. As my father recounted years later, "It was a sense that this home . . . didn't accept me and had kicked me out . . . I would put it that way. That I just didn't feel comfortable in California or the West Coast."[4]

My father had grown up in California in a Japanese American community and spoke wistfully of his days in California, of how he once ate a dozen hot dogs at the state fair, how he fished in the Sierra Mountains for trout, and how he loved the vibrancy of San Francisco. Every day that he worked outside in the yard, tending his beloved pachysandra, he wore a faded leather belt with a big buckle adorned with the state symbol: a giant bruin. But Cal would not welcome my father back to resume his studies, and so he completed his undergraduate degree at Temple University, with the help of the Quakers who worked to place Nisei students in colleges and universities outside of the West.[5] After receiving clearance from the FBI and War Department, my father left Tule Lake accompanied by armed military personnel as he traveled through the expanse of West Coast soil from which he was banned. The document certifying his right to leave "camp," as he always referred to it, was titled, "Citizen's Indefinite Leave."

He moved to Philadelphia, where, because he was accustomed to the low skyline of Sacramento, the skyscrapers shocked his senses. After finishing his degree, he entered Temple Medical School, where he would study alongside one of Masuo Yasui's sons, Shu (Robert). Only after he died, when looking through his WRA file, would I learn that he had also been accepted to Duke Medical School, but his clearance to attend Duke, my brothers' alma mater, did not come until over a year after he had applied.

Like that of many Nisei, his migration meant settlement in an area virtually devoid of a Japanese American community, consistent with the WRA's expressed goal to "impose upon the evacuees a policy of sprinkling them unnoticeably across the length and breadth of the country."[6] These pioneers not only moved eastward into the nation but also across its divisions of class and race, as large numbers of Nisei, like my father and Bob Yasui, eventually moved into the upper-middle class and married outside their race. The end result of the internment had not been containment but redistribution across geographic, economic, and social borders.[7]

Despite their attainment, it is shortsighted to point to the story of Japanese Americans as an iconographic success story, the narrative of a model minority, which has been used by the media and others to define their post–World War II experience and the more general Asian American experience.[8] Numerous internees could never recover the property, homes, farms, communities, status, or even the peace of mind they had once enjoyed. This was especially true for the Issei. As one internee recalled: "The poor old folks, they had no job. And all they could do was get a menial job in American farms, you see. . . . Oh, it was pretty rotten."[9] After the war, Min Yasui earned a precarious living as an attorney in Denver until his death in 1986, and despite intense efforts by himself, his family, and Japanese American groups, the Supreme Court refused to reconsider his original case.[10]

The lives of those of us not confined to those camps, but who exist only in their shadow image, also remain bordered, restricted, or directed: the communities we can't live in, the families we can't join, and the places where we can't travel safely. Though Japanese Americans, especially Nisei, have worked to move on with life and to emphasize the positive in their experiences and even willfully to forget, the claim in Idaho's official history that "many 'Japanese' are grateful for the evacuation experience" is a misrepresentation that obscures the long-term effects on evacuees and the larger Japanese American community.[11]

A Land Made More Tenuous

Outside the car window, the view now was of rolling brown plains with impossibly green patches of corn, hay, and sugar beets bordering the river. Tall lines of poplars. Occasionally the big green Snake River appeared where the road cut into the river plain, and its water sprayed out of the sprinklers that rested in the fields. Outside of Twin Falls, I occasionally caught glimpses of the unmistakably long flat shapes that tell of Idaho's World War II history: the former barracks at Minidoka that were sold by the federal government and moved across the plains of southern Idaho to become storage sheds and cheap housing. People still live in some of these former barracks. And I wondered, as I followed their migration, "Do they ever imagine the lives within these walls fifty years ago?"

I fidgeted with the radio dial, and a voice blared out in that cheery spokesperson tone: "This is our homeland! So, if you're thinking of sprucing up your home in time for the big Pioneer Day celebration, hitch up the wagon and visit your neighborhood Ponderosa Paint and Wallpaper Store!" Pioneer. Like "patriot" back in New England, the word "pioneer" resonates to some assumed collective root; we name holidays, sports teams, and even paint stores after these ancestors and line the highway with markers to note their passage. Yet, like Nikkei before me, I was moving eastward, heading the opposite direction. Signs frequently reminded me that I was passing along the Oregon Trail Auto Tour Route; and as I headed north toward Pocatello on I-86, I came across a site, Massacre Rocks, that recalled the travails of our putative Western ancestors.

In August 1862, pioneers and Shoshone Indians engaged in a series of skirmishes near here that left ten pioneers dead. The Indians attacked two separate wagon trains on consecutive days and were then pursued by a party of men from both wagon trains, who sought to recover their stolen stock, cash, and provisions. They attacked the Indian camp but were forced to retreat, losing three men in the running battle. The brochures I picked up here had an etching on the cover of a wagon passing through the desert, and they detailed the battle and its locale. But the Indian dead and wounded were left unknown. As historian Brigham Madsen notes in his book about the Shoshone leader, Pocatello, "There was no Shoshoni reporter to record the Indian loss for posterity."[12] Although the waves of migrants westward that began in the 1840s only passed through Idaho, they left an indelible mark upon the homeland of Idaho's Indians, and this environmental impact was the primary reason for the events at Massacre Rocks and similar skirmishes that eventually led to the removal of the Shoshone, the loss of most of their lands, and the costliest battle in Native American history, "variously called the Battle of Bear River and the Bear River Massacre."[13]

The Shoshone, who believed wolves were their ancestors, lived in the Snake River Plain region and followed a pattern of seasonal migration that allowed them to utilize the variety of resources the region offered. Because they did not practice agriculture, they had to make use of the natural food sources most abundant at any given time. They collected camas root in regions of southern Idaho, harvested salmon in the fall along the river basins, and hunted buffalo out in the Great Plains. By the time of the mass migration of Euro-Americans into Idaho during the mid-1800s, this migratory lifestyle was already influenced by earlier contact with Europeans. During the 1700s, the Shoshone acquired horses from the Spanish, which gave them increased mobility and allowed them to widen the range of their seasonal migrations and to move eastward to the Great Plains, where they were eventually pushed out by Blackfeet and other competing tribes.[14] In fact, it was the rich horse stocks of the Shoshone that caused Captain Meriwether Lewis to seek them out during his transcontinental trek in 1805, for he desperately needed horses to pass over the Continental Divide. Despite the scarcity of food among this tribe whom, Lewis noted, "suffered as we then saw great hardships for the want of food," a member of the Corps who "had had a good view of their horses estimated them at 400. most of them are fine horses."[15]

The Shoshone were wary. They feared that these odd travelers might be associated with their enemies, and Lewis fretted that "the state of the expedition . . . appeared at this moment to depend in a great measure upon the caprice of a few savages who are ever as fickle as the wind."[16] When Lewis, accompanied by these Shoshone, reunited with William Clark and a group of the men who had scouted out a potential water course up the newly named Jefferson River, a providential event occurred that helped assuage the suspicions of the Shoshone. Accompanying Clark was Sacajawea, a Shoshone girl owned by their French interpreter Toussaint Charbonneau; she had been captured by the Hidatsa in a raid and was later sold by them to Charbonneau. Among the band of Shoshone, she immediately recognized a woman who had been with her the day of her capture and later her brother, Cameahwait, the leader of this band.

Lewis's plan to obtain several horses was still threatened by the more immediate concerns of the Shoshone, who were on the move to meet up with other bands of Indians in preparation for their annual buffalo hunt. Lewis had refused them what they most desired: guns to tip the balance of power more in their favor in contestations with neighboring tribes who had already traded for large numbers of weapons. In the end, the Corps obtained their horses and, just as important, information about the land west of them. Cameahwait drew a map in the ground of the local river drainages and used heaps of sand to represent the formidable mountains that surrounded them—information that discouraged Lewis. From an older member of the band, they learned that the region to the southwest, today's southern Idaho, was "a dry and parched sandy desert . . . in which [they] must suffer if not perish for the want of water," and that there was indeed a "river below the rocky mountains that it ran a great way toward the setting sun and finally lost itself in a great lake of water which was illy taisted."[17] Finally, Lewis felt the Pacific was at hand. The Shoshone provided them with a guide to lead them across the mountain pass to the region inhabited by the "persed nosed Indians." In return, they bestowed Cameahwait with a medal bearing the likeness of Thomas Jefferson and promised him that "it would not be many years before the whitemen would put it in the power of his nation to live in the country below the mountains where they might cultivate corn beans and squashes."[18] Earlier Lewis had promised that "whitemen would come to them with an abundance of guns and every other article necessary to their defence and comfort."[19]

During the first few decades after Meriwether Lewis's stay with this band of Northern Shoshone, his promised goodwill between whites and Indians was a fairly accurate portrayal of their relations. Indians traded with travelers and trappers in a mutually beneficial arrangement, and the relatively small number of white settlers and migrants moving into Indian lands posed only a limited threat to traditional lifestyles. Although they did not actively gather furs, Idaho's Shoshone and Bannock Indians traded foodstuffs and horses with fur trading operations until this business petered out in the 1840s. This period of limited cross-cultural contact has been defined as a "cultural golden age" for Northern Shoshone.[20] But while Shoshone surely benefited from the access to material goods, firearms, and wealth that this trade provided, the contact with white civilization also came with devastating consequences. This was apparent even to Lewis and Clark at the turn of the century, when they stayed amidst the

Sheepeaters, as this band of Shoshone was called. In his journal entry of August 19, 1805, Lewis noted that, despite their isolation, "these people have suffered much by the small pox which is known to be imported and perhaps those other disorders [referring to syphilis and gonorrhea] might have been contracted from other indian tribes who by a round of communication might have obtained from the Europeans."[21]

To the Shoshone, Euro-Americans represented a plague—despite the anti-Indian and later anti-immigrant rhetoric that argued for the need to protect the white race from contagion.[22] In fact, the population losses resulting from such epidemics are a likely cause of Shoshone loss of power in the Plains and of their retreat westward. Within sixty years, places where Shoshone and whites met had charted a disastrous course from the early promise of Lewis and Clark's "Camp Fortunate" to the violent conflict at Massacre Rocks. Historian Peter G. Boag sets 1851 as the date marking this transition, based on portrayals of Indians that trail emigrants recorded in their overland journals.[23] Based on his reading of seventy emigrant journals, he sees in the mid-nineteenth century a shift in white attitudes toward the Indians of southern Idaho from a more balanced and at times positive view—"We have two Indians and a squaw with us tonight. They are friendly, and gave us some information relative to the country"[24] —to one that emphasizes their danger: "They are filthy in the extreme & their women, those that I saw were very homely & dirty, being a perfect burlesque on the sex."[25] In the 1860s the relative peace amongst whites and Indians in this region would end, and a period of raids and eventually warfare would come to the Snake River Plain. Lewis was correct in predicting that whites would come "with an abundance of guns," and that the Sheepeater band would come "to live in the country below the mountains," but neither occurrence would be for their comfort or defense.

At Massacre Rocks State Park was a little wooden pavilion with displays of pioneer life: a wagon, tools, and campsite. On the deck overlooking the Snake River and the volcanic outcroppings once inundated by the great Bonneville Flood that swept across the landscape was a diagram of the Oregon Trail. The panel representing this part of the trail included an account by a member of the Applegate Group of 1843: "It is nothing else, than a wild, rocky, barren, wilderness, of wrecked and ruined Nature; a vast field of volcanic desolation."[26] As many travelers before and after this group of pioneers saw it, the Snake River Plain, with its lava flows, sage flats, and open spaces, was only hostile. Yet if it was "wrecked nature," much of that, even in the early 1840s, was not the work of nature, but of the pioneers. As early as 1843 the cartographer for John Frémont, Charles Preuss, noted, "The white people have ruined the country of the Snake Indians and should therefore treat them well. Almost all the natives are now obliged to live on roots; game can scarcely be seen any more."[27] That even today the wagon tracks of these sojourners can still be seen in many places in Idaho indicates the fragility of such desert regions and the fiction of the West as an untainted landscape in the 1800s. The impact of thousands of wagons and livestock—horses, cows, oxen, and mules—moving through such a dry region was enormous: "During the peak migration, 10,000 wagons crossed the Oregon Trail in 1852. Travelers reported 200 wagons in one day. Diarists reported the Snake River Valley was destitute of grass for 700 miles."[28] Because Idaho included both the Oregon Trail and the start of the California Trail, massive numbers of emigrants crossed through southern Idaho. From 1849 to 1860, nearly 250,000 people are believed to have passed through these plains.[29] A journey through barren and open plains may more accurately be described as an ongoing environmental disaster if historical perspective is situated from the Shoshone point of view.

Because of the limited resources available to them in this region, Shoshone were, as noted earlier, a highly mobile group who utilized a variety of food sources. All of these food sources were affected as traffic on the overland trails increased. The destruction of grasslands not only threatened the survival of Shoshone pony herds but destroyed several food sources as well, particularly grass seeds, which, as Brigham Madsen notes, were "a very important part of the diet of all Shoshoni."[30] Of course, grasslands destruction also impacted native game animals that the Indians hunted. The depletion of firewood and water sources also threatened the well-being of Idaho's native residents.

One of the most important food sources for Shoshone, including Sacajawea's band, was the camas root, the perennial flower with an edible bulblike root also harvested by the Nez Perce. Large fields of camas grew in the south central plains of Idaho, and Shoshone, as well as Bannock bands, their closely associated neighbors, commonly migrated to this region to harvest camas. The influx of immigrants threatened not only the native species that Indians relied upon but also the mobility of the Indians to harvest these resources. The open West grew increasingly closed around them, and their attacks upon whites in the 1860s directly resulted not from an abstract threat to their way of life or an inherent deviltry but from a need to insure their survival. Richard N. Holmer notes that the flexible and migratory lifestyle that characterized traditional Shoshone culture "made them able to handle dramatic environmental change better than other groups, enabling the Shoshone to expand throughout the Desert West while other groups retreated to more productive areas."[31] This very adaptation to their environment, however, made them vulnerable when such unnatural forces claimed the land. Not only were nearby food sources and other staples destroyed by emigrants, but the inability of the Indians to migrate freely prevented them from adjusting to these depletions and fully utilizing the land's food resources. Madsen and others suggest that the violent incidents of the 1860s and the subsequent wars between Idaho Indians and government forces were caused by these factors.[32] As a result of the changes brought to the land by the pioneers, the Native Americans of Idaho "now inhabited a physical world made more tenuous."[33]

A New Zion

Eventually, the various bands of the Shoshone ended up confined to the Fort Hall Indian Reservation in southwestern Idaho. The band known as Sheepeaters that Lewis and Clark traded with were originally granted a reservation in their mountain homeland along the Idaho and Montana border, near the town of Lemhi. However, whites, especially miners, encroached on their lands, and the government eventually resettled them at Fort Hall. What remains of their presence in this section of Idaho are the names of places they left behind, such as the town of Tendoy, named after their leader during this tumultuous period. Their original designation, Sheepeaters, would also be lost, as they would become known as Lemhi Shoshone, just as the major landmark of their homeland, the Lemhi River, would forever be known by another name. Instead of the principal element of their diet, a part of their homeland, they would take the name of a character from the Book of Mormon.

Perhaps no group of Westerners more profoundly illustrates both the implementation and the denial of Jefferson's vision of the West than the Mormons. Although they did "make the desert bloom," and their canonical religious text frequently uses the very phrase, their agricultural success in the dry regions of the West was not the result of independent efforts by small farmers but of the collective implementation of a vision—a religious one. Jefferson had heralded farmers as "the chosen people of God," but for Latter-day Saints, their role as farmers was simply the work of those already chosen by God. While Jefferson saw God in the land, Mormons reshaped and worked the land as an act to please God. Having escaped persecution in the Midwest, they came to the dry valleys of Utah and later some of them moved northward into Idaho to build the new Zion. As their spiritual leader, Brigham Young, stated, "We have no business but to build up the kingdom of God, and preserve it and ourselves in it. Whether it is ploughing, sowing, harvesting, building, going into the kanyons, or whatever it is we do, it is all within the pale of the kingdom of God, to forward his cause on earth, to redeem and build up Zion."[34]

The common notion that the West represents autonomy, at times an almost asocial character, gets deconstructed when Mormons are placed within its canyons and plains. Mormon communities relied upon a highly ordered social structure, and the church often directly mandated individual acts, including land use practices. The communal nature of Mormons also made them objects of suspicion in the land that epitomized individualism. As Dean May notes in his book *Three Frontiers: Family, Land, and Society in the American West, 1850–1900*, the Mormons' "greatest blasphemy was to advocate and doggedly attempt to realize a society where individual freedoms would be compromised by the needs of the broader community."[35] Like other groups before and after them, Mormons would be defined as a threatening horde, and legislatures, at both local and federal levels, would work to restrict their opportunities in the West.

The immediate limitation upon Mormon settlement was the environment. Brigham Young had led his followers into the Great Basin Desert of Utah, where agricultural production, as in similar regions of Idaho, was dependent upon extensive irrigation. As recounted by a contemporary Mormon poet, the Mormon settlement of the West was a battle against aridity, which, if religiously inspired, was accomplished by human hands:

> I was born in the desert
> Brigham made bloom.
> I was reared among the dry grass.
> Measured water
> came each two weeks,
> and even God
> could not make it reach
> to the far fence corners.[36]

Unlike the other various irrigation projects in the West, Mormon water projects were funded neither by private business interests, like the failed Boise River Project of Arthur Foote, nor by the federal government. Thus, agricultural development by Mormons was at first limited, for only massive irrigation projects could insure the volume of water needed to practice large-scale agriculture in such regions, and only the federal government had the resources to complete such works. Moreover, Mormon doctrine espoused a limited use of the land that paralleled the small-scale production of Jefferson's yeoman farmer, and Mormon leadership developed a system of land distribution that awarded relatively small plots of land to followers. The system derived from a philosophy that Latter-day Saints should only work as much land as they needed to meet their individual needs. [37]

The Mormon hierarchy directed the settlement of Idaho—an expansion of Zion across space.[38] It was common practice for church hierarchy to choose specific members to settle new regions, and the church leaders picked particular men to lead the push into Idaho. The movement of these pioneers followed the earlier migration pattern of the Shoshone, spreading north from Utah into the southeast corner of Idaho, and their lives would eventually entwine with the people who had passed along this corridor over three thousand years before them.[39] Mormon pioneers established the town of Lemhi in 1855, but it was later abandoned and not until 1862 was the first permanent settlement—Idaho's first white settlement—established at Franklin. It was from these original white settlers of their home range, who five years later abandoned the region, that Sacajawea's band of Shoshone derived their name, Lemhi.

In Mormon theology, North American Indians were descendants of the Israelites, more specifically their fallen descendants, the Lamanites. Mormon doctrine held that the Lamanites' wickedness was signified by their darkness. The Book of Mormon proclaims, "For behold, they had hardened their hearts against him, they had become like unto a flint; wherefore, as they were white, and exceedingly fair and delightsome, that they might not be enticing unto my people the Lord God did cause a skin of blackness to come upon them."[40] Despite this portrayal of nonwhites, Mormon relations with Idaho's native inhabitants often contrasted markedly with the treatment they received from other pioneers. In her study of Mormon life stories, Susan Hendricks Swetman notes the relative absence of negative portrayals of Idaho's Indians, a contrast to the overland journals studied by Peter Boag.[41]

After the tumultuous period of Indian and white relations that included incidents like those at Massacre Rocks and the eventual establishment of the Fort Hall Reservation at the site of a traditional Indian wintering ground, Shoshone followed a varying pattern of settlement on the reservation and reliance on treaty rations, seasonal migrations to traditional hunting grounds, occasional raiding, and assistance from Mormon communities. Brigham Young had espoused a policy of feeding Indians, and as the federal presence in Utah grew, Young attempted to persuade the Indians to settle down and become members of the Mormon church.[42] Although many have questioned the motives of Mormon leaders for their more lenient Indian policy, at times the expressed opinions of these men displayed a radical perspective about western lands. Writing in a Utah newspaper in response to recent stories about the Shoshone's most notorious leader, Pocatello, church leader Peter Maughan defended the Church's policy by claiming that it derived from "a sense of humanity, realizing that they [Shoshone] look upon the very lands we occupy as a portion of their inheritance."[43] Of course, what Maughan's statement also pointed out was that the expansion of Zion, the very touchstone of the Mormon mission, meant forcing the Indians, "the Lamanites," out of their inherited homeland.

Nevertheless, the more generally benign treatment of Mormons attracted many Shoshone, especially as pressure from the federal government forced more and more of them onto the Fort Hall Reservation, where, despite treaty obligations laid out in the late 1860s, food supplies were often grossly inadequate. From its inception, the town of Franklin attracted Indians who survived off the handouts of the local Mormons. Eventually, in 1874, the Mormon Church decided to convert the Indians and to establish them as farmers. A farm was begun in Franklin, as well as in northern Utah, and several Shoshone were baptized in nearby waters. Soon large numbers of Shoshone began to flock to missionary George W. Hill, who in the summer of 1875 alone baptized 574 of these new saints.[44]

Despite the Book of Mormon's proscription against race-mixing— "cursed shall be the seed of him that mixeth with their seed"[45]— Mormon leader Brigham Young sanctioned Indian-Mormon marriages as a means of improving relations among the groups. Another church leader had told him that church founder Joseph Smith had experienced a revelation that foresaw the mixing of Indians and whites, similar to Thomas Jefferson's vision of America's future. This was also, of course, a means by which the tainted darkness of the Lamanites could be removed. The unique relationship between Mormons and Indians created suspicion among other settlers and the federal government. The Ghost Dance revival of the late 1800s, for example, was often blamed on Mormon influence.[46] Pocatello, Idaho's most reviled Shoshone leader, eventually became a Mormon. Federal government officials and local gentiles became increasingly alarmed by the Mormon outreach to the local Shoshone and eventually ordered Shoshone to return to the reservation under threat of military force. Pocatello returned to the reservation, and in October of 1884, he died there, his body laid to rest inside a spring on the Snake River Bottoms.

Toia

Continuing along the Oregon Trail Auto Tour Route, I passed by American Falls Reservoir, one of the massive federal water projects that allowed for the agricultural production that now defines this region: the transformation of Idaho from "dreary sagebrush . . . into irrigated wonderlands."[47] Built during the 1920s, the American Falls Dam resulted in the creation of a nearly twenty-five-mile-long reservoir and required the acquisition of nearly 35,000 acres of the Fort Hall Indian Reservation. As I neared the reservation, a large billboard announced the "Shoshone-Bannock Peak Casino and Truck Stop." Gambling, tax-free cigarettes, and cheap gas are now the markers of these traditional homelands. The truck stop was painted a pastel blue with geometric designs. Alongside the highway now were the tracks of the Union Pacific Railroad, and I followed them east into Idaho's second largest city, Pocatello.

The Utah and Northern Railroad stretched northward from Ogden into southeastern Idaho, and this spot made a natural connecting point to the Oregon Short Line that provided rail service all the way to the Pacific coast. The Fort Hall Indians agreed to a right-of-way across their reservation in 1881; in 1887, this easement was increased to 1,840 acres, the original site of Pocatello. Pocatello, named after the chief, whose name in the Federal Writers' Projects publication *Idaho: A Guide in Word and Picture* is translated as "road not to follow," became the largest rail center west of the Mississippi and was known as the "Gate City."[48] Today, railroads are still a dominant feature in the landscape, and the Union Pacific Railroad is one of the city's largest employers. Driving through the old downtown, I heard the loud screech of train wheels and could not imagine any place in this town where one could not hear the sounds of trains—the scream of steel wheels or the clanking of ties underneath passing trains—even in the large ranch style homes that now spread out from the town center and into the surrounding mountains. Although it is no longer the "Gate City," it retains the name of this Shoshone chief, despite the views of his descendants who claim that he never used it. There is no letter L in the Shoshone language.[49]

Like the Shoshone who preceded them, the Japanese who came to Pocatello had no means of translating directly the notorious chief's moni-

ker; the Japanese language also lacks an L. They called this area, eastern
Idaho, "Toai." Japanese emigrants first moved eastward into Toai as railroad workers on the Oregon Short Line, establishing communities along
its stops, as they had done in southwestern Idaho. According to accounts
collected by the local Nikkei community, there were over 400 Japanese
workers in Pocatello by 1911.[50] Upon the settlement of a general strike two
years later, however, the company replaced nearly all its Japanese railroad
workers. Some of these early Nikkei spread out to other regions of the
West, while others began to work in the state's growing agriculture industry, especially its important sugar beet sector. Eventually, some of them,
despite restrictions like the Alien Land Law, established themselves as
prosperous farmers and contributed immensely to the growth of Idaho's
renowned potato crop. To meet the needs of Toai's burgeoning Nikkei
population, a Japanese hospital, boarding houses, motels, and other businesses such as groceries, barber shops, billiard halls, and restaurants
opened in the area. The 1916 *Idaho State Gazetteer and Business Directory* lists
dozens of Nikkei-operated businesses in the state, most along the Oregon
Short Line.

Laying Low

I, however, had not come to seek out the sites of old businesses. I came to
see rocks. On the campus of Idaho State University in Pocatello is the
Idaho Museum of Natural History, a modest display of Idaho's creation, its
flora and fauna. I walked through the glass doors to that warm "Hello!" so
easily offered in the West. A graduate student in a T-shirt manned the
desk. The recorded sounds of owls boomed from across the hall. I was invited to take photographs and "to take my time." The Nature of Idaho display began with a layout of the state's often dramatic geologic history. En-
cased in glass were rocks that chronicled these changes in the land and
the variety of minerals and gems found in the Gem State: pahoehoe, lava
bombs, geodes, topaz, agates, and gypsum. What was not noted is that
many of these specimens were collected by Henry Fujii, that early immigrant to southwestern Idaho in whose home I sat one afternoon the previous summer as his daughter showed me some of the rewards of his rock-
hunting sojourns during the latter years of his life, after he retired from
farming. It was the irony that appealed to me, those fissures in the dominant pull of history that outline the illogic of our enforced ideas about
what is natural and about who or what a native is: a man who for so long

was denied the legal right to possess any of Idaho's land had offered all its residents the opportunity to learn it—to know the terra firma itself.

Earlier in the year I had read the account of an internee traveling through Idaho en route to the Minidoka Relocation Center: "I thought how ironic it was that we should see . . . Japanese who were free to do as they pleased while we, by trainloads, were being herded to camps."[51] Recent decades have seen an impressive amount of scholarship on the experiences of Japanese American relocatees, what they saw from the trains and barbed wire–enclosed camps, but little attention has been paid to the view from that platform. How did Idaho's Nikkei view the irony of their situation? They were free within a state that contained ten thousand Nikkei who suffered imprisonment because of the one trait they had in common: ethnicity. And were they really "free to do as they pleased"? The wartime experiences of the Fujii family and of Nikkei from Toai suggest that they, too, suffered a shrinking of the democratic space of the American West, if one far less severe and costly.

Henry Fujii and his family were not simply part of an ethnic enclave, as the wartime policies of the federal government assumed. As the only Japanese family in the area, their lives were bound both to their white neighbors and their social institutions and also to the local Nikkei community of southwestern Idaho. Mr. Fujii cooperated with neighboring farmers and was a member of the Rotarians and a trustee in the local Methodist church. In a 1971 interview, he was asked if he had any trouble with neighbors during the war period. "No," he answered, but what he did reveal was the close monitoring of his movements by the authorities: "No, they prohibit, limit travels to twenty-five miles I think from home." Because he needed to travel to sell his produce, Fujii recalls obtaining a permit from the local district attorney that allowed him to "move anytime anywhere in Idaho."[52] That authorities closely watched local Nikkei, including such seemingly harmless citizens as Mr. Fujii, was not surprising given federal policies, the statements of Idaho's xenophobic governor at the time, Chase Clark, and the long history of Americans' racialization of Asians.

Governor Clark had earlier prevented the voluntary migration of coastal Nikkei to Idaho, and his wartime rhetoric was at times aimed at his state's own Japanese Americans, most of them citizens. By 1940, more than sixty percent of Idaho Nikkei were native-born Americans.[53] Although the first Idaho man to register for the Selective Service after Pearl Harbor was of

Japanese descent, Clark admitted during the 1942 conference to develop a plan for relocation: "I am so prejudiced that my reasoning might be a little off, because I don't trust any of them. I don't know which ones to trust and so therefore I don't trust any of them."[54] Although Clark admitted to the potentially irrational basis of his anti-Japanese feelings, he still used familiar racist rhetoric to describe his fellow Idahoans. Nikkei were a contagion, comparable to the vermin that, although introduced into America from Europe, was most closely associated with disease—rats. In a speech before the Grangeville Lions Club, he claimed Japanese Americans "act like rats" and that the solution to the "Jap problem" was to "send them all back to Japan and sink the island."[55]

As on the West Coast, FBI officials searched the homes of prominent Idaho Issei and closely monitored their movements. Historian Robert Sims notes that by the end of winter in 1942, the FBI had searched about one hundred homes in southwestern Idaho alone. Mary Fujii Henshall recalled to me the somewhat amusing persistence of FBI officials who searched the attic of their home, painstakingly sifting through the onion skins left over from the harvest with which her father had lined the attic for insulation.[56] While Henry Fujii's response to his interviewer suggested a more peaceable existence around his farm than Chase's rhetoric suggested, his daughter's recollections portray a time of restrictions, of "laying low" as she phrased it to me, and of periodic violent intimidation.

On the hill just up the street from the Fujii farm, someone placed a sign that stayed up during the war: No Japs Welcome Here. Since the Fujiis were the only Japanese in the neighborhood, it was clear that the sign's creator had intended a personal message. One night, someone shot out the window of the kitchen where Mary and her small child were, and on another night, white-hooded visitors burned a cross in the family's yard. Although such incidents are dramatic examples of racist intimidation and may not accurately reflect the experience of all Idaho's Nikkei during World War II, the less dramatic containment of the Fujiis' mobility, both geographically and socially, is typical of the community's wartime recollections.

Government policies limited the movement of Nikkei in Idaho during the war, but they, themselves, also chose to "lay low," to make themselves less visible. In some instances, friends and associates asked them to do so. Despite his reputation as a respected member, Henry Fujii was asked not to attend Rotary meetings; his fellow members feared repercussions from others in the white community. Although Mary found work coloring photographs for a local store, she had to park behind the store and slip in the back door, where she then did her work hidden from customers. Of course, the racial fault lines in the social space of American democracy had existed before the war. Public space was not available to all. In an article written in the 1980s, Mary recalled how she had attempted to enroll in Red Cross lifesaving classes at the city pool. "I did not understand when the man said, 'We can't let you in the pool.' I still feel the terrible hurt when I realized what the man meant." Mary did eventually get to take those classes because her father immediately approached the mayor, and the next day she "got in and had a good swim, the only Japanese American who ever contaminated their water."[57]

After the war, the lives of the Fujiis soon returned to the increasingly wider realm of contacts and challenges that had characterized them before the attack on Pearl Harbor. Henry Fujii returned to the Rotary Club, becoming president of the local chapter in 1951. Among his fellow Rotarians was the legislator who introduced the Alien Land Law in Idaho; he became Mr. Fujii's lawyer. He soon retired and began his active pursuit of rock collecting. The Fujiis spent hours writing poetry, and both received several prizes for their traditional Japanese poems. Mary pursued a career in teaching, returning to the family farm after thirty years in Arizona. At the ceremony honoring Mr. Fujii's donation of his rock collection to the state, Governor Cecil Andrus said of the Fujiis: "We honor them for their contributions to international understanding. . . . Their lives epitomize the American Dream. . . . You have helped build Idaho to the great state it is."[58] For Henry's funeral service in November of 1976, the following poem of his was chosen for the program.

> I have come to the sea
> The ocean that reaches out to Japan
> is deep and blue.

Below it appears a sketch of the ocean, Mt. Fuji, and birds in flight.

Haunted by Waters

At the ending of his novella, "A River Runs through It," which recounts his family's lives amidst the fabled trout waters of western Montana, Norman Maclean provides an evocative final sentence: "I am haunted by waters."[59] That sentence could serve to define the lives of many Americans, especially Idahoans, who rely so greatly upon the life-sustaining waters their rivers provide, who are joined because of them, and who also commonly display a less pragmatic, at times spiritual, attachment to the Lochsa, Snake, and Big Wood rivers. Reading Henry Fujii's poem, I think that he, too, was haunted by waters. Having left Japan as a young man and become a part of the "American Dream," the ocean that separated him from his native Japan had become both an imposing barrier and a source of inspiration. It was a physical representation of the tranquil nostalgia he felt as he looked westward in old age from his new home of Idaho. Yet, even if he was an American—a pioneer—to express this feeling he relied on a Japanese poetic form thousands of years old.

I, too, am haunted by waters. I guess anyone who flyfishes so much that he elicits consternation from others, who has stood all day in the rain, who has driven across the country to fish one river, and who has taken unreasonable risks to reach just the right spot on a river, is haunted. I can list a plethora of reasons why I fish, but what draws me to some places remains beyond language. I wish that I could ask Fumiko Fujii, also an avid angler, what about waters haunted her. Her story, that of Issei women in general, is one left out of the master narratives about Western spaces.[60] She wrote:

> The limit I caught
> I wash my hands
> In the river
> At the end of the fishing day.

Mary Fujii Henshall, when writing of her parents in her article "Pioneer Portraits: Henry and Fumiko Fujii," noted that her mother "has climbed every mountain at his side in rock hunts and often lands bigger trout than he does!"[61]

I recently filled out a questionnaire from an Idaho group that works to protect its rivers, and as I plowed through the predictable questions about age, occupation, and income, I was suddenly confounded by the question: "What emotions come to mind when you think of Idaho rivers?" I paused. I struggled. I had to come back the next day with a partial and unsatisfactory list: awe, desire, humility, loss, excitement, freedom. As with people, different rivers fill our lives over time, haunt us. I am haunted now by one river in particular, the Little Wood.

As I drove west across the desert from Pocatello, the sky was hazy; ahead a giant brown cloud pushed east. The desert was burning. Brush fires were burning all over the West that summer, and firefighters had battled this fire in the desert for days. In the flat plains of southeastern Idaho, the cloud appeared to be just a few miles away, but as I drove, it took forty minutes before I reached its edge and the burnt sagebrush by the highway. My eyes watered.

The usual impossibly blue sky was more the hazy summer sky of my childhood in Pittsburgh, and the Big Lost Mountains were hard to make out in the distance. Ahead was INEL, the Idaho National Engineering Laboratory—an odd array of clumps of white buildings, blocked-off roadways, barbed wire, massive power lines, and radio towers atop buttes out in the middle of a desert. It is the perfect fodder for the conspiracy theorists and antifederalists with whom Idaho is so often associated, mostly by those outside its borders. Plutonium has been detected here deep in the ground, and in the 1950s and 1960s, the government intentionally leaked radioactive gas.[62] A badger sat waiting for something by the highway. Outside of the little town of Arco, where the mountains above chronicle the high school class years of local daredevils, going back to 1932, a sign proclaimed: "The first town lit by nuclear energy."

As I got closer to the river, my anticipation made it harder to contain my speed, and questions flooded my mind. What would the water be like? Low? High? Clear? Were the golden stoneflies still hatching? What pulled me to this particular river is hard to explain. It was not the fishing. I had been here the year before, and after I caught a few fish, a storm soon blew in from Utah and knocked me off the river. In that open country, with no windbreaks and miles of flat terrain, the wind can come up in an instant and knock you to your knees. I had fought merely to stand.

It may be that what drew me to this small river out in the sage flats was the very thing that repelled earlier travelers—the desert. Idaho poet Jane Goldbeck could be describing the Little Wood with the opening lines of her poem "Rivers":

> Each subtle curve and slope of earth
> suggests a possibility
> of moving water inherent in the smallest rain
> A river sudden from a rolling land
> deep-cut canyon, red-grey
> at the feet of sagebrush hills[63]

Though often only a short distance from the highway, the river remained almost entirely hidden as it wound out in the sage flats dotted by volcanic rocks and large basalt outcroppings, where the water fell into deep cool pools. It was to me full of possibilities, different as can be from the heavily wooded mountain streams of my childhood in the Allegheny Mountains.

Plants I had never seen lined the banks, and what once appeared to me a uniform landscape was now full of variegated shapes, angles, and colors. A narrative.

I strapped on my backpack, with its quarts of water, sunblock, and food, and walked to the river. The dry cheatgrass shook and clicked all around me; hoppers, and big dark katydids, what are also sometimes referred to as "Mormon crickets," were everywhere. Just as I had hoped. The traditional enemy of Idaho farmers, having ruined entire harvests, hoppers are one of the most welcomed signs to flyfishers. Their calorie potential is irresistible to trout, and even the most habitually cautious brown trout will slam a well-presented hopper pattern. I had read earlier in the week about their latest invasion. Idaho's director of agriculture, Pat Takasugi, a third-generation Japanese American, was quoted, "This [infestation] is shaping up to be a very bad one. We have heard some rumors that this has the potential to be the sixth worst one we've had in history."[64] In 1985, government agencies declared a "hopper war" in Idaho and utilized military aircraft to spray over six million acres of Idaho with insecticides. Such measures were not being considered now. War had yet to be declared.

I saw the rise of a small trout under a willow and rolled my grasshopper to its lair. It slammed the fly. After I moved out into the river and scooped up the brown and golden trout, I offered it above, to show my father, with whom I can no longer fish here in this time. As the day progressed, and I carefully fished the river, I realized this fish had showed me the method to success. To escape the hot sun and the predatory birds that skim above the river, the brown trout were under the shade of the willows, holding tight on the far bank. A cast made against the bank in an area with rocks for cover and current to carry food to the fish nearly always got a rise. At times the richly mottled fish exploded from the shade or rocks at the masked grasshopper and leaped madly. More commonly, they rushed for the cover of their home bank. In one short stretch, I caught twenty. By the end of the day I had landed at least sixty wild trout in a river out in the desert and had not seen another person. Just a coyote. Some rattlesnakes. It was likely the best fishing I have ever had. As night fell and the desert glowed outside the car window from the burning sagebrush, I drove back across the Arco desert with the bends and banks of the Little Wood there to fill my dreams, to haunt me even now.

Taters

The next day I drove north to Blackfoot, the car covered in dust. As I pulled off the highway and into town, a sign proclaimed: WELCOME TO BLACK-FOOT, WORLD POTATO CAPITAL. Nothing is more closely associated with the state of Idaho than potatoes. Famous Potatoes is stamped into thousands of license plates that roam the state's roadways. Step into any supermarket in the country, and you will find bags of potatoes that display the Grown in Idaho label, a registered trademark. Idaho leads the United States in the production of potatoes, and probably every American has consumed a Gem State tuber. McDonalds makes about half of its french fries from Idaho russets. By the outbreak of World War I, Idaho was already known for potatoes. And this region of southeastern Idaho is Potato Central. The elevation that creates warm summer days and cool nights provides ideal growing conditions for potatoes here. In addition, the volcanic ash in this region provides a perfect soil type because potatoes need good drainage. Thirty percent of the nation's potatoes, more than anywhere else on earth, are produced in Idaho, much of it here. The sign is no hype; this is the potato capital of the world.

I visited the Idaho Potato Expo there, housed in the old Oregon Short Line train station. Outside of it sat a giant russet potato sculpture with "Idaho" on it. It was even topped with butter and sour cream. A seven-foot-tall potato with a crown on its head and holding a welcome sign stood outside the entrance. The price of admission got you a free baker. Inside the museum was a map with colored pins for visitors to mark their hometowns. Nobody from my side of the state seemed to have made it out here. I stuck a yellow pin into western Massachusetts. The museum had the expected displays on the history of potatoes and potato production, but also some quirky items: a burlap potato sack Marilyn Monroe wore, the world's largest potato chip—an impressive twenty-five-by-fourteen-inch snack—and a potato autographed by the spelling-challenged former vice president, Dan Quayle. I learned from a sign on the wall by the drinking fountain that the first president to serve potatoes in the White House was none other than Thomas Jefferson.

In a glass case was another display of snacks: potato chips from Japan. And as I looked up to the high ceiling above me, I noticed brightly colored banners draping the tops of the walls. Reading them I realized that these, too, like Henry Fujii's poem and a can of potato chips, connected the home of the Potato Capital of the World to islands across the ocean. Mat-surra, Wada, Tsukamoto: all Japanese names. The banners were sold as a fundraiser for the museum, and many of these benefactors were local farmers, Japanese American potato farmers. In the next room of the museum was a display of potato farming equipment: diggers, harvesting belts, and a planter shoe. The sign next to it told me that "the shoe is designed to lift the dry loose soil up and out of the groove it cuts without compacting the soil. . . . Invented and donated by Masa Tsukamoto."

When I pulled up into the Tsukamoto's driveway, a shiny black pickup sat in the driveway facing me. A bug guard with "EZ Tarp" written on it was mounted on the front end. The EZ Tarp is another one of Mr. Tsukamoto's inventions: a device that allows a driver to pull a tarp over a load automatically without leaving the truck cab. Masa Tsukamoto attributes his knack for inventing to a simple habit of identifying a need, of seeing a better way of doing something; and these visions have all grown out of his work as a farmer. His first invention was the "water saver wheel," a device that allowed farmers to conserve water by creating small pockets in the soil.[65] He was one of the first in the area to utilize water conservation practices on his land, but as he noted to me, "A farmer isn't really environmentally friendly."[66] Irrigation is simply too harmful an act, and farmers use almost twice as many pesticides, measured in terms of weight per acre, on potato crops than on any other crop.[67] Since his retirement in 1993, he has devoted himself to his inventions and the business that sprouted from them. His most recent invention allows farmers to clean and disinfect rapidly the tubes that are used in potato cellars to force air and moisture into the cellars, as potatoes require very high humidity in storage.

As I admired the rosebushes outside the front door, a little girl with dark bangs and a shy grin answered the door, a granddaughter. It had taken me a few days to chase Masa down. His son, who now runs the family business, kept telling me, "He's fishing." He had spent the last few days taking his grandkids bluegill fishing. He is a short man, youthful, with a quick laugh and a steady measured way of speaking.

Like many Nikkei in Idaho, his roots go back to the railroads; his father, Kuniichi Tsukamoto, came from Hiroshima to Idaho in 1900 to work as a contract laborer on the Oregon Short Line but lost his job after the railroad strike. He then opened up a boarding house, where he and his wife raised their family until he began leasing land in the area to farm. This was during the beginning of the Depression, and the family struggled. In the spring of 1942, rumors began circulating that the government would soon seize Issei assets in Idaho, so Mr. Tsukamoto transferred his assets to his son. Because of the Alien Land Law, the Tsukamotos had always leased land, and not until the 1960s did they begin to purchase property. They grew potatoes and grain. Eventually, they owned a maximum of 640 acres, larger than the average farm size in Idaho today. Despite the spread of agribusiness and the corresponding spread of large-scale farming in America—farms measured in the thousands of acres—much of Idaho's landscape retains the Jeffersonian vision of small independent farms spread across the land. The majority of Idaho's 25,000 farms are still owned by individuals or families with net incomes under $30,000.[68]

Like the Fujiis across the state, Japanese Americans in the area suffered restrictions upon their lives during World War II. Mr. and Mrs. Tsukamoto recounted those times: "Anytime when you went out of town you didn't know whether to stop at a gas station or not. . . . Cafes the same way. You didn't know whether to go into the cafe. You just go in and kind of look around and slide into the first seat and hope you get waited on. Sometimes you got thrown out." The Tsukamotos recalled how their families limited their trips into town and how both their mothers burned most anything Japanese out of fear: "She threw them in the dump and covered them up with dirt." Neighbors held a meeting to discuss what to do about the "Japs." The local police gathered up guns and ham radios. Idaho's governor helped fan the hysteria with his anti-Japanese rhetoric, language they still vividly recall. Although many Nisei would eventually serve in the armed forces during the war and the first Pocatelloan to volunteer was a local Nisei, fear and outright intimidation persisted. The Yamashita family displayed a five-star flag in their window during the war. One night someone shot that window out. Nevertheless, like many Nikkei who were not relocated, Masa Tsukamoto noted his relative good fortune: "It wasn't real rough like being evacuated."[69]

Better Americans

Like Mary Fujii Henshall, Masa and Midori Tsukamoto recalled their lives returning to normal fairly soon after the war. The uncertainty and hysteria of their neighbors that ruled where they could go and what they could do dissipated. One day a neighbor came to apologize to Masa. He continued farming and developing his inventions, and he and his wife enjoyed fishing trips to local waters. They both gleefully told me of the nine-pound rainbows each of them caught one recent season in a friend's lake. But

Masa also noted how much his native state had changed, how its open spaces had been closed off for those who enjoyed its hunting and fishing: "Used to be you could go about anywhere. Now even the guys, if you ask them, won't let you in."[70]

One activity that Masa has been deeply involved with is the JACL, the Japanese American Citizens League. JACL history traces back to an informal regular gathering of Nisei professionals in San Francisco in 1918. One of these men was my uncle, Tokutaro Hayashi. This small group later banded with other similar organizations to form the JACL, which held its first convention in 1930 in Seattle.[71] The Pocatello-Blackfoot chapter of the JACL was chartered in 1941 and grew out of an earlier organization, the Pocatello Nisei League. As the name suggests, the JACL marked the transition of power within the Nikkei community from Issei to Nisei. As its hymn displays, the JACL has emphasized assimilation by Nikkei into American life, becoming "better Americans," as the title of a 1960s publication notes. The JACL official hymn encapsulates these values and provides a uniform vision of Japanese American identity.

> There was a dream my father dreamed for me,
>   A land in which all men are free;
> Then the desert camps with watch-towers high
>   Where life stood still, 'mid sand and brooding sky.
> Out of the war in which my brothers died—,
>   Their muted voices with mine cried;
> This is our dream that all shall be free.
>   This is our creed we'll live in loyalty.
> God help us rid the land of bigotry
>   That we may walk in peace and dignity[72]

The JACL booklet from the 1960s further describes the members' parents, the Issei, as unrecognized "pioneers of the still undeveloped West. . . . They were peaceful, hard-working, self-reliant Americans in every way."[73] The JACL emphasis on following such a standard plan of Americanism and especially its failure to protest the evacuation have made it a controversial organization within the Nikkei community. Its leaders, men such as Mike Masaoka, espoused full cooperation with federal authorities during the relocation and even presented the WRA's former director, Dillon Myer, with an award after the war. As a result, JACL members were targets of derision for some Nikkei in the camps, and JACL leaders were even assaulted. The rift between those who complied with evacuation and those who resisted, especially the so-called no-no boys, men who resisted the draft, remains unhealed. Not only did these men experience ostracism within the larger Nikkei community after the war, as recounted in John Okada's novel No-No Boy, but the focus on the outstanding accomplishments and sacrifices of the 442nd Regimental Combat Team has threatened to wipe their protest out of Nikkei history and eclipse the total history of Japanese in America.[74]

The JACL has obfuscated the historical record as well through its reluctance to divulge the extent of its cooperation with federal authorities. In the late 1980s, it commissioned an investigation of JACL wartime activities but then tried to suppress the damaging findings that documented the relationship between JACL leaders and the federal government. The report revealed a disturbing willingness to discredit and even punish fellow Japanese Americans whom JACL deemed subversive. In a letter to Dillon Myer, Mike Masaoka, a wartime JACL official, argued: "Immediate action should be taken whereby, without warning or hearing, known agitators and troublemakers are moved out of the relocation centers and placed in special camps of their own."[75]

However, JACL did later prove itself an effective civil rights organization, working to dissolve the barring of Issei from citizenship, which was finally achieved in 1952. In Idaho, they lobbied to repeal the 1923 Alien Land Law, which came off the books in 1955. And later, in 1967, they helped realize amendments to the state constitution, which originally barred "Chinese, or persons of Mongolian descent, not born in the United States" from voting, holding office, and serving as jurors. This section of the constitution had also barred Indians who had not "severed their tribal relation" from the same rights.[76] In the 1980s, they helped lead the movement for redress, and Mike Masaoka was a pivotal figure as a lobbyist on Capitol Hill.[77] The federal government eventually commissioned an investigation of the internment that concluded: "The promulgation of Executive Order 9066 was not justified by military necessity, and the decisions which followed from it . . . were not driven by analysis of military conditions. The broad historical causes which shaped these decisions were race prejudice, war hysteria and a failure of political leadership."[78] Surviving internees received an apology signed by the President of the United States and a tax-free $20,000 payment in restitution, a result of the Civil Liberties Act of 1988. Also in the 1980s, the JACL sought to replace and even enact history onto Idaho's landscape itself, but this, too, would raise controversy.

More Worthy Pioneers

As noted, resettlement led to the spread of Nikkei all across the country. Although my grandfather never lived to settle elsewhere, my aunt and her husband left Minidoka and joined with other internees to form a mushrooming Japanese American community in Chicago.[79] My father moved to Philadelphia, served in the Army in Germany, and finally settled in the suburbs of Pittsburgh. Only my uncle returned to Sacramento. The success of the War Relocation Authority's experiment of creating "pioneer communities" for these individuals would be analyzed and debated. Minidoka's project director, Harry Stafford, who had received much criticism for his lenient treatment of Minidoka's residents, had already come to his own conclusion: "I believe the ramifications of evacuation, incarceration, relocation, and resettlement to have been a most unfortunate experience for evacuees and government alike."[80] Gradually, the land surrounding the former camps reclaimed them by natural forces—wind, rain, erosion. Today, little remains of them. Most of the camps became quickly neglected and remained so for decades. At Minidoka, however, the pioneering tradition that the federal government attempted to create at a concentration camp housing its own citizens remained alive, at least for a short time.

"Most people think pioneers exist today only in history books." So begins a 1987 newspaper article from the Twin Falls Times-News.[81] Shortly after the end of the war, the Bureau of Land Management opened up the site of the former Hunt Relocation Center to returning veterans, and in 1947 a lottery was held in which the government awarded forty-three land allotments to former servicemen. The only payments required of the veterans were a one-dollar-per-acre fee to the Bureau of Reclamation and fifty cents to the American Falls Reservoir District. The plots varied from 69 to 170 acres. Two years later, another drawing was held and another forty-six lots were awarded to veterans whom the lieutenant governor assured would "prove to be worthy pioneers of Idaho."[82] Along with the land, each veteran also received two of the former barracks to use as housing or storage, some of which still stand today. The local Hunt Latter-day Saints chapel was made from two of these former barracks.

The recollections of those who homesteaded the former camp under this plan strangely echo the experiences of their predecessors. They recount the struggle to clear the sagebrush, to fight off rabbit infestations, and to endure the physical deprivations, especially during their first days, when adequate housing was not yet available. The newspaper article notes, "The settlers first lived in one group of barracks at the old Hunt internment camp known as 'block 30' until they could get their barracks moved to their own farms. They had to share a common wash house, and Kenner recalls that 'some of the wives were upset to have to use community shower facilities.'"[83] Like former internees, they also had to learn to cook on hotplates and to cope with the incessant dust. One former settler recalled in the 1987 article that the barracks were "hot in summer and cold in winter." By then only a handful of the original veterans still remained. One of these summarized his experience: "I said then that all we were given was a fine opportunity to earn and pay for a piece of land from which we could make a living and a home. And that is all any of us wished to be given."[84] For those who had preceded "these worthy pioneers," this was exactly what had been taken from them.

By the time the article about these pioneering veterans was written, little of the original camp remained on the site. The lava stone structure of the guardhouse and an old potato cellar were the only prominent signs of this place's past. Nothing on the nearby highway led travelers to this site. Coupled with the still pervasive misunderstanding about the wartime treatment of Japanese Americans, the site's invisibility helped to reinforce the putative rationale for this injustice. When, in the late 1970s, Congress recognized the site of the former Manzanar Relocation Center as a National Historic Landmark, this inspired the local JACL chapter to investigate the long-neglected site of Idaho's former relocation center.[85] Masa Tsukamoto approached the local JACL president, Bob Endo, who agreed that something should be done, and Masa began to investigate a similar plan for Minidoka. His first task was to find out who actually owned the land. He was surprised to find that the Bureau of Reclamation was the owner of much of the site.

The Bureau was willing to offer help, and the JACL raised money through its organization and its publications. On August 18, 1979, the Minidoka Relocation Center was nominated to the National Register of Historic Places.[86] The Bureau of Reclamation's accompanying Statement of Significance was direct in its interpretation of the site's meaning and resisted the still dominant view that the relocation was either a military necessity or a protective measure for the benefit of Nikkei. Such views are evident in this excerpt from an interview with one Idaho resident in 1991: "I felt that it was for their own protection. . . . And as far as I have ever heard, they received good treatment. They were not brutally beaten or any of that type of treatment that our people received in their camps."[87] The

Bureau document was blunt. It stated, "Ruins of Camp Minidoka, a Japanese American internment camp during World War II, are tangible reminders of one of the most serious and painful contradictions of our country's philosophy of freedom. Through a nefarious legal fiction, over 110,000 loyal Americans were wrenched from their homes and forcefully detained without due process of law, in bleak, barbed-wire enclosed camps scattered over isolated inland areas on desolate tracts of Federal land."[88] The dedication ceremony included a presentation of colors, a recitation of the Pledge of Allegiance, and playing of "The Star Spangled Banner" and the JACL hymn. JACL representatives spoke, along with Idaho politicians, including United States Senator Frank Church. Other JACL members who had originally planned to be present, however, stayed home.

The Seattle JACL chapter, which included many former Minidoka internees, had planned a very different ceremony for October 13 of that year. They envisioned a much more dramatic act, a performance in which they would both reenact and deconstruct their lives as internees and the camp itself: "At Minidoka, we will remember those of us who died in camp with a memorial service at the camp rock garden. We will wear our family name and number tags we were required to wear. . . . We will build a replica guard tower. Then former captives and former keepers will chop, tear and burn the tower down. Whites who once put the tags on us will collect them from us and toss them into the fire. Together we will release each other from the camps and send them into history."[89] The Seattle chapter's plan met with strong opposition from the Pocatello-Blackfoot chapter, which feared how such a theatrical display would be received by the local community. "These Seattle people are going to come in here, burn a tower and then leave. But we've built a good relationship with the people in this area, and we don't want to disturb it," Masa Tsukamoto noted in an interview with Idaho's largest newspaper. Martin Matsudaira, president of the Seattle chapter, criticized the validity of the Idaho JACL members' right to shape the commemoration, claiming, "They are not the custodians of history of Minidoka."[90] Due to the controversy, the Seattle JACL did not attend the dedication ceremony in August and eventually abandoned its plan, which the national JACL also refused to support.

Just who the custodian of this history should be was clearly the crucial question and was never fully answered. What is promising is that the contestation at least includes a debate within the Nikkei community and that they now possess the ability to participate in shaping their history. It is true that the local JACL chapter of southeastern Idaho has a minority of members who actually lived at Minidoka. However, through their publications, their outreach and education programs, and their work at making Minidoka a visible part of the state's history, they have helped to establish a public history for these "pioneer communities" where Seattle residents, my family members, and others were sent.

Still, this unique history of an ethnic group, which illustrates the historical stain of racism inherent to the dominant vision of American democracy, can be obscured when it is commemorated in a fashion that only seems to confirm ideals of American patriotism. Even the perquisites awarded as a result of military service were historically denied ethnic Japanese, who had to fight in the courts to achieve the right of naturalization that other alien veterans enjoyed. Issei had served in the American armed forces since the Spanish-American War but had little success in obtaining naturalization through legislation that offered it to alien veterans. In 1925, a case involving a Japanese World War I veteran entered the Supreme Court. The Court based its interpretation of the relevant amendment, which offered naturalization to apparently "any alien" who had served in the armed forces, upon the more general naturalization laws that offered naturalization to the limited class of individuals debated earlier in the Ozawa case, "free white persons." It ruled that this earlier legislation superceded the apparent plain language of the later amendment since "it has long been the national policy to maintain the distinction of color and race, radical change is not lightly to be deemed to have been intended."[91] Only in 1935, when Congress passed the Nye-Lea Act, would Japanese veterans finally be guaranteed their service would win them the right to citizenship. Therefore, even such apparently reaffirming ceremonies, such as the one at Minidoka, can be interpreted as more than an affirmation of democratic ideals. As Lucy Salyer notes, in relation to the JACL's use of the political coinage of Nisei combat service, "the JACL's strategy for inclusion rested precariously on glorification of military ideals, and even then the ultimate sacrifice—death in combat—could not dispel the persistent tensions between martial and racialist citizen ideals."[92] Moreover, the degree of personal trauma and fracturing of the Japanese American community that are a direct result of this event remain hidden from the public. Americans must know that these were concentration camps where people and communities suffered, many never regaining the place they had in America or the feelings of attachment to their native West and to each other that they once enjoyed.

Mixed Blood

Emiko Omori's recent documentary film, *Rabbit in the Moon*, brought this rift within the Nikkei community, particularly the debates within the JACL, to the forefront. Issues of the JACL newspaper, *Pacific Citizen*, were filled with editorials and letters staking out claims for and against the wartime actions of JACL as it debated and eventually agreed to a public apology for the draft resisters it once vilified. During this debate, Seattle JACL member and author Frank Chin wrote, "The JACL owes Japanese America an apology for the egregious white racist behavior of the JACL under the leadership of Mike Masaoka. The JACL owes an apology to all of America for forcing Japanese America to submit to a white racist hysteria that did not exist."[93] The Tsukamotos' and Mary Fujii Henshall's recollections certainly contradict Chin's claim that "a white racist hysteria" did not exist during the war. Masa Tsukamoto views Chin as a revisionist who cannot accurately factor the impact of events from such a distance. What is intriguing about Chin's editorial is his assumption that race is not a "natural" category. One can ostensibly adopt or reject "white" or "Japanese" traits of identity. Race is a matter of self-representation. In that manner, he eerily echoes the WRA planners and men like them who sought to remake Indians and Japanese into truer, whiter Americans.

After we had been talking for some time, Masa posed a question to me that also highlighted the complexity of the racial landscape in America, the tangled strands of American identity that are obscured and that its planners sought to avoid: "I notice you refer to yourself as Japanese American. Why? You are only half—right?" No one had ever asked me this question. And a little uncertain then of the direction our interview was heading, I relied on the assumed safety of my inherent sarcasm: "Well, no one ever called me a damn Kraut." They laughed.

When I tell people I am going to Idaho, they often make some snide reference to backwoods yahoos, white supremacists running around in the woods with white hoods and swastikas. When I flew into Boise last summer, a woman in the seat in front of me opined to another fellow Idahoan, "Everybody back East has this image of everyone in Idaho running around in a white cape." I satisfy my questioners by assuring them I plan to visit the Panhandle enclaves of the Christian Identity movement and confront its members—tell them they give the Aryan race a bad name. For I am, I would insist to them, likely more Aryan than they are, my mother's parents having immigrated from Hamburg and Bremen. I am what Hawaiians refer to as "hapa," one of partial Asian ancestry, and this phenomenon of mixed-race marriages has become more and more common among Japanese Americans, who have one of the highest outmarriage rates of any ethnic minority.[94] This, too, is the result of the Relocation, as Nisei like my father moved away from the largely Japanese communities of their youth and entered predominately white communities and social institutions, where they were encouraged to blend into the community, not to be too Japanese.

This hybrid character of Nikkei further problematizes the definition of race that American institutions have relied on to divide access to American geographic and social space, and the multiracial reality of American identity, "an overlapping of races" as the Supreme Court forebodingly described in *Ozawa*, is, thus, a source of societal anxiety. As Marilyn Halter notes in her discussion of Cape Verdean Americans, "When significant numbers of people cannot be readily categorized, it threatens to undermine the entire system of social classification."[95] In Idaho, this breakdown of discrete racial categories has historically incited legislative attempts to fight it, so that at the time of their wedding in 1953, my parents' marriage was illegal in Idaho.[96] For Japanese Americans, this phenomenon raises pressing questions about what will define them in generations to come, as their collective story becomes more and more fractured, complicated by a wide array of inherited historical trajectories. In fact, it may be that Japanese Americans' persistent attachment to the story of World War II combat service may be in response to a perceived sense of dissolution, as they become increasingly diverse in ethnic and racial identity and generational affiliation, the traditional marker of Japanese American ethnicity.[97]

Fears of miscegenation, of course, have plagued other groups in the West and appeared in the early written accounts of the travelers on the Oregon Trail. Although the baby that Sacajawea carried with her into Idaho, during the first white exploration of the region, was of mixed race, unions between Indians and whites were outlawed in 1867. During the territorial period and into early statehood, Idaho's marriage laws were used to control another group as well: the Mormons. The federal government explicitly outlawed the practice of polygamy with the Morrill Anti-Bigamy Act of 1862. Idaho's Mormon settlers, however, made it virtually impossible to enforce, because local juries would not convict those tried under the Act. Further legislation did not prove much more effective, and Latter-day Saints worked to prevent members from being arrested, often hiding them within their communities. Even their work of making the "desert bloom" could yield such opportunities. A recent article on polygamy in southeastern Idaho includes the recollection of a local Mormon woman who claimed that in one Idaho town the grain was grown high around the temple to provide a hiding place for the men.[98] A more pragmatic reason for such restriction of Mormon marriage practices was the political threat Mormons posed to Idaho politicians. Mormons, voting as a block, helped the Democratic Party dominate Idaho politics. Thus, in 1885, the territory adopted the Test Oath Act, which barred anyone who supported the practice of polygamy from voting. Mormons challenged the act, but it was upheld, both by the territorial courts and eventually by the United States Supreme Court in 1890. Until the repeal of this legislation in 1893, Mormons were effectively barred from participating in Idaho politics because of the "unnatural acts" they committed or condoned.

Laying Out the City

That evening after I left the Tsukamotos' home in Blackfoot, I drove north to Lewisville, and dusk appeared as an eerie orange glow through the brown clouds in the west, the desert still burning. When I pulled off of the interstate, I passed a sign for the TV Museum, a surprising site in the rural upper Snake River Valley of Idaho, but intriguing as it was, I passed on until I finally saw the small sign backgrounded by huge poplars: "Entering Lewisville. Population 471." The part of the sign with 471 was lighter, indicating a recent adjustment to the town's size. I assumed the number was revised downward, for as I drove through its streets, Lewisville seemed asleep. No one was outside. I came to an intersection. The road sign said SE Jefferson, an apt name for this town that in many ways so faithfully displayed what the architect of America's democracy imagined across these Western spaces.

Lewisville is laid out in a grid, one oriented north-south, as if fixed to the system that Jefferson attempted to lay out across the continent. What directed this town's development, however, was not the edict that directed America's first official geographer under Jefferson but the vision of another man, Brigham Young, who upon arrival in Salt Lake City declared that it "be laid out perfectly square, north and south, east and west."[99] Young's vision was inherited from Joseph Smith, the original Mormon spiritual leader, whose inspiration was the Bible's book of Numbers.[100] It became the basic design principle for all Mormon towns in the West. And, in a town such as Lewisville, the center of town represents the lives of its saints: at the center is the church and its related institutions.[101] Other traits are distinctly Mormon and reflect what were once explicit church directives, such as wide streets and irrigation ditches. In Lewisville, the ditches were long gone, but their outlines remained along the wide weedy streets without sidewalks. The massive Lombardy poplars around the town were also characteristic of Mormon town planning, and although common in non-Mormon areas, they became so closely associated with Mormons that they have often been referred to as "Mormon poplars." In his work, The Mormon Landscape, Richard Francaviglia notes that "by the 1880s virtually all areas settled by the LDS were visually dominated by poplars."[102] Francaviglia lists several traits that typify the Mormon landscape, but more intriguing is his argument that one can interpret these landscape and architectural practices as symbolic, representing the cultural characteristics of Latter-day Saints. Some of the more anachronistic architectural elements of Mormon settlements reflect the attachment to the old world ways of Mormon settlers, many of whom were recent immigrants from northern European countries, including Welsh, whom others had expected to find here decades ago.

Francaviglia's observation that the West represented a haven, a hideout for the Mormons, raises questions about how their perceptions of the West's natural landscape may differ from that of other pioneers. I remember a Mormon friend telling me that when he moved to New England, the landscape felt "claustrophobic," as if there were "always something hiding behind that next tree." There were no vistas. Given the fact that other Westerners experience a similar disorientation when first confronted with the vastly contrasting topography and vegetation of the more temperate East, was his reaction in any way Mormon? Mormon elder George Smith described my friend's native Utah as a kind of rocky fortress: "If the mountains were covered with beautiful timber, and plenty of grain could be raised without irrigation, there is no doubt but our enemies would overrun us, or at least make us a great deal of trouble; but as it is, we inherit the chambers of the mountains: the rocks are our protection, and the oases of the desert our homes."[103] These Americans were fleeing, and Brigham Young described the Mormon exodus westward as a quest for sanctuary: "Ourselves and our friends can find a place for many years to come amid these wild mountain regions, where surrounds the health inspiring atmosphere, and the clear cool mountain rivulet winds its way from lofty and rugged eminences, presenting a scenery bold, grand and beautiful, to some sequestered vale, where downtrodden liberty shall feel exalting aspirations, and contentment find repose."[104] In his imagined West, Jefferson's yeoman was more inclined to find his place in the valley with the mountains as a backdrop, as in Idaho's state seal. Brigham Young's saints, however, would be hidden somewhere up in those mountains out of sight. Yet, both would likely end up joined by their dependence on the waters of that "clear cool mountain rivulet."

A Web of Water

From Lewisville I headed back east and got on Highway 20 North. In Rigby I saw a sign for Roberts Idaho Potatoes and passed by a branch of the Zion Bank, which advertised a 24-hour ATM. On my right, ran the tracks of the Union Pacific Railroad, the line that Japanese immigrants followed in their migration up into the valley. Just west of me lay the Snake River, flowing almost due south from its headwaters across the Teton Range. As with so many places here in the West, that water ties the lives of people together. Aridity, Wallace Stegner wrote, is the defining characteristic of the American West. Aridity determined settlement patterns, flora and fauna, and the role of the federal government in Western development.[105] While Stegner's thesis may be overly broad, it certainly applies to large areas of the intermountain West. The need for water has driven Idaho's history and bound the lives of its various groups together, so that at the beginning of the twenty-first century, a life of self-reliance and individual freedom out here seems more and more an act of the imagination, not grounded in the earth. The study of one local resident helps to outline some of the ways that environmental conditions in the Snake River Valley have made even small family farmers reliant upon larger forces and each other.

Masayoshi Fujimoto was born in 1916 in Rexburg, a town named after Thomas Ricks, a Mormon leader who was directed by the church to settle this area. After spending much of his childhood in Japan, where his parents had returned to care for their aging parents, Fujimoto began his career as a farmer. Until 1937, the family had leased land, but that year and the following year he, his uncle, and his wife purchased a total of 180 acres in the Sugar City area. Fujimoto's diary and life history detail the evolution of his connections to the community around him, his reliance and interdependence upon others, and the limits of traditional categories of identity.[106]

As one might expect, Fujimoto relied upon the aid of his fellow Nikkei to operate his farm. He recounted all-Nikkei crews that harvested the potatoes of individual Japanese American farmers. Any expectation that cooperation was based upon ethnicity and was solely altruistic is complicated, however, by the revelation that these labor exchanges entailed obligations that were attached to monetary value. This cooperative arrangement gave "him an early advantage in growing potatoes," but Fujimoto would later come to rely more upon his white neighbors.[107] As the experiences of other Idaho Nikkei farmers illustrates, the boundaries of race seem more permeable in the history of Western rural communities than prior studies of Japanese Americans suggest.[108]

Fujimoto's life directly connects two groups that have generally been discussed separately: Mormons and Nikkei. In 1954, Fujimoto joined the local LDS church, where he was the only member of Japanese ancestry. At the same time, he began to rely more and more on the help of his neighboring white farmers, also Latter-day Saints. Eric Walz notes how the varied production sources of the Fujimoto farm and Fujimoto's business decisions insured a small-scale subsistence operation. He explains Fujimoto's lack of capitalist motives: "This noneconomic attachment has been described by several agricultural historians and undoubtedly had its roots in the Jeffersonian ideal that 'those who labor in the earth are the chosen people of God.'"[109] The roots of Fujimoto's views of farming, however, are complicated because of the variety of influences upon him: traditional Japanese beliefs and agricultural practices, Mormonism, and the American mythos of the self-reliant yeoman. Furthermore, his diaries help to unravel the fiction behind any notion of self-reliance as the defining characteristic of such individuals' lives. Not only did he rely upon the labor and help of others, including financial support from the Mormon church as he grew more and more financially insolvent in the 1960s, but the occupation of farming itself meant participation in a web of complex relationships—a web of water: "The water in canal rise and flooded my potatoes. It really made me mad."[110] This diary entry of Fujimoto's reveals the often precarious relationships that arose from so many people relying upon one vital commodity.[111] The canal that brought water to local farmers created a complex mesh of connections that ultimately could not be handled to everyone's liking. Both the city of Rexburg and local farmers derived their water from the same canal. One day of the week was restricted to the city's water use. When the water was available to farmers, however, the situation was further complicated.

One's proximity to the floodgates affected how much water he would receive; and the lay of the land, soil composition, and crop type also affected water distribution and water needs. As Fujimoto's diary notes, simply watering one's fields could lead to accidental harm to others. If one was not careful, he could easily flood his neighbor's fields. Droughts further complicated matters. Those water users downstream were at the mercy of earlier users due to Idaho's reliance on the law of prior appropriation, and measures to address this set of interconnections often proved unsatisfactory and undemocratic. The Rexburg Canal Company formed a board of directors to manage the operations of the canal. Because the board was controlled by those who held the most shares, however, "This meant that large farmers enjoyed a proportionally greater influence on the election of directors and thus the hiring of a water master."[112] Although water users invested power to control the canal's water in a water master, "there always remained an underlying feeling that all was not equitable."[113] Furthermore, all the careful planning and built-in guarantees of fairness on the part of the board and its members could not overlook the fact that basic environmental conditions, such as the amount of rainfall, could not be predicted or altered. The overall amount of water available from year to year would always depend on factors outside of their control.

Here, as in Valerie Matsumoto's work on the all-Nikkei community of Eden, California, "assumptions of autonomy and choice linked with a golden past inhabited by Euro-American settlers" lose credibility.[114] As Eric Walz points out, the practices of local farmers that have created this rural landscape are the result of a variety of influences including, "such considerations as the irrigation community, geographic location, local climate, tradition, personal preference, and financial position."[115] The farmers in Madison County came from many different countries with unique cultural beliefs and practices, but common influences, including the Mormon church, brought them here, and the land itself bound them in complex and varied ways. This suggests the need for a more complicated model for understanding environmental and social development that allows one to chart how the Western landscape has evolved, including in relation to race and ethnicity.

Small Potatoes

There is something about this region, especially the mountains of the West, "those lofty rugged eminences," as Brigham Young described them, that pulls one. As I drove east on Highway 33 on my way to fish the upper Teton River, my respiration raced, and my chest tightened as I looked toward the Teton Range, where the warm air of the plain rode up into the cool mountain air, forming white water-laden clouds. Perhaps no other place in the West better illustrates the common habit of gendering this landscape—making it feminine, fit to be conquered. French trappers named this mountain range after a part of the female body; *teton* meaning breast in French. Like the waters that flow out of these mountains, that name spread out to the surrounding land, providing the name for a river, two towns, a county, and eventually a dam.

Between the towns of Teton and Tetonia, was a strange undulating landscape, pockmarked and green with crops. Large fields of potatoes and potato storage sheds dotted the view from the highway. In places, the fields stretched out beyond my sight. Eventually, the road headed down into a valley that ran up against the Tetons, massive and still covered in thick glaciers from the deep snow pack of that year. Over the pass was the resort town of Jackson Hole. But I had fish on my mind; for months my head had been flooded with images of this river and the giant cutthroat that swim in this desolate canyon stretch of the Teton River.

New homes, built to offer magazine-cover views of the Tetons, sat with their large glass windows glimmering. I pulled off onto a dirt road and passed a small creek that was all stones, drawn dry by irrigation. It was a bumpy and slow drive in my rental car, but I was determined to see this water. I passed a farmhouse, and the road made a perfect right angle turn, where a man stood tinkering with his irrigation pump. I waved in that slow manner of country places. Finally, down in the basalt canyon, I saw the cut of the river, and I pushed the car along, the gravel spitting from the wheels and clanking off the car's undercarriage. Finally, I came to the last narrow stretch of road and headed through a field and down to the river. The road worsened. The small gravel had become small rocks and the surface a series of deep ruts. I knew it was another two miles at least, and finally I admitted that I had to abandon this trip, this water I had dreamt of for months. I told myself to adjust and adapt to what came my way. The West had taught me that. I turned around and headed back to Rexburg.

On the way back, I passed by another one of those signs that the state put up: TETON FLOOD, it read. For decades, the Bureau of Reclamation had proposed a dam on the Teton River just north of here. In the 1970s, the project came to life through the lobbying of local farmers. Although Brigham Young and Thomas Jefferson had imagined a West occupied by individual farmers producing little more than what they needed for themselves, many of these "chosen people of God" had also become people of wealth. As recently as the early 1990s, Idaho had the highest percentage of millionaires of any state in the nation.[116] In *Cadillac Desert*, Marc Reisner describes how one such man, Willis Walker, a Mormon farmer, was able to rally local support for the dam and with the backing of local newspapers get the project moving. The only real opposition to the dam came from lo-cal environmental groups, one of which was formed to combat the dam. The local chapter of Trout Unlimited, a national organization that works to protect and preserve trout fisheries, formed in 1972 as a response to the dam proposal.[117] The Teton River is home to a unique strain of native Yel-lowstone cutthroat trout, and this chapter named itself the Upper Snake River Cutthroats Chapter.

Recent droughts had provided local dam boosters with evidence to sup-port the need for such a project, although the Bureau's own figures indi-cated that the impact of the dam on overall irrigation levels would be min-imal. Moreover, the area already enjoyed a generous water supply, an average annual rainfall of 132 inches, "five times the annual rainfall of farmland in Iowa."[118] In addition, geologists working for the United States Geological Survey who worked as consultants on the dam project pointed to serious problems with the proposed site. As the Nature of Idaho display in Pocatello illustrates, much of Idaho's landscape, especially this region, is the result of volcanic activity, which formed a pockmarked landscape composed of porous rock, and is prone to earthquakes. One of the Geo-logical Survey's scientists, in a memo to the Bureau noted that "flooding in response to seismic or other failure of the dam—probably most likely at the time of highest water—would make the flood of February 1962 look like small potatoes."[119] The Bureau refused to change course, and local support for the project remained strong. Reisner includes in his text an ex-cerpt sent to a local newspaper that illustrates how deeply ingrained ideas about the natural progress of the West had become in the minds of some of its residents: "Those who would cramp and belittle America's dream and who labor to stalemate needed natural development have plans for a singularly small and feeble nation."[120]

Eventually, the Bureau started its work. Environmentalists had lost their battle in the courts. In the fall of 1975, Teton Dam stood completed. But that spring, a deep snowpack began to melt and filled the dam at a rate far beyond projected thresholds. On June 3, the dam began to leak. Over the next few days the leaks grew, until by the morning of June 5, Caterpillars began pushing earth back across the dam in a frantic attempt to fill the gaping holes. It was too late. Shortly before noon, the crest toppled into the reservoir behind it, and shortly after the largest flood in North America since the great Bonneville Flood crashed down the Snake River Canyon. For the first time, the Bureau of Reclamation had attempted to dam a river and failed.

Despite the still persistent calls of some locals to rebuild the dam, it sits broken and chained off. It is an almost pyramid-shaped mound 300 feet high. On the far side of the river, the earth tore away due to water filling in large spaces of the porous rock. The concrete spillway on the north side is filled with graffiti, and local kids run used tires down it for sport. Though it was two hours before sunset, it was preternaturally dark here. The sky was purple and gray with hazy clouds from the brushfires that blocked the sun. Looking downriver, I saw tree trunks, gravel, and stones that had washed out onto the banks. It seemed a scene out of a war.

The flood created a twenty-foot-high wall that crashed through the nearby towns, literally wiping the town of Wilford forever off the map. Masayoshi Fujimoto's hometown of Sugar City, which he had left by then, was nearly washed away. Rexburg residents fled to the high ground near the college and watched the sweep of brown muddy water filled with homes, trees, and cars crash into town. The water would finally be contained behind the dam at American Falls, but not before thousands of homes were destroyed and eleven people killed, some of whom had been out fishing when the flood hit. It was this flood that left that strange landscape I had seen as I drove west to the Tetons that afternoon: "Nothing, however, was as startling as what the flood had done to the land. The topsoil was gone from tens of thousands of acres—stripped off as if a plow a mile and a half wide had come along, scraping the earth down to the bedrock."[121] The dam affected the land in other ways, too. After the flood, the area was inundated with swarms of flies and mosquitoes. The fishery below the dam was ruined and will never recover. Wildlife in this once treasured canyon also disappeared. In compensation for the flood damage, the Bureau paid Idaho Fish and Game $1.7 million, which it has used to restore the upper stretches of the river. Although this area is above the original dam site and escaped flooding, the dam also had a major impact on this section of the river. The disruption of the natural flow of the river and creation of a large reservoir prevented the river from discharging silt and other debris, so that even today siltation is a problem in this section of the river.[122]

Haunted Again

Surprisingly, there were some able to find something good out of the Teton Dam disaster. One Latter-day Saint recalled that he was dispirited by the loss of his completed autobiography in the floodwaters. However, when he began rewriting his story, "he realized that he *should* be revising it, for in this reconstructive research he encountered many previously over-looked sources, and the second history was not only much more accurate, but six times as long as the first version."[123] Perhaps, the story of this man can act as a model for us as we attempt to tell the history of these places, of how ideas about race and environment have played out upon the landscape of the American West. Our definitions about what is natural and how progress should occur have created a dominant story that has been any-thing but natural or complete. At the least, the story must be longer, re-vised. Maybe it is this that haunts me, what I find in these waters.

Standing in the cool water of the Little Wood, I can look around at the open sage plains with no barbed wire in sight and only the mute blue sky of Idaho overhead and imagine a place open and free for me. But it is only illusion, I know. Even the forested banks of the clear Lochsa can no longer seem pure to me now that they are filled with the markers of time and tied to the ideas that drove its exploration and development. And the Little Wood? I still can see the marks where cattle grazed along the banks and know that only a few miles upstream from here the river runs dry in the summer, when irrigation demands drain it. Downstream a company was caught dumping waste into the river.

When I stand here, flailing a small hook covered in feathers and fur to mimic a life, relying upon my sense of all the natural rhythms and cycles—season, wind, insect activity, fish behavior—I fall out of time. I can free myself from other barriers, those that left my grandfather to die on this desert plain a prisoner of the government I was raised to honor. I can for-get how in grade school, looking up at the alphabet circling the wall and the flag before us, I could never say that whole pledge, could never, know-ing what I did, utter that last word: "all."

For being naturalized as an other in America has always meant moving in its spaces conscious of borders, of places where you cannot or should not venture. Standing here in the cool rich water of this river, with the desert breeze and skittering of birds my only company, moving at a pace only limited by the trace of the sun in the clear sky of Idaho, may be as close as I can come to the dream of America. Is it any wonder so many of us are haunted by these places?

Library at Minidoka with display of resettlement materials, January 1944.

The Naming of Sacajawea by T. P. Dunlap.

Color guard at Minidoka Pilgrimage, June 2003.
COURTESY NATIONAL PARK SERVICE.

Little Wood River, August 1999.

PHOTO BY ROBERT T. HAYASHI.

NOTES

Introduction

1. Merchant, "Shades of Darkness," 381.

2. In her introduction to *The Ecocriticism Reader*, Cheryl Glotfelty notes, "Ecocriticism has been predominately a white movement. It will become a multi-ethnic movement when stronger connections are made between the environment and issues of social justice, and when a diversity of voices are encouraged to contribute to the discussion." Glotfelty and Fromm, eds., *Ecocriticism Reader*, xxv. Recently, T. V. Reed has argued for a more expansive range of voices in the study of literary representations of the environment. See Reed, "Toward an Environmental Justice Ecocriticism."

3. Omi and Winant, *Racial Formation*.

4. The general connection between human identity and place has been explored by the work of numerous cultural geographers, and many are increasingly studying the specific relation between race and place. See, for instance, Berry and Henderson, eds., *Geographical Identities of Ethnic America*.

5. Cronon, *Changes in the Land*, and Merchant, *Ecological Revolutions*.

6. See Espiritu, *Asian American Panethnicity*. Marilyn Halter also discusses this racialization of ethnicity in her work on Cape Verdeans; see Halter, *Between Race and Ethnicity*.

7. Patricia Limerick and others have made such an argument about Mormon identity. See Limerick, "Peace Initiative."

8. Lopez, *White by Law*, 17.

9. Sze, "From Environmental Justice Literature,"166.

10. Joyce, *Portrait of the Artist*, 203.

11. Freedman and Frey, eds., *Autobiographical Writing across the Disciplines*, 2.

12. See Limerick, "Dancing with Professors," and Balakian, "How a Poet Writes History."

13. Nikkei is a general term that refers to Japanese immigrants and their descendants.

14. Okihiro, "Is Yellow Black or White?" in *Margins and Mainstreams*.

CHAPTER 1 | The Innocence of Our Intentions

1. Clark, September 12, 1805, in Moulton, ed., *Journals of Lewis and Clark*. (All footnote references to *Journals of Lewis and Clark* are to this edition.)

2. My "reading" of the Idaho environment depends on methodologies more

commonly associated with cultural geography. A recent essay by historian William L. Lang outlines the application of such approaches to the field of environmental history. Lang outlines three important areas of investigation: how places have been perceived, how they have been symbolized, and how these cultural definitions have incorporated or discarded other earlier meanings of place. See Lang, "The Sense of Place and Environmental History."

3. Whitehorse, September 5–6, 1805, *Journals of Lewis and Clark*.

4. Jefferson, *Portable Thomas Jefferson*, 309–311.

5. Ibid., 78.

6. Ibid., 94–96.

7. Jefferson, *Writings of Thomas Jefferson*, 452.

8. Linklater, *Measuring America*, 111. Linklater provides a detailed discussion of the evolution of America's system of weights and measures. He also asserts that Jefferson's reliance on a uniform system based on the square and decimal was a manifestation of Jefferson's political philosophy.

9. Jefferson, *Portable Thomas Jefferson*, 309.

10. Linklater, *Measuring America*, 83.

11. Bedini, "Scientific Instruments of Lewis and Clark," 93.

12. See Ronda, "A Chart in His Way."

13. Nabokov, "Orientations from Their Side," 242.

14. In *Order upon the Land*, Hildegard Binder Johnson provides a detailed history of the development of the American land surveying system and its impact upon the nation's geography.

15. Stegner, *Wolf Willow*.

16. Schwantes, *In Mountain Shadows*, 5.

17. See Morrissey, *Mental Territories*. Katherine Morrissey's text emphasizes the kind of cultural studies approach to understanding place that I deploy. Morrissey focuses on how various groups, mainly Euro-Americans, characterized this region as a distinct place.

18. Carolyn Merchant notes, "The history of spatial changes is a history of power changes." *Ecological Revolutions*, 50. More specifically, in a recent essay, Mark Spence traces the environmental degradation of the Western environment, and the American government's mistreatment of the Indian nations encountered by Lewis and Clark, to their initial journey. See "Let's Play Lewis and Clark."

19. Spence, "Let's Play Lewis and Clark," 223.

20. See Knobloch, *Culture of Wilderness*. Knobloch outlines the process by which agricultural production, bolstered by the rationalism of science and technology, masked the colonization of the West. She pays particular attention to the discourse of this process that defined it as natural. In her book, she does note the impact of this process upon minority peoples, and I use her ideas as a jumping-off point.

21. For instance, Goetzmann, *Exploration and Empire*; Ronda, *Lewis and Clark among Indians*; Allen, *Passage through the Garden*; Furtwangler, *Acts of Discovery*; Botkin, *Our Natural History*; Burroughs, *Natural History of Lewis and Clark*; and Ambrose, *Undaunted Courage*.

22. For an example of such work, see Ronda, *Thomas Jefferson and the Changing West*. This collection includes essays that outline the environmental history of the West in relation to Jeffersonian principles.

23. Jefferson, *Portable Thomas Jefferson*, 217.

24. Gass, September 19, 1805, *Journals of Lewis and Clark*.

25. See Allen, "Imagining the West."

26. Jefferson, *Portable Thomas Jefferson*, 432.

27. In his journalism, however, Whitman often expressed nativist views that contradict the optimistic universalism that characterizes his verse. See Reynolds, *Walt Whitman's America*.

28. Geographer Nicholas K. Blomley argues that law is a fundamental means by which societies organize physical space and control geographic and social mobility. Therefore, the combined study of legal history and human geography outlines the relationship of political and social power in societies. In this work, I deploy Blomley's basic arguments to explore how space has been organized in Idaho in relation to its minority residents and the various institutions most responsible for organizing and shaping its physical space. See Blomley, *Law, Space, and Geographies*.

29. United States, Naturalization Act, March 26, 1790, Ch. 3, 1 Stat. 103.

30. Jefferson, *Portable Thomas Jefferson*, 186.

31. See Ceasar, "Natural Rights and Scientific Racism."

32. See de Crèvecoeur, *Letters from an American Farmer*; Smith, *Virgin Land*; Turner, *The Frontier in American History*.

33. Allen, *Passage through the Garden*, 305.

34. See Edward Casey, "How to Get from Space." Casey explains that Western modes of knowledge typically assume a homogeneous conception of locales as fixed and formed by human perception. Instead, Casey proposes that both experience and perception are bound to specific places and that places are the repositories of meanings, including history and memory. Casey, therefore, argues that places are best understood when experienced via the physical body. The inclusion of my personal journeys through Idaho are meant to function as an example of Casey's general thesis.

35. Knobloch, *Culture of Wilderness*, 124.

36. Botkin, *Our Natural History*, 134.

37. Jefferson, *Portable Thomas Jefferson*, 311.

38. Ordway, May 29, 1805, *Journals of Lewis and Clark*.

39. Jefferson, *Portable Thomas Jefferson*, 183.

40. For a history of American attitudes to the wolf, see McIntyre, *War against the Wolf*. The Corps of Discovery killed animals, of course, to survive. Donald Worster has pointed out, however, that the magnitude of their killings often clearly exceeded their dietary needs, and they killed therefore for a variety of potential reasons: science, sport, and conquest. Worster, *Unsettled Country*, 60–63.

41. Lewis, August 15, 1805, *Journals of Lewis and Clark*.

42. Ordway, December 29, 1804, *Journals of Lewis and Clark*.

43. "House Sends Batch of Messages to Feds," *Idaho Statesman*, March 27, 2001.

44. Travis Brewer, letter to the editor, *Idaho Statesman*, February 27, 2001.

45. Central Idaho Wolf Coalition, www.usa4id.com/ciwc, accessed July 30, 2001.

46. "Chenoweth Hears the Grizzly Truth," *Lewiston Tribune*, September 21, 1995.

47. See Clarke, "Constructing Conflict."

48. Cheater, "Wolf Spirit Returns."

49. Jefferson, *Portable Thomas Jefferson*, 135.

50. Miller, *Jefferson and Nature*, 200.

51. See Smith, *Virgin Land*, chapter 12.

52. *Statutes at Large of the United States*, vol. 2, p. 277.

53. William Cronon's *Changes in the Land* provides an excellent explication of the contrasting notions of property in Indian and Euro-American societies and the environmental repercussions of Indian and Euro-American contact in New England due to the contrasting ideologies that defined these societies.

54. Spalding to Reverend David Greene, October 17, 1845, in Drury, *Diaries and Letters*, 338.

55. See James, "The Allotment Period."

56. For a general discussion of the Dawes Act, see Carlson, *Indians, Bureaucrats, and Land*. Not only did the Act result in their loss of land, but almost immediately Nez Perce farm productivity declined.

57. Smohalla in McFarland and Studebaker, *Idaho's Poetry*, 10.

58. Marshall, "Unusual Gardens," 173.

59. At the time of Lewis and Clark's journey, it is estimated that annual adult salmon populations in the Columbia and Snake river drainages approached sixteen million. See Scarce, *Fishy Business*, 5.

60. For a detailed history of recent federal environmental practices in the region, see Moore, *Lochsa Story*. Moore is both a longtime resident of the area and a former U.S. Forest Service employee.

61. For further information on this incident, see Owens, "Pierce City Incident."

62. Bureau of the Census, 1870.

63. See Limerick, "Disorientation and Reorientation." Limerick forcefully makes this point in her piece—that historians have ignored the Asian American perspective when discussing the West's environmental history.

64. Jefferson, *Portable Thomas Jefferson*, 125.

65. See Knobloch, *Culture of Wilderness*, 141. While Knobloch applies the definition of "weeds" to American Indian peoples, I am expanding that to, in particular, Asian immigrants in the West.

66. James O'Meara qtd. in Derig, "Celestials in the Diggings," 2.

67. F. B. Gault, *Gem State Rural*, November 1895.

68. Boone, *Idaho Place Names*, 77–78.

69. Couch, "Topophilia and Chinese Miners." For more information on Chinese miners in northern Idaho, see Wegars, "History and Archaeology"; Wikoff, "Chinese in Idaho Gold Fields"; and Stapp, "Ethnography of Chinese Mining Community." Priscilla Wegars is curator of the University of Idaho's Asian American Comparative Collection and also has researched the Kooskia Internment Camp in

northern Idaho, which contained Nikkei men who helped construct the section of Highway 12 along the Lochsa River. See Wegars, "Japanese at Kooskia Internment Camp."

70. Department of Agriculture, *Forest Service Manual 2300*.

71. See Jess Walter, *Every Knee Shall Bow*, for more on Weaver.

72. See Blank, *Individualism in Idaho*, and Gaboury, *Dissension in the Rockies*.

73. Tiffany Hardy in "Idaho Seeking a More Tolerant Image," *New York Times*, February 20, 2000.

74. For a discussion of Idaho's white separatist movement, see Aho, *Politics of Righteousness*. For a detailed discussion of the movement in the United States, see Dobratz and Shanks-Meile, *White Separatist Movement*.

75. Aryan Nations, *Attention White Men*.

76. U.S. Bureau of the Census, 2000.

77. Dan Pena in "Nampa Now 2nd Largest City; Hispanic Population Rising," *Idaho Statesman*, March 24, 2001.

CHAPTER 2 | Matching the Hatch

1. The Pink Albert imitates a mayfly unique to the region, the Pink Albert Cahill, *Epeorus albertea*. See Retallic and Barker, *Flyfisher's Guide*, 194.

2. Lewis, August 14, 1805, *Journals of Lewis and Clark*.

3. Idaho Commerce and Labor, *Idaho at a Glance*.

4. Peter Boag has argued that the Snake River Plain is not only a unique geographic region but one that has shaped the consciousness of its diverse inhabitants. Peter Boag, "Mountain, Plain, Desert, River."

5. Schwantes, *In Mountain Shadows*, 14–16.

6. Clark, October 17, 1805, *Journals of Lewis and Clark*.

7. Schwantes, *In Mountain Shadows*, 41.

8. Rodman W. Paul qtd. in Foote, *Victorian Gentlewoman*, 2.

9. Foote, *Victorian Gentlewoman*, 265.

10. Ibid., 275.

11. Ibid., 276.

12. As noted by Benay Blend, Mary Hallock Foote's relation to centers of power complicates the traditional understanding of Western women's writing as articulated by contemporary critics. See Blend, "A Victorian Gentlewoman." Also Etulian, *Re-imagining the Modern American West*, 10–15.

13. Foote, *Victorian Gentlewoman*, 328.

14. Arthur Foote had acquired a total of one thousand acres of property through the Homestead Act, the Desert Land Act, and the Timber Culture Act, which permitted a settler to obtain an additional one hundred sixty acres in return for planting trees.

15. Foote, *Victorian Gentlewoman*, 329.

16. George Wheeler, "Idaho Retrospective," in McFarland and Studebaker, *Idaho's Poetry*, 48.

17. Ordway, May 26, 1805, *Journals of Lewis and Clark*.

18. Worster, *An Unsettled Country*, 1–30. For more on Powell, see Goetzmann, *Exploration and Empire*, 530–76, and Stegner, *American West as Living Space*, 31–60. Stegner also wrote a biography of Powell, *Beyond the Hundredth Meridian*.

19. Robbins, *Colony and Empire*, 78.

20. Knobloch, *Culture of Wilderness*, 3. For more discussion of federal water policy in the West, see Pisani, *Water, Land and Law*; Worster, *Rivers of Empire*; Reisner, *Cadillac Desert*; and Ingram and Wallace, "An Empire of Liberty." Ingram and Wallace directly connect natural resource policy to Jeffersonian democracy. In addition, Charles Miller, in *Jefferson and Nature*, portrays Jefferson as the intellectual founder of modern resource management. For information specific to Idaho, see Fiege, *Irrigated Eden*, and Hugh Lovin, "The Carey Act in Idaho," "Free Enterprise," and "Water, Arid Land, and Visions."

21. Schwantes, *In Mountain Shadows*, 166.

22. W. V. Doyle qtd. in Pisani, *To Reclaim a Divided West*, 293.

23. "Irrigation: A Life Line to Success," *Idaho Press-Tribune*, July 12, 1990.

24. Foote, *Victorian Gentlewoman*, 284.

25. Arrington, *History of Idaho*, vol. 1, 482–484.

26. *Evening Capital News*, October 4, 1915.

27. Idaho Commerce and Labor, *Idaho at a Glance*.

28. Fiege, *Irrigated Eden*, 204.

29. Idaho Constitution, Article XV, Section 3. For more on the Idaho Constitution and Constitutional Congress, see Dennis C. Colson, *Idaho's Constitution*.

30. Josephson, "Historical Geography of Idaho Water," 72.

31. Chief Justice James Beatty in *Drake et al. v. Earhart*.

32. This was amended in 1928, allowing the state to appropriate and divert water for power generation. See Josephson, "Historical Geography of Idaho Water," 120.

33. U.S. Bureau of the Census, 1900 Census.

34. Wheeler, "Idaho Retrospective" in McFarland and Studebaker, *Idaho's Poetry*. 49.

35. See, for instance, Walt Whitman's "Starting from Paumanok" in which Whitman writes that American Indians remain only names in the landscape, "Leaving such to the States they melt, they depart, charging the / water and the land with names." Whitman, *Leaves of Grass*, 26.

36. "The State Seal: Designed by a Woman," *Idaho Press-Tribune*, July 12, 1990.

37. Ibid.

38. Foote, *Victorian Gentlewoman*, 308, 289.

39. U.S. Bureau of the Census, 1870.

40. Idaho Constitution, Article VI, Section 3.

41. See Wunder, "The Courts and the Chinese," 25.

42. "Chinatown to Go," *Idaho Daily Statesman*, September 21, 1901.

43. John F. Miller qtd. in Takaki, *Strangers from a Different Shore*, 101.

44. *Laws of Idaho 1867*, Chapter 11, Section 3, p. 72.

45. *Idaho Revised Codes*, Section 2616.

46. U.S. Bureau of the Census, 1910 Census.

47. See Hseu, "Chinese Women in Idaho."

48. Boone, *Idaho Place Names*, 150.

49. Dunbar interview, January 1, 1971.

50. "A Lonely Man" aired January 2, 1972.

51. Idaho's antimiscegenation laws were rescinded by the state legislature in 1959. *Idaho Session Laws*, 1959, Ch. 44, Section 1, p. 89.

52. *Idaho Session Laws*, 1921, Ch. 115, Section 4596, p. 291.

53. Retallic and Barker, *Flyfisher's Guide*, 191.

54. Lewis, August 19, 1805, *Journals of Lewis and Clark*.

55. Retallic and Barker, *Flyfisher's Guide*, 294.

56. For a detailed discussion of fisheries management and a similar manipulation of salmon species, see Scarce, *Fishy Business*.

57. Retallic and Barker, *Flyfisher's Guide*, 191–192.

58. Boone, *Idaho Place Names*, 280–281. See also Arrington, *History of Idaho*, vol. 1, 94–95.

59. For information on Japanese associations, see Ichioka, "Japanese Associations and Japanese Government." For information on Japanese associations in Idaho and Idaho's Japanese in general, see Sims, "Japanese Experience in Idaho," and Simon-Smolinski, "Idaho's Japanese Americans."

60. Hisashi, *America-Bound*, 166–170, and Iwata, *Planted in Good Soil*, vol. 1, 176.

61. Sims, "Japanese American Contributions," 3. Sims's work remains the definitive research on Japanese in Idaho. For information on Japanese railroad workers in the region, see Ryan, "The Rising Son."

62. Sims, "Japanese American Contributions," 5.

63. Henshall, "Pioneer Portraits," 22.

64. Arrington, *History of Idaho*, vol. 2, 281.

65. *Idaho Revised Codes*, Section 1458. This legislation was made void in 1911 due to the state Supreme Court's holding in a case involving a Greek immigrant. See *Ex parte Case*, 20 Idaho 128.

66. "Japanese Run Out," *Idaho Daily Statesman*, July 9, 1892.

67. "Caldwell People Fearful That the Scourge Will Spread," *Idaho Daily Statesman*, July 27, 1892.

68. "All Japanese Peremptorily Ordered to Leave Boise," *Idaho Daily Statesman*, July 28, 1892.

69. "Strike of Japanese," *Idaho Daily Statesman*, August 5, 1897.

70. Qtd. in Simon-Smolinski, 58.

71. Simon-Smolinksi, 59. The author notes that Japanese railroad workers received the lowest pay of any race of workers. That their racial status was the reason is indicated by the fact that companies recorded pay based upon race.

72. "Jap Strike at an End," *Idaho Daily Statesman*, August 7, 1897.

73. Sims, "Japanese American Contribution," 7.

74. Ibid., 8–9. See also Arrington, *Beet Sugar in West*.

75. Clark, *Nampa Idaho*, 49.

76. Ibid., 10.

77. Arrington, *History of Idaho*, vol. 2, 281.

78. "Japanese Discharged," *Idaho Daily Statesman*, September 2, 1903.

79. Mary Fujii Henshall qtd. in Fujii interview, June 17, 1981.

80. Nisei refers to second-generation Japanese Americans.

81. Idaho Fish and Game, *Fishing Seasons and Rules*, 71.

82. Idaho Power, *Fun Country!*

83. For example, see Hwang's *M Butterfly* or, for a scholarly discussion, Ma, *Deathly Embrace*.

84. For information on Japanese American women, see the following: Ichioka, "Amerika Nadeshiko"; Sarasohn, *Issei Women*; Nakano, *Japanese American Women*; Glenn, *Issei, Nisei, War Bride*; Nomura, "Tsugiki"; and von Hassell, "Issei Women."

85. See Spencer, "We Are Not Dealing."

86. Whitman, *Leaves of Grass*, 244–245. See also Schueller, *U.S. Orientalisms*, for a discussion of Whitman and orientalism.

87. Ibid., 243.

88. Ibid., 246.

89. Takaki, *Strangers from a Different Shore*, 43.

90. Issei refers to first-generation Japanese immigrants. For a detailed history of Issei, see Ichioka, *Issei*.

91. Takaki, *Strangers from a Different Shore*, 45.

92. Fujii interview, August 23, 1971.

93. "The Japs Are Coming," *Elmore Bulletin*, June 7, 1900.

94. Henshall interview, August 26, 1998.

95. "Comes to Idaho to Start Colony," *Idaho Daily Statesman*, May 15, 1907.

96. *Idaho Revised Codes*, Sections 2609, 2610. Despite these laws, Idaho's Supreme Court tended to rule in favor of Chinese seeking such rights, which were guaranteed by treaty agreements between the Chinese and American governments. One scholar has attributed the relative leniency of Idaho's highest court during the territorial period to Idaho's unique geography, the region's resulting isolation and internal divisions. See Wunder, "Courts and Chinese."

97. Iwata, *Planted in Good Soil*, vol. 2, 623.

98. "State Senate Defeats Alien Land Measure," *Idaho Daily Statesman*, March 1, 1921.

99. *Idaho Session Laws 1923*, ch. 122, Section 1–12, p. 160.

100. "Shall Japanese-Americans in Idaho . . . ," 3.

101. Ibid., 8–10.

102. Takao Ozawa qtd. in Ichioka, "Early Japanese Immigrant Quest," 10–11.

103. Freed blacks were also eligible for citizenship, but "free white persons" was the only term potentially applicable to Ozawa or to other Asians.

104. *Ozawa v. U.S.* For more on the Ozawa case, see Chuman, *The Bamboo People*; Carrott, "Prejudice Goes to Court"; Kim, *Legal History of Asian Americans*; McClain, *Japanese Immigrants and American Law*; and Lopez, *White by Law*.

105. Fujii interview, June 17, 1981.

106. Idaho Department of Commerce, *Idaho Facts*.

107. Fujii interview, August 23, 1971.

CHAPTER 3 | O Pioneers

1. Derig, *Roadside History of Idaho*, 107.

2. Niering and Olmstead, *Audubon Guide to Wildflowers*, 383–384.

3. For information on the Yasui family, see Kessler, *Stubborn Twig*, and Yasui, *Yasui Family of Hood River*.

4. Limerick, "Disorientation and Reorientation," 1025.

5. Kessler, *Stubborn Twig*, 11.

6. Limerick, "Disorientation and Reorientation," 1035.

7. See Ambrose, *Undaunted Courage*, 457–458. See also Betts, *In Search of York*.

8. Executive Order 9066, *Authorizing the Secretary of War to Prescribe Military Areas*, title 3, CFR 1092 (1938–1943).

9. *San Francisco Examiner*, January 29, 1942.

10. Kessler, *Stubborn Twig*, 182.

11. The ACLU later changed its position. The JACL, however, continued to offer no support to Min Yasui.

12. Minoru Yasui to Miss Shipps, April 22, 1943. War Relocation Authority Records, Record Group 210, National Archives Building, Washington, D.C.

13. For accounts of Yasui's original case, see Irons, *Justice at War*; Kim, *Asian Americans and Supreme Court* and *Legal History of Asian Americans*; and Chuman, *Bamboo People*.

14. Clark qtd. in Sims, "Japanese American Experience," 6.

15. "Don't Sell Japs Land Says Clark," *Idaho Daily Statesman*, March 15, 1942.

16. Department of the Interior, *Relocation Program*, 13.

17. Matsuda, "Evacuation Diary," published as a serial in *Times-News*, 1975.

18. "Report Reveals Census Bureau Data on JAs Used in Internment Process," *Pacific Citizen*, March 24–30, 2000. See also, "Census Bureau Aided Removal of Japanese, Report Says," *New York Times*, March 17, 2000.

19. For general histories of Minidoka, see Jessup, "Minidoka Relocation Center," and Hausler, "History Japanese-American Relocation Center."

20. Yamada, "In the Outhouse," in *Camp Notes*, 17.

21. Kaneko, "Family Album," in *Coming Home from Camp*, unpaginated.

22. Martha Inouye Oye qtd. in Tsuchida, *Reflections*, 292.

23. Sone, *Nisei Daughter*, 191.

24. Ibid., 192.

25. Yamada, "Desert Storm," in *Camp Notes*, 20.

26. Elmer R. Smith, "Community Analysis Section Final Report," October 3, 1945. War Relocation Authority Records, hereafter NARC, DC.

27. Yamada, "Harmony at the Fair Grounds," in *Camp Notes*, 15.

28. Hayashida interview, September 7, 1989.

29. Okubo, *Citizen 13660*, 136.

30. Fisher, "Democratic Social Space," 74.

31. See Drinnon, *Keeper of Concentration Camps*.

32. Milton Eisenhower qtd. in Drinnon, *Keeper of Concentration Camps*, 63.

33. Okubo, *Citizen 13660*, 15.

34. Greg Robinson, in his book on Franklin Roosevelt and the Relocation, discusses John Collier's plan for agricultural development and Relocation. Collier, an unsuccessful candidate for the directorship of the War Relocation Authority, was at the time director of Indian Affairs and planned an extensive program of desert reclamation utilizing internee labor. Robinson, *By Order of the President*, 132–133.

35. Campbell qtd. in Weglyn, *Years of Infamy*, 85.

36. Daniels, *Decision to Relocate*, 36.

37. Sims, "Japanese-Americans in Idaho," 104.

38. Department of the Interior, *WRA*, 27.

39. Ibid., 32.

40. "Myer Stresses Necessity of Active Participation in Agricultural Program," *Minidoka Irrigator*, May 22, 1943.

41. Vernon Kennedy to Dillon S. Myer, April 25, 1943, NARC, DC.

42. *Northside News*, April 22, 1943.

43. Commission on Wartime Relocation and Internment of Civilians, *Personal Justice Denied*, 163.

44. *Minidoka Interlude*.

45. Minidoka Evacuee Issei Representatives, "Minidoka Center Residents' Report to the Spanish Consul," December 22, 1943. Private Papers of Harry L. Stafford. College of Southern Idaho, Twin Falls, Idaho.

46. R. S. Davidson, "Agriculture's First Year at Minidoka," Japanese American Evacuation and Resettlement Records, hereafter JERS, BANC.

47. Takahashi interview, August 16, 1984.

48. "Yearly Summary Report—Agriculture 1944," JERS, BANC.

49. Sims, "Japanese-Americans in Idaho," 105.

50. Department of the Interior, *Relocation Program*, 12.

51. Amalgamated Sugar Company, "The Sugar Beet: The Root of Success," December 1942, NARC, DC.

52. John Bigelow to Bernard Mainwaring, January 19, 1944, NARC, DC.

53. Mainwaring to Bigelow, February 3, 1944, NARC, DC.

54. Author unknown, "Community Analysis Section Field Report 262," January 10, 1944, NARC, DC.

55. Elmer R. Smith, "Community Analysis Section Report 316," June 27, 1944, NARC, DC.

56. Elmer R. Smith," Community Analysis Section Final Report," October 3, 1945, NARC, DC.

57. Elmer R. Smith, "Community Analysis Section Report 316," June 27, 1944, NARC, DC.

58. Joseph G. Beeson to Harry L. Stafford, November 5, 1943, private papers of Henry L. Stafford, hereafter CSI.

59. Mas Okada, *Hunt Hi-Lites*, October 1, 1943, NARC, DC.

60. *Minidoka Irrigator*, September 10, 1942.

61. John de Young, "Community Analysis Section Report 143," July 15–17, 1943, NARC, DC.

62. John de Young, "Community Analysis Report 160," August 5, 1943, NARC, D.C.

63. Ibid.

64. Ibid.

65. Commission on Wartime Relocation and Internment of Civilians, *Personal Justice Denied*, 165.

66. Niiya, *Japanese American History*, 233.

67. Jessup, "Minidoka Relocation Center," 27.

68. Harry L. Stafford to Charles Welteroth, March 18, 1943, NARC, DC.

69. Author unknown, "Windbreaks," JERS, BANC.

70. Harry L. Stafford to Y. Fujii, April 17, 1944, NARC, DC.

71. "Ranchers Open Fight to Halt Diversion of Water for Japs," *Times-News*, April 30, 1942.

72. *Idaho Daily Statesman*, February 24, 1942.

73. Harry L. Stafford to Charles H. Welteroth, March 18, 1943, NARC, DC.

74. Charles H. Welteroth to Harry L. Stafford, April 15, 1943, NARC, DC.

75. Harry L. Stafford to Y. Fujii, April 17, 1944, NARC, DC.

76. Ibid.

77. Newlands Act of 1902, Public Law 161, 57th Cong., 1st sess. (June 17, 1902), Ch. 1093.

78. Amendment to Newlands Act of 1902, May 10, 1956, Ch. 256, 70 Stat. 151.

79. Stene, "The Owyhee Project."

80. Minidoka Evacuee Issei Representatives, "Minidoka Center Residents' Report to the Spanish Consul," December 22, 1943, CSI.

81. Daniel Sheehan to S. Hara, June 28, 1943, NARC, DC.

82. John de Young, "Community Analysis Report 177," July 1943, NARC, DC.

83. *Area B News*, March 9, 1944, NARC, DC.

84. Takahashi interview, August 16, 1984.

85. Author unknown, "Community Analysis Section Report," April 28, 1943, NARC, DC.

86. Sojin Takei, untitled poem in Nakano, *Poets behind Barbed Wire*, 41.

87. Author unknown, "Community Analysis Section Report," April 28, 1943, NARC, DC.

88. "Memorandum of Understanding," signed by Harry L. Stafford and Chairman of Minidoka Consumers' Coop, June 11, 1943, NARC, DC.

89. Author unknown, "Community Analysis Section Report," April 28, 1943, NARC, DC.

90. Ibid.

91. Ibid.

92. Ibid.

93. Yamada, *Camp Notes*, 25.

94. "Looking Back through the Files," *Minidoka Irrigator*, September 25, 1943. The incident occurred on December 3, 1942.

95. Yamada, *Camp Notes*, 19.

96. Limerick, *Desert Passages*.

97. Matsuda, "Evacuation Diary."

98. *Ikebana* is a form of flower arrangement, *bonsai* the art of manipulating the growth of trees, and *bon-kei* involves the construction of miniature landscapes.

99. Eaton, *Beauty behind Barbed Wire*, 34.

100. For a discussion of Japanese gardens and landscaping in the relocation centers, see Tamura, "Gardens below the Watchtower." The National Park Service has also completed an archeological survey of the Minidoka site. See Burton and Farrell, *This Is Minidoka*.

101. Hayashida interview, September 7, 1989.

102. Ibid., 23. Mrs. Hayashida was most likely referring to Fujitaro Kubota, a well-known Seattle landscape designer. See Tamura, "Gardens below the Watchtower," 79.

103. Mary Tsukamoto qtd. in Tateishi, *And Justice for All*, 14.

104. William Maxey Jr. to R. A. Pomeroy, April 27, 1944, NARC, DC.

105. Telegram, Leland Barrows to Harry L. Stafford, February 6, 1943, CSI.

106. Harry L. Stafford to R. S. Davidson, March 22, 1943, NARC, DC.

107. "Twin Falls Residents Donate Bulbs, Shrubs, Flower Seeds to Hunt," *Minidoka Irrigator*, March 27, 1943.

108. G. Mizuki qtd. in "Improvements Now Being Made on Wild Life Preserve," *Minidoka Irrigator*, July 1, 1944. This area was commonly referred to as Nitta Gardens, as it was constructed by a Mr. Nitta.

109. Drinnon, *Keeper of Concentration Camps*, 126.

110. Dillon S. Myer qtd. in Drinnon, *Keeper of Concentration Camps*, 29.

111. Memorandum, R. S. Davidson to Harry L. Stafford, May 18, 1943, NARC, DC.

112. Sims, "Japanese American Experience in Idaho," 10.

113. C. Sumida, T. Takasugi, and S. Muraoka, "Cooperative Colonization," August 1, 1944, CSI.

114. Dillon S. Myer, "A Message to the Residents of Relocation Centers," in *When You Leave the Relocation Center*, NARC, DC.

115. Department of the Interior, *Relocation Program*, 45.

116. Ibid., 93.

117. Elmer R. Smith, "Weekly Analysis Summary: April 8–14, 1945," April 15, 1945, NARC, DC.

118. Kleinkopf, *Relocation Center Diary*, 600–601.

119. Spicer, et al. *Impounded People*, 43.

120. Memorandum, Elmer R. Smith, April 8, 1943, NARC, DC.

121. Another example of this collapsing of Indian and Asian identities among federal administrators is found in Lewis Meriam's *The Problem of Indian Administra-*

tion, a federally authorized investigation of the state of American Indian affairs that was issued in 1928. Meriam noted, "Some people assert that the Indians prefer to live as they do; that they are happier in their idleness and irresponsibility. The question may be raised whether these persons do not mistake for happiness and content an almost oriental fatalism and resignation." Meriam, *Problem Indian Administration*, 6.

122. Drinnon, *Keeper of Concentration Camps*, 265.

CHAPTER 4 | Haunted by Waters

1. For a brief history of the development of Sun Valley and the Union Pacific's role, see Rothman, *Devil's Bargains*, 186–201.

2. Average mean value of single-family housing in the Ketchum/Sun Valley area was $685,117 in 2004. Idaho Department of Commerce and Labor, *Idaho at a Glance*.

3. Daniels, "Quantifies Forced Migrations," 420.

4. Teruo Terry Hayashi qtd. in Hayashi, *Face of the Enemy*, 138.

5. For a detailed account of the National Student Relocation Council, see Okihiro, *Storied Lives*.

6. Minidoka Evacuee Issei Representatives, "Minidoka Center Residents' Report to the Spanish Consul," December 1943, CSI.

7. For a discussion of Japanese American ethnicity in relation to geography, see Miyares, Paine, and Nishi, "Japanese in America."

8. For a recent critique, see Cheng and Yang, "'Model' Minority Deconstructed."

9. Takahashi interview, August 16, 1984.

10. In 1984 Min Yasui filed a petition for a *writ of coram nobis* with a court in Portland, Oregon. The judge in the case sided with the government's position to have Yasui's conviction vacated. Yasui, however, wanted the court to rule that the government had committed misconduct by withholding information about the necessity for the evacuation. Yasui appealed the dismissal of his writ to the Ninth District Court, but he died before his appeal could be heard. For information on Yasui's case and that of other relocation cases, see Irons, *Justice Delayed*.

11. Arrington, *History of Idaho*, vol. 2, 91.

12. Madsen, *Chief Pocatello*, 49.

13. Arrington, *History of Idaho*, vol. 1, 267. For information on the Bear River Massacre, see Madsen, *Shoshoni Frontier*.

14. Schwantes, *In Mountain Shadows*, 14. For a more complete history of the Shoshone, see Madsen, *Northern Shoshoni*.

15. Lewis, August 14, 1805, *Journals of Lewis and Clark*.

16. Lewis, August 16, 1805, *Journals of Lewis and Clark*.

17. Lewis, August 14, 1805, *Journals of Lewis and Clark*.

18. Lewis, August 22, 1805, *Journals of Lewis and Clark*.

19. Lewis, August 14, 1805, *Journals of Lewis and Clark*.

20. Madsen, *Northern Shoshoni*, 23–25.

21. Lewis, August 19, 1805, *Journals of Lewis and Clark*.

22. In *Ecological Imperialism*, Alfred Crosby argues that the introduction of dis-

eases, plants, and animals that accompanied European migration into the Americas was another kind of imperialism, a biological one that enormously impacted American Indian societies.

23. Boag, "Indians of This Place."

24. Parke, *Dreams to Dust*, 55.

25. Perkins, *Gold Rush Diary*, 90–91.

26. Johnson and Winter, *Route across the Rocky Mountains*, 30.

27. Preuss, *Exploring with Fremont*, 86.

28. Tydeman, "No Passive Relationship," 24.

29. Arrington, *History of Idaho*, vol. 1, 152.

30. Madsen, *Pocatello*, 16.

31. Holmer, "Prehistory of the Northern Shoshone," 55.

32. See Madsen, *Shoshoni Frontier*.

33. Boag, "Indians of This Place," 26.

34. Young, "Providence—Ignorance."

35. May, *Three Frontiers*, 18.

36. Philip White, "Seed," in England and Clark, *Harvest*, 239.

37. May, *Three Frontiers*, 154.

38. For a brief history of early Mormon settlement in Idaho, see Coates, Boag, Hatzenbuehler, and Swanson, "Mormon Settlement of Southeastern Idaho"; Nash, "Salmon River Mission"; and Coates, "Spalding-Whitman Lemhi Missions."

39. For recent research on Shoshone migration, see Holmer, "Prehistory Northern Shoshone," 52–53.

40. *The Book of Mormon*, 2 Nephi 5:21.

41. Swetman, *Lives of the Saints*.

42. See Madsen, *Pocatello*, 35. For more on Mormon and Indian relations, see Arrington and Bitton, *Mormon Experience*.

43. Peter Maughan qtd. in Madsen, *Pocatello*, 72–73.

44. Madsen, *Pocatello*, 98.

45. *The Book of Mormon*, 2 Nephi 5:23.

46. See Bennett, "Cousin Laman," and Smoak, "Mormons and Ghost Dance."

47. Arrington, *History of Idaho*, vol. 1, 160.

48. Federal Writers' Projects, *Idaho*, 284.

49. Madsen, *Pocatello*, 24.

50. "The Japanese in Idaho . . . as told in Pocatello," *Pacific Citizen*, December 20, 1957.

51. Unknown writer qtd. in Sims, "Japanese American Experience," 8.

52. Fujii interview, August 23, 1971.

53. Bureau of the Census, *1940 Census*.

54. Chase Clark qtd. in Sims, "Fearless, Patriotic," 78.

55. "Clark Bitterly Denounces Japs," *Idaho Daily Statesman*, May 23, 1942.

56. Henshall interview, August 26, 1998.

57. Henshall qtd. in Clark, *Nampa Idaho*, 216–217.

58. Cecil Andrus qtd. in Henshall, "American Dream."

59. Maclean, *River Runs through It*, 104.

60. Historian Peggy Pascoe has noted the need for "a history of women in the West that is multicultural, cross-cultural, and intercultural." Peggy Pascoe, "Western Women," 43. Discussions of women's writing and the western landscape have tended to focus solely on the writings of Euro-Americans. See, for instance, Kolodny, *Land before Her*. Fumiko Fujii's Christian vision and recreational use of Western spaces conflict with Kolodny's contention that women sought an "idealized domesticity" in the frontier.

61. Henshall, "Pioneer Portraits," 27.

62. Schwantes, *In Mountain Shadows*, 219.

63. Jane Goldbeck, "Rivers," in Wyndham, *Famous Potatoes*, n.p.

64. "Federal Agencies Will Help Arm Idaho Farmers in Fight to Kill Hoppers," *Idaho Statesman*, July 23, 1999.

65. "U.S. Potato Industry Honors Idaho Nisei," *Pacific Citizen*, December 1997.

66. Tsukamoto interview, July 23, 1999.

67. "NRC Report Calls for Making Safer Pesticides," *Wall Street Journal*, July 19, 2000.

68. Dept. of Agriculture, "Idaho Statistics."

69. Tsukamoto interview, July 23, 1999.

70. Ibid.

71. For information on the early JACL, see Niiya, *Japanese American History*, 182–183.

72. "JACL Hymn," words by Marion Tajiri and music by Marcel J. Tyrell.

73. JACL, *Better Americans*, 4.

74. Okada's novel is a rare treatment of this division within the community, though his novel portrays a utopian reunification of Japanese America along patriotic lines.

75. Mike Masaoka qtd. in Lim, "Research Report," 69.

76. Idaho Constitution, Article VI, Section 3.

77. For a detailed discussion of the political lobbying involving the redress legislation, see Naito and Scott, "Against All Odds," and Maki, Kitano, and Berthold, *Achieving Impossible Dream*.

78. Commission on Wartime Relocation and Internment of Civilians, *Personal Justice Denied*, 18.

79. See Charlotte Brooks, "In the Twilight Zone."

80. "Japanese Relocation Center Remembered in Film," *Times News Review*, March 17, 1974.

81. *Twin Falls Times-News*, June 14, 1987.

82. Donald S. Whitehead qtd. in "Japanese Relocation Center Remembered in Film," *Times News Review*, March 17, 1974.

83. *Twin Falls Times-News*, June 14, 1987.

84. Carlyle Butler qtd. in *Twin Falls Times-News*, June 14, 1987.

85. For information on the historical invisibility of the relocation centers in the public realm and their role in Nikkei history, see Hayashi, "Transfigured Patterns."

86. On January 17, 2001, Minidoka was designated a national monument via presidential proclamation under the auspices of the Antiquities Act of 1906. The National Park Service has been working with individuals and groups, including the JACL, to develop a management plan for the site.

87. Haakonstad interview, October 9, 1991.

88. Qtd. in Shrontz, Hunt for Idaho, 156.

89. Martin Matsudaira qtd. in Idaho Statesman, September 13, 1979.

90. "Idaho Japanese-Americans Reject Tower-Burning," Idaho Statesman, September 24, 1979.

91. Toyota v. United States, 268 U.S. 402 (1925).

92. Salyer, "Baptism by Fire," 876.

93. "JACL Owes Japanese America an Apology," Pacific Citizen, August 13–19, 1999.

94. Bureau of the Census, 2000 Census.

95. Halter, Between Race and Ethnicity, 18.

96. For a general history of miscegenation laws in the United States, see Moran, Interracial Intimacies, and Wallenstein, Tell the Court.

97. Notable works that discuss the formation of Japanese American identity include: Takahashi, Nisei/Sansei; Yoo, Growing Up Nisei; and Kurashige, Japanese American Celebration. The role of a shared narrative in defining ethnicity is discussed by Stephen Cornell in his essay, "That's the Story of Our Life" in Spickard and Burroughs, We Are a People. Cornell asserts that through a process of selection, plotting, and interpretation, ethnic groups fashion a narrative that defines them, but the formation of these stories also entails internal struggles over which and whose version assumes dominance. In this sense, the JACL can be seen as an influential shaper of the Japanese American story, one that has helped create an identity for Japanese Americans that is neither accurate nor inclusive. Patricia Limerick has noted the role of narrative in shaping and maintaining a coherent Mormon ethnic identity. She asserts that "perhaps more than anything, the told and retold stories of Mormon history, made it very unlikely that Mormons would lose their distinctive ethnicity and disappear into a homogeneous, mainstream, American whole." Limerick, "Peace Initiative," 20.

98. Bennett, "Mormon Polygamy," 28. See also Wells, "Idaho Anti-Mormon Test Oath."

99. Brigham Young qtd. in Woodruff, Journal, July 28, 1847.

100. Linklater, Measuring America, 181.

101. Francaviglia, Mormon Landscape, 29.

102. Ibid., 89. See also Stegner, Mormon Country, and Norton, "Mormon Identity."

103. Smith, "Prosperity of Zion."

104. Brigham Young qtd. in Nibley, Brigham Young, 181.

105. Stegner, American West Living Space, 3–27.

106. Walz, "Idaho Farmer" and "Masayoshi Fujimoto." See also Walz, "Japanese

Immigration and Community" for information on the Nikkei community in Rexburg, Idaho.

107. Walz, "Masayoshi Fujimoto," 76–77, 114–116.

108. Gary Okihiro notes that "our notion of community, molded by seminal works of towns, must be reformulated to take into account the findings revealed by rural studies. . . . The rural model also grapples with the concepts of ethnic identity and solidarity so confidently asserted in urban studies." Okihiro, "Fallow Field," 9.

109. Walz, "Masayoshi Fujimoto," 81.

110. Masayoshi Fujimoto qtd. in Walz, "Masayoshi Fujimoto," 91.

111. In *Irrigated Eden*, Mark Fiege provides a detailed picture of the complicated relations marked by both conflict and cooperation that defined the agricultural community of the Upper Snake River Valley due to its reliance on irrigation.

112. Walz, "Masayoshi Fujimoto," 93.

113. Ibid., 96.

114. Matsumoto, *Farming the Home Place*, 10.

115. Walz, "Masayoshi Fujimoto,"164.

116. Reisner, *Cadillac Desert*, 384.

117. Trout Unlimited, "Upper Snake River Cutthroats Chapter."

118. Reisner, *Cadillac Desert*, 387.

119. David Schleicher qtd. in *Cadillac Desert*, 391.

120. Ibid., 388.

121. Ibid., 407.

122. Retallic and Barker, *Flyfisher's Guide*, 70.

123. Swetman, *Lives of the Saints*, 74.

BIBLIOGRAPHY

Archives

Idaho State Historical Society. Boise, Idaho.

Japanese American Evacuation and Resettlement Records. BANC MSS 67/14c. The Bancroft Library, University of California, Berkeley (JERS, BANC).

Private Papers of Harry L. Stafford. College of Southern Idaho, Twin Falls, Idaho (CSI).

War Relocation Authority Records. Records Group 112. National Archives, Washington, DC (NARC, DC).

War Relocation Authority Records. Records Group 112. National Archives, College Park, MD.

Newspapers

Christian Science Monitor
Elmore (ID) Bulletin
Evening Capital (ID) News
Gem (Caldwell) State Rural
Idaho Daily Statesman
Idaho (Caldwell) Press-Tribune
Lewiston (ID) Tribune
Minidoka (ID) Irrigator
New York Times
Northside (ID) News
Pacific Citizen
San Francisco Examiner
Times News Review
Twin Falls (ID) Times-News
Wall Street Journal

Books and Articles

Aho, James A. *The Politics of Righteousness: Idaho Christian Patriotism.* Seattle: University of Washington Press, 1990.

Allen, John Logan. "Imagining the West: The View from Monticello." In *Thomas Jefferson and the Changing West,* edited by James P. Ronda. Albuquerque: University of New Mexico Press, 1997. 3–23.

———. *Passage through the Garden.* Urbana: University of Illinois Press, 1975.

Ambrose, Stephen E. *Undaunted Courage: Meriwether Lewis, Thomas Jefferson, and the Opening of the American West*. New York: Simon & Schuster, 1996.

Arrington, Leonard J. *Beet Sugar in the West: A History of the Utah-Idaho Sugar Company, 1891–1966*. Seattle: University of Washington Press, 1966.

———. *History of Idaho*. Vols. 1 and 2. Moscow: University of Idaho Press, 1994.

Arrington, Leonard J., and Davis Bitton. *The Mormon Experience: A History of the Latter-day Saints*. New York: Knopf, 1979.

Aryan Nations. *Attention White Men: Declaration to Regain a National State*. n.d.

Balakian, Peter. "How a Poet Writes History without Going Mad." *Chronicle of Higher Education*, May 7, 2004. 10–13.

Bedini, Silvio A. "The Scientific Instruments of the Lewis and Clark Expedition." In *Mapping the North American Plains*, edited by Frederick Luebke, Frances W. Kaye, and Gary E. Moulton. Norman: University of Oklahoma Press, 1987. 93–110.

Bennett, Dana. "Mormon Polygamy in Early Southeastern Idaho." *Idaho Yesterdays* 28, no. 1 (Spring 1984): 24–30.

Bennett, Richard Edmond. "Cousin Laman in the Wilderness: The Beginnings of Brigham Young's Indian Policy." *Nebraska History* 67, no. 1 (1986): 69–82.

Berry, Kate A., and Martha L. Henderson, eds. *Geographical Identities of Ethnic America: Race, Space, and Place*. Reno: University of Nevada Press, 2002.

Betts, Robert B. *In Search of York: The Slave Who Went to the Pacific with Lewis and Clark*. Boulder: University of Colorado Press, 2000.

Blank, Robert H. *Individualism in Idaho: The Territorial Foundations*. Pullman: Washington State University Press, 1988.

Blend, Benay. "A Victorian Gentlewoman in the American West: Ambiguity in the Work of Mary Hallock Foote." In *Reading under the Sign of Nature: New Essays in Ecocriticism*, edited by John Tallmadge and Henry Harrington. Salt Lake City: University of Utah Press, 2000. 85–100.

Blomley, Nicholas K. *Law, Space, and the Geographies of Power*. New York: Guilford Press, 1994.

Boag, Peter G. "'The Indians of This Place Are Snakes in the Grass': The Overlander Perspective on Native Americans in Southeastern Idaho, 1836–1860." *Idaho Yesterdays* 27, no. 3 (Fall 1993): 16–26.

———. "Mountain, Plain, Desert, River: The Snake River Region as a Western Crossroads." In *Many Wests: Place, Culture, and Regional Identity*, edited by David Wrobel and Michael C. Steiner. Lawrence: University Press of Kansas, 1997. 177–203.

Boone, Laila. *Idaho Place Names: A Geographical Dictionary*. Moscow: University of Idaho Press, 1988.

Botkin, Daniel B. *Our Natural History: The Lessons of Lewis and Clark*. New York: Perigee, 1995.

Brooks, Charlotte. "In the Twilight Zone between Black and White: Japanese American Resettlement and Community in Chicago, 1942–1945." *Journal of American History* 86, no. 4 (March 2000): 1655–1687.

Bruchac, Joseph, ed. *Songs from this Earth on Turtle's Back: Contemporary American Indian Poetry.* Greenfield Center, NY: Greenfield Review Press, 1983.

Burroughs, Raymond Darwin, ed. *The Natural History of the Lewis and Clark Expedition.* East Lansing: Michigan State University Press, 1961.

Burton, Jeffrey F., and Mary M. Farrell. *This Is Minidoka: An Archeological Survey of Minidoka Internment National Monument, Idaho.* Tucson: Western Archeological and Conservation Center, National Park Service, U.S. Department of the Interior, 2001.

Carlson, Leonard A. *Indians, Bureaucrats, and Land: The Dawes Act and the Decline of Indian Farming.* Westport, Connecticut: Greenwood Press, 1981.

Carrott, Browning M. "Prejudice Goes to Court: The Japanese and the Supreme Court in the 1920s." *California History* 62, no. 2 (Summer 1983): 122–138.

Casey, Edward. "How to Get from Space to Place in a Fairly Short Stretch of Time." In *Senses of Place*, edited by Steven Feld and Keith H. Basso. Sante Fe: School of American Research Press, 1996. 13–52.

Ceasar, James W. "Natural Rights and Scientific Racism." In *Thomas Jefferson and the Politics of Nature*, edited by Thomas S. Engeman. Notre Dame, Indiana: University of Notre Dame Press, 2000. 165–190.

Cheater, Mark. "Wolf Spirit Returns to Idaho." *National Wildlife Magazine*, August–September, 1998. http//www.nwf.org/nationalwildlife/article.cfm, accessed July 17, 2006.

Cheng, Lucie, and Philip Q. Yang. "The 'Model' Minority Deconstructed." In *Contemporary Asian America: A Multidisciplinary Reader*, edited by Min Zhou and James V. Gatewood. New York: New York University Press, 2000. 459–482.

Chuman, Frank F. *The Bamboo People: The Law and Japanese-Americans.* Del Mar, California: Publisher's Inc., 1976.

Clark, Lynda Campbell, ed. *Nampa Idaho, 1885–1985: A Journey of Discovery.* Nampa: Pacific Press Publishers, 1985.

Clarke, Tracylee. "Constructing Conflict: The Functioning Synedoche in the Endangered Wolf Controversy." *Wicazo SA Review* 14, no. 1 (Spring 1999): 113–127.

Coates, Lawrence G. "The Spalding-Whitman and Lemhi Missions: A Comparison." *Idaho Yesterdays* 31, nos. 1–2 (Spring 1987): 38–46.

Coates, Lawrence G., Peter G. Boag, Ronald I. Hatzenbuehler, and Merwin R. Swanson. "The Mormon Settlement of Southeastern Idaho." *Journal of Mormon History* 20, no. 2 (1994): 45–62.

Colson, Dennis C. *Idaho's Constitution: The Tie That Binds.* Moscow: University of Idaho Press, 1991.

Cornell, Stephen. "That's the Story of Our Life." In *We Are a People: Narrative and Multiplicity in Constructing Ethnic Identity*, edited by Paul Spickard and W. Jeffrey Burroughs. Philadelphia: Temple University Press, 2000. 41–53.

Couch, Samuel L. "Topophilia and Chinese Miners: Place Attachment in North Central Idaho." PhD diss., University of Idaho, 1996.

Cronon, William. *Changes in the Land: Indians, Colonists, and the Ecology of New England.* New York: Hill and Wang, 1983.

Crosby, Alfred W. *Ecological Imperialism: The Biological Expansion of Europe, 900–1900.* Cambridge, England: Cambridge University Press, 1986.

Daniels, Roger. *The Decision to Relocate the Japanese Americans.* Malabar, Florida: Robert E. Krieger Publishing, 1975.

———. "Roger Daniels Quantifies the Forced Migrations of Japanese Americans, 1942–1946." In *Major Problems in the History of the American West*, edited by Clyde A. Milner II, Anne M. Butler, and David Rich Lewis. Boston: Houghton Mifflin, 1997. 417–420.

———, ed. with Sandra Taylor and Harry Kitano. *Japanese Americans: From Relocation to Redress.* Salt Lake City: University of Utah Press, 1986.

de Crèvecoeur, J. Hector St. John. *Letters from an American Farmer.* Gloucester: P. Smith, 1968.

Derig, Betty. "Celestials in the Diggings." *Idaho Yesterdays* 16, no. 3 (Fall 1972): 2–23.

———. *Roadside History of Idaho.* Missoula, Montana: Mountain Press Publishing, 1996.

DeVoto, Bernard, ed. *The Journals of Lewis and Clark.* Boston: Houghton Mifflin, 1953.

Dobratz, Betty A., and Stephanie L. Shanks-Meile. *White Power, White Pride!: The White Separatist Movement in the United States.* Baltimore: Johns Hopkins University Press, 2000.

Drake et al. v. Earhart, 2 Idaho 750 (1890).

Drinnon, Richard. *Keeper of Concentration Camps: Dillon S. Myer and American Racism.* Berkeley: University of California Press, 1987.

Drury, Clifford Merrill, ed. *The Diaries and Letters of Henry H. Spalding and Asa Bowen Smith Relating to the Nez Perce Mission, 1838–1842.* Glendale, California: Arthur H. Clark, 1958.

Dunbar, Henrietta C. Interview by Esther F. Gibson. Boise: Idaho Oral History Center. January 1, 1971.

Earle, Steve. *Guitar Town.* MCA, MCAD-31305.

Eaton, Allen H. *Beauty behind Barbed Wire: The Arts of the Japanese in Our War Relocation Camps.* New York: Harper, 1952.

Engeman, Thomas S., ed. *Thomas Jefferson and the Politics of Nature.* Notre Dame, Indiana: University of Notre Dame Press, 2000.

England, Eugene, and Dennis Clark, eds. *Harvest: Contemporary Mormon Poems.* Salt Lake City: Signature Books, 1989.

Espiritu, Yen Le. *Asian American Panethnicity: Bridging Institutions and Identities.* Philadelphia: Temple University Press, 1992.

Etulian, Richard. *Re-imagining the Modern American West: A Century of Fiction, History, and Art.* Tucson: University of Arizona Press, 1996.

Federal Writers' Projects of the Works Progress Administration. *Idaho: A Guide in Word and Picture.* Caldwell, Idaho: Caxton Publishers, 1937.

Fiege, Mark. *Irrigated Eden: The Making of an Agricultural Landscape in the American West.* Seattle: University of Washington Press, 1999.

Fisher, Philip. "Democratic Social Space: Whitman, Melville, and the Promise of

American Transparency." In *The New American Studies: Essays from Representations*, edited by Philip Fisher. Berkeley: University of California Press, 1991. 70–111.

Foote, Caleb. *Outcasts! Story of America's Treatment of the Japanese-American Minority*. New York: Fellowship of Reconciliation, n.d.

Foote, Mary Hallock. *A Victorian Gentlewoman in the Far West: The Reminiscences of Mary Hallock Foote*, edited by Rodman W. Paul. San Marino, California: Huntington Library, 1972.

Francaviglia, Richard V. *The Mormon Landscape: Existence, Creation, and Perception of a Unique Image in the American West*. New York: AMS Press, 1978.

Freedman, Diane P., and Olivia Frey, eds. *Autobiographical Writing across the Disciplines*. Durham, North Carolina: Duke University Press, 2003.

Fujii, Henry, and Fumiko Fujii. Interview by Mrs. Robert Alexander and Mrs. Cecil Hungerford. Boise: Idaho Oral History Center. August 23, 1971.

———. Interview. Boise: Idaho Oral History Center. June 17, 1981.

Furtwangler, Albert. *Acts of Discovery: Visions of America in the Lewis and Clark Journals*. Urbana: University of Illinois Press, 1993.

Gaboury, William Joseph. *Dissension in the Rockies: A History of Idaho Populism*. New York: Garland Publishing, 1988.

Glenn, Evelyn Nakano. *Issei, Nisei, War Bride: Three Generations of Japanese American Women in Domestic Service*. Philadelphia: Temple University Press, 1986.

Glotfelty, Cheryl, and Harold Fromm, eds. *The Ecocriticism Reader: Landmarks in Literary Ecology*. Athens: University of Georgia Press, 1996.

Goble, Dale D., and Paul W. Hirt, eds. *Northwest Lands, Northwest Peoples: Readings in Environmental History*. Seattle: University of Washington Press, 1999.

Goetzmann, William H. *Exploration and Empire: The Explorer and the Scientist in the Winning of the American West*. New York: Norton, 1966.

Haakonstad, Audrey. Interview by Teresa R. Funke. Boise: Idaho Oral History Center. October 9, 1991.

Halter, Marilyn. *Between Race and Ethnicity: Cape Verdean American Immigrants, 1860–1965*. Urbana: University of Illinois Press, 1993.

Hausler, Donald E. "History of the Japanese-American Relocation Center at Hunt, Minidoka County, Idaho." MA thesis, Utah State University, 1964.

Hayashi, Ann Koto. *Face of the Enemy: Heart of a Patriot*. New York: Garland Publishing, 1995.

Hayashi, T. Robert. "Transfigured Patterns: Contesting Memories at the Manzanar National Historic Site." *Public Historian* 25, no. 4 (Fall 2003): 51–71.

Hayashida, Seichi, and Chiyeko Hayashida. Interview. Boise: Idaho Oral History Center. September 7, 1989.

Henshall, Mary Fujii. "American Dream." *Idaho Press-Tribune*, February 27, 1998.

———. "Pioneer Portraits: Henry and Fumiko Fujii." *Idaho Yesterdays* 19, no. 1 (Spring 1975): 20–27.

———. Interview with the author. August 26, 1998.

Hisashi, Tsurutani. *America-Bound: The Japanese and the Opening of the American West*. Tokyo: Japan Times, 1989.

Holmer, Richard N. "Prehistory of the Northern Shoshone." In *Fort Hall and the Shoshone Bannock*, edited by E. S. Lohse and Richard N. Holmer. Pocatello: Idaho State University Press, 1990. 41–57.

Hseu, I-hsien. "Chinese Women in Idaho during the Anti-Chinese Movement." MA thesis, University of Idaho, 1994.

Hwang, David Henry. *M Butterfly*. New York: Plume, 1993.

Ichioka, Yuji. "Amerika Nadeshiko: Japanese Immigrant Women in the United States, 1900–1924." *Pacific Historical Review* 49, no. 2 (1980): 339–357.

———. "The Early Japanese Immigrant Quest for Citizenship." *Amerasia* 4, no. 2 (1977): 1–22.

———. *Idaho Facts*. n.d.

———. *The Issei: The World of Japanese Immigrants, 1885–1924*. New York: Free Press, 1988.

———. "Japanese Associations and the Japanese Government: A Special Relationship, 1909–1926." *Pacific Historical Review* 46, no. 3 (1977): 408–437.

Idaho Department of Commerce and Labor. *Idaho at a Glance*. n.d.

Idaho Fish and Game Department. *2006–2007 Fishing Seasons and Rules—Including Steelhead*. n.d.

Idaho Power. *Fun Country!* n.d.

Ingram, Helen M., and Mary G. Wallace. "An Empire of Liberty: Thomas Jefferson and Governing Natural Resources in the West." In *Thomas Jefferson and the Changing West*, edited by James P. Ronda. Albuquerque: University of New Mexico Press, 1997. 93–108.

Irons, Peter. *Justice at War: The Story of the Japanese American Internment Cases*. New York: Oxford University Press, 1983.

———, ed. *Justice Delayed: The Record of the Japanese American Internment Cases*. Middletown, Connecticut: Wesleyan University Press, 1989.

Iwata, Masakazu. *Planted in Good Soil: A History of the Issei in United States Agriculture*. Vols. 1 and 2. New York: Peter Lang, 1992.

James, Elizabeth. "The Allotment Period on the Nez Perce Reservation: Encroachments, Obstacles, and Reactions." *Idaho Yesterdays* 37, no. 1 (Spring 1993): 11–23.

Japanese American Citizens League. *Better Americans in a Greater America*. Spokane, Washington: Litho Art Printers, n.d.

Jefferson, Thomas. *The Portable Thomas Jefferson*, edited by Merrill D. Peterson. New York: Penguin Books, 1977.

———. *The Writings of Thomas Jefferson*. Vol. 16, edited by Andrew A. Lipscomb and Albert Ellery Bergh. Washington: Thomas Jefferson Memorial Foundation, 1903.

Jessup, Rex E. "The Minidoka Relocation Center." MA thesis, California State University, Dominguez Hills, 1996.

Johnson, Hildegard Binder. *Order upon the Land: The U.S. Rectangular Land Survey and the Upper Mississippi Country*. New York: Oxford, 1976.

Johnson, Overton, and William D. Winter. *Route across the Rocky Mountains: Narratives of the Trans-Mississippi Frontier*. Princeton, New Jersey: Princeton University Press, 1932.

Josephson, Theron. "An Historical Geography of Idaho Water: A Legal Ecological Approach." PhD diss., University of Nebraska, 1996.

Joyce, James. *A Portrait of the Artist as a Young Man.* New York: Viking Press, 1959.

Kaneko, Lonny. *Coming Home from Camp.* Waldron, Washington: Brooding Heron Press, 1984.

Kessler, Lauren. *Stubborn Twig: Three Generations in the Life of a Japanese American Family.* New York: Plume, 1993.

————, ed. *Asian Americans and the Supreme Court: A Documentary History.* Westport, Connecticut: Greenwood Press, 1992.

Kim, Hyung-chan. *A Legal History of Asian Americans, 1790–1990.* Westport, Connecticut: Greenwood Press, 1994.

Kingston, Maxine Hong. *China Men.* New York: Vintage Books, 1989.

Kleinkopf, Arthur. *Relocation Center Diary.* Unpublished manuscript.

Knobloch, Frieda. *The Culture of Wilderness: Agriculture as Colonization in the American West.* Chapel Hill: University of North Carolina Press, 1996.

Kolodny, Annette. *The Land before Her: Fantasy and Experience of the American Frontiers, 1630–1860.* Chapel Hill: University of North Carolina Press, 1984.

Kurashige, Lon. *Japanese American Celebration and Conflict: A History of Ethnic Identity and Festival, 1934–1990.* Berkeley: University of California Press, 2002.

Lang, William L. "The Sense of Place and Environmental History." In *Northwest Lands, Northwest Peoples,* edited by Dale D. Goble and Paul W. Hirt. Seattle: University of Washington Press, 1999. 79–94.

Lim, Deborah. *Research Report Prepared for the Presidential Select Committee of JACL Resolution #7.* 1990. Available online at www.resisters.com/study/LimTOC.htm.

Limerick, Patricia Nelson. "Dancing with Professors: The Trouble with Academic Prose." *New York Times Book Review,* October 31, 1993. A3, 23.

————. *Desert Passages.* Albuquerque: University of New Mexico Press, 1985.

————. "Disorientation and Reorientation: The American Landscape Discovered from the West." *Journal of American History* 79, no. 3 (December 1992): 1021–1049.

————. "Peace Initiative: Using Mormons to Rethink Ethnicity in American Life." *Journal of Mormon History* 21, no. 2 (1995): 1–29.

Linklater, Andro. *Measuring America: How an Untamed Wilderness Shaped the United States and Fulfilled the Promise of Democracy.* New York: Walker and Company, 2002.

Lopez, Barry. *Arctic Dreams: Imagination and Desire in a Northern Landscape.* New York: Charles Scribner's Sons, 1986.

Lopez, Ian F. Haney. *White by Law: The Legal Construction of Race.* New York: New York University Press, 1996.

Lovin, Hugh. "The Carey Act in Idaho, 1895–1925: An Experiment in Free Enterprise Reclamation." *Pacific Northwest Quarterly* 78, no. 4 (October 1987): 122–133.

————. "Free Enterprise and Large-scale Reclamation on the Twin Falls–North Side Tract, 1907–1930." *Idaho Yesterdays* 29, no. 1 (Spring 1985): 2–14.

————. "Water, Arid Land, and Visions of Advancement on the Snake River Plain." *Idaho Yesterdays* 35, no. 1 (Spring 1991): 3–18.

Ma, Sheng-Mei. *The Deathly Embrace: Orientalism and Asian American Identity*. Minneapolis: University of Minnesota Press, 2000.

Maclean, Norman. *A River Runs through It and Other Stories*. Chicago: University of Chicago Press, 1976.

Madsen, Brigham D. *Chief Pocatello: "The White Plume."* Salt Lake City: University of Utah Press, 1986.

———. *The Northern Shoshoni*. Caldwell, Idaho: Caxton Publishers, 1980.

———. *Shoshoni Frontier and the Bear River Massacre*. Salt Lake City: University of Utah Press, 1985.

Maki, Mitchell T., Harry H. Kitano, and S. Megan Berthold. *Achieving the Impossible Dream: How Japanese Americans Obtained Redress*. Urbana: University of Illinois Press, 1999.

Marshall, Alan G. "Unusual Gardens: The Nez Perce and Wild Horticulture on the Eastern Columbia Plateaus." In *Northwest Lands, Northwest Peoples: Readings in Environmental History*, edited by Dale D. Goble and Paul W. Hirt. Seattle: University of Washington Press, 1999. 173–187.

Matsuda, Ted. "Evacuation Diary." *Twin Falls Times-News*, December 29–31, 1975.

Matsumoto, Valerie J. *Farming the Home Place: A Japanese American Community in California, 1919–1982*. Ithaca, New York: Cornell University Press, 1993.

May, Dean L. *Three Frontiers: Family, Land, and Society in the American West, 1850–1900*. Cambridge, England: Cambridge University Press, 1994.

McClain, Charles, ed. *Japanese Immigrants and American Law: The Alien Land Law and Other Issues*. New York: Garland Publishing, 1994.

McFarland, Ronald E., and William Studebaker, eds. *Idaho's Poetry: A Centennial Anthology*. Moscow: University of Idaho Press, 1988.

McIntyre, Rick, ed. *War against the Wolf: America's Campaign to Exterminate the Wolf*. Vancouver: Voyageur Press, 1995.

Merchant, Carolyn. *Ecological Revolutions: Nature, Gender, and Science in New England*. Chapel Hill: University of North Carolina Press, 1989.

———. "Shades of Darkness: Race and Environmental History." *Environmental History* 8, no. 3 (2003): 380–394.

Meriam, Lewis. *The Problem of Indian Administration*. Baltimore: Johns Hopkins University Press, 1928.

Miller, Charles A. *Jefferson and Nature: An Interpretation*. Baltimore: Johns Hopkins University Press, 1988.

The Minidoka Interlude. Reprint of 1943. Portland, Oregon: Thomas Takeuchi, 1989.

Minthorn, Philip. "This Earth." In *Songs from This Earth on Turtle's Back: Contemporary American Indian Poetry*, edited by Joseph Bruchac. Greenfield Center, New York: Greenfield Review Press, 1983. 156.

Miyares, Ines M., Jennifer A. Paine, and Midori Nishi. "The Japanese in America." In *Ethnicity in Contemporary America: A Geographical Appraisal*, edited by Jesse O. McKee. Lanham, Maryland: Rowman & Littlefield, 2000. 263–282.

Moore, Bud. *The Lochsa Story: Land Ethics in the Bitterroot Mountains*. Missoula, Montana: Mountain Press Publishing, 1996.

Moran, Rachel F. *Interracial Intimacies: The Regulation of Race and Romance*. Chicago: University of Chicago Press, 2003.

Morrissey, Katherine G. *Mental Territories: Mapping the Inland Empire*. Ithaca, New York: Cornell University Press, 1997.

Moulton, Gary E., ed. *The Journals of the Lewis and Clark Expedition*. Lincoln: University of Nebraska Press, 2002. Also available online at http://lewisandclarkjournals .unl.edu, accessed August 12, 2006, through September 5, 2006.

Nabokov, Peter. "Orientations from Their Side: Dimensions of Native American Cartographic Discourse." In *Cartographic Encounters: Perspectives on Native American Mapmaking and Map Use*, edited by G. Malcolm Lewis. Chicago: University of Chicago Press, 1998. 241–269.

Naito, Calvin, and Esther Scott. *Against All Odds: The Campaign in Congress for Japanese American Redress*. Case Program, John F. Kennedy School of Government, 1990.

Nakano, Jiro, and Kay Nakano, eds. *Poets behind Barbed Wire*. Honolulu: Bamboo Ridge Press, 1984.

Nakano, Mei T. *Japanese American Women: Three Generations, 1890–1990*. Berkeley, California: Mina Press, 1990.

Nash, John D. "The Salmon River Mission of 1855." *Idaho Yesterdays* 11, no. 1 (Spring 1967): 22–31.

Nibley, Preston. *Brigham Young: The Man and His Work*. Salt Lake City: Deseret News Press, 1937.

Niering, William A., and Nancy C. Olmstead. *The Audubon Society Field Guide to North American Wildflowers*. New York: Knopf, 1979.

Niiya, Brian, ed. *Japanese American History: An A-to-Z Reference from 1868 to the Present*. New York: Facts on File, 1993.

Nomura, Gail M. "Tsugiki, A Grafting: A History of a Japanese Pioneer Woman in Washington State." In *Writing the Range: Race, Class, and Culture in the Women's West*, edited by Elizabeth Jameson and Susan Armitage. Norman: University of Oklahoma Press, 1997. 493–512.

Norton, William. "Mormon Identity and Landscape in the Rural Intermountain West." *Journal of the West* 37, no. 3 (July 1998): 33–43.

Okada, John. *No-No Boy*. Seattle: University of Washington Press, 1979.

Okihiro, Gary. "Fallow Field: The Rural Dimensions of Asian American Studies." In *Frontiers of Asian American Studies: Writing, Research, and Commentary*, edited by Gail Nomura, Russell Endo, Stephen H. Sumida, and Russell C. Leong. Pullman: Washington State University Press, 1989. 6–13.

———. *Margins and Mainstreams: Asians in American History and Culture*. Seattle: University of Washington Press, 1994.

———. *Storied Lives: Japanese American Students and World War II*. Seattle: University of Washington Press, 1999.

Okubo, Mine. *Citizen 13660*. Seattle: University of Washington Press, 1983.

Omi, Michael, and Howard Winant. *Racial Formation in the United States: From the 1960s to the 1990s*. 2nd ed. New York: Routledge, 1994.

Omori, Emiko. *Rabbit in the Moon*. Wabi-Sabi Productions, 1999.

Owens, Kenneth. "Pierce City Incident." In *Chinese on the American Frontier*, edited by Arif Dirlik. Lanham, Maryland: Rowman & Littlefield, 2001. 259–266.

Ozawa v. United States, 260 U.S. 178 (November 13, 1922).

Parke, Charles Ross. *Dreams to Dust: A Diary of the California Gold Rush, 1849–1850*, edited by James Davis. Lincoln: University of Nebraska Press, 1989.

Pascoe, Peggy. "Western Women at the Cultural Crossroads." In *Trails: Toward a New Western History*, edited by Patricia Nelson Limerick, Clyde A. Milner II, and Charles E. Rankin. Lawrence: University Press of Kansas, 1991. 40–58.

Perkins, Elisha Douglass. *Gold Rush Diary*, edited by Thomas D. Clark. Lexington: University of Kentucky Press, 1967.

Pisani, Donald J. *To Reclaim a Divided West: Water, Law and Public Policy, 1848–1902*. Albuquerque: University of New Mexico Press, 1992.

———. *Water, Land and Law in the West: The Limits of Public Policy*. Lawrence: University Press of Kansas, 1996.

Preuss, Charles. *Exploring with Fremont: The Private Diaries of Charles Preuss, Cartographer for John C. Fremont on His First, Second, and Fourth Expeditions to the Far West*, edited and translated by Erwin G. Gudde and Elizabeth K. Gudde. Norman: University of Oklahoma Press, 1958.

Reed, T. V. "Toward an Environmental Justice Ecocriticism." In *The Environmental Justice Reader*, edited by Joni Adamson, Mei Mei Evans, and Rachel Stein. Tucson: University of Arizona Press, 2002. 145–162.

Reisner, Marc. *Cadillac Desert: The American West and Its Disappearing Water*. New York: Penguin Books, 1993.

Retallic, Ken, and Rocky Barker. *Flyfisher's Guide to Idaho*. Gallatin, Montana: Wilderness Adventure Press, 1996.

Reynolds, David S. *Walt Whitman's America: A Cultural Biography*. New York: Vintage Books, 1996.

Robbins, William G. *Colony and Empire: The Capitalist Transformation of the American West*. Lawrence: University Press of Kansas, 1994.

Robinson, Greg. *By Order of the President: FDR and the Internment of Japanese Americans*. Cambridge, Massachusetts: Harvard University Press, 2001.

Ronda, James P. "A Chart in His Way." In *Mapping the North American Plains: Essays on the History of Cartography of North America*, edited by Frederick Luebke, Frances W. Kaye, and Gary E. Moulton. Norman: University of Oklahoma Press, 1987. 81–92.

———. *Lewis and Clark among the Indians*. Lincoln: University of Nebraska Press, 1984.

———, ed. *Thomas Jefferson and the Changing West*. Albuquerque: University of New Mexico Press, 1997.

Rothman, Hal K. *Devil's Bargains: Tourism in the Twentieth-Century American West*. Lawrence: University Press of Kansas, 1996.

Ryan, John. "The Rising Son." *Yardbull: Inland Empire Railway Historical Society Newsletter* 26, no. 1 (Spring 1992): 2–20.

Salyer, Lucy E. "Baptism by Fire: Race, Military Service, and U.S. Citizenship Policy, 1918–1935." *Journal of American History* 91, no. 3 (December 2004): 847–876.

Sarasohn, Eileen Sunada. *Issei Women: Echoes from Another Frontier.* Palo Alto, California: Pacific Books, 1998.

Scarce, Rik. *Fishy Business: Salmon, Biology, and the Construction of Nature.* Philadelphia: Temple University Press, 2000.

Schueller, Mailini Johar. *U.S. Orientalisms: Race, Nation, and Gender in Literature, 1790–1890.* Ann Arbor: University of Michigan Press, 2001.

Schwantes, Carlos A. *In Mountain Shadows: A History of Idaho.* Lincoln: University of Nebraska Press, 1991.

"Shall Japanese-Americans in Idaho Be Treated with Fairness and Justice or Not?" Addresses and Proceedings at First Congregational Church in Boise, Idaho. January 23, 1921.

Shrontz, Bessie M. *Hunt for Idaho.* Self-published, 1994.

Simon-Smolinski, Carole. "Idaho's Japanese Americans." Working paper, Idaho State Historical Society.

Sims, Robert C. "A Fearless, Patriotic, Clean-Cut Stand: Idaho's Governor Clark and Japanese-American Relocation in World War II." *Pacific Northwest Quarterly* 70, no. 2 (April 1979): 75–81.

———. "Japanese American Contributions to Idaho's Economic Development." Working paper, Boise State University.

———. "The Japanese American Experience in Idaho." *Idaho Yesterdays* 22, no. 1 (Spring 1978): 2–10.

———. "Japanese-Americans in Idaho." In *Japanese Americans: From Relocation to Redress,* edited by Roger Daniels, Sandra C. Taylor, and Harry H. L. Kitano. Salt Lake City: University of Utah Press, 1986. 103–111.

Smith, George A. "Prosperity of Zion, &c: A Discourse Delivered in the Tabernacle, Great Salt Lake City, March 10, 1861." *Journal of Discourses* 9:66. http://www.journalofdiscourses.org, accessed September 5, 2006.

Smith, Henry Nash. *Virgin Land: The American West as Symbol and Myth.* Cambridge, Massachusetts: Harvard University Press, 1978.

Smoak, Gregory E. "The Mormons and the Ghost Dance." *South Dakota History* 16, no. 3 (1986): 269–294.

Sone, Monica. *Nisei Daughter.* Seattle: University of Washington Press, 1979.

Spalding, Henry. *The Diaries and Letters of Henry H. Spalding and Asa Bowen Smith Relating to the Nez Perce Mission, 1838–1842,* edited by Clifford Merrill Drury. Glendale, California: Arthur H. Clark, 1958.

Spence, Mark. "Let's Play Lewis and Clark: Strange Visions of Nature and History at the Bicentennial." In *Lewis and Clark: Legacies, Memories, and New Perspectives,* edited by Kris Fresonke and Mark Spence. Berkeley: University of California Press, 2000. 219–238.

Spencer, John. "We Are Not Dealing Entirely with the Past: Americans Remember Lewis and Clark." In *Lewis and Clark: Legacies, Memories, and New Perspectives,* edited by Kris Fresonke and Mark Spence. Berkeley: University of California Press, 2000. 159–183.

Spicer, Edward H., Asael T. Hansen, Katherine Luomala, and Marvin K. Opler. Impounded People: Japanese Americans in the Relocation Centers. Tucson: University of Arizona Press, 1969.

Stapp, Darby Campbell. "The Historic Ethnography of a Chinese Mining Community in Idaho." PhD diss., University of Pennsylvania, 1990.

Stegner, Wallace. The American West as Living Space. Ann Arbor: University of Michigan Press, 1987.

———. Beyond the Hundredth Meridian: John Wesley Powell and the Second Opening of the West. Boston: Houghton Mifflin, 1954.

———. Mormon Country. New York: Duell, Sloan and Pearce, 1942.

———. Wolf Willow: A History, a Story, and a Memory of the Last Plains Frontier. New York: Viking Press, 1962.

Stene, Eric A. "The Owyhee Project." Bureau of Reclamation History Program (Denver, 1996). www.usbr.gov/dataweb/projects/oregon/Owyhee/history.html, accessed September 14, 2001.

Swetman, Susan Hendricks. Lives of the Saints in Southeast Idaho: An Introduction to Mormon Pioneer Life Story Writing. Moscow: University of Idaho Press, 1991.

Sze, Julie. "From Environmental Justice Literature to the Literature of Environmental Justice." In The Environmental Justice Reader, edited by Joni Adamson, Mei Mei Evans, and Rachel Stein. Tucson: University of Arizona Press, 2002. 163–180.

Takahashi, C. T. Interview by Judith Austin. Boise: Idaho Oral History Center. August 16, 1984.

Takahashi, Jere. Nisei/Sansei: Shifting Japanese American Identities and Politics. Philadelphia: Temple University Press, 1997.

Takaki, Ronald. Strangers from a Different Shore: A History of Asian Americans. New York: Penguin Books, 1989.

Tamura, Anna H. "Gardens below the Watchtower: Gardens and Meaning in WWII Japanese American Internment Camps." MLA thesis, University of Washington, 2002.

Tateishi, John. And Justice for All: An Oral History of the Japanese American Detention Camps. New York: Random House, 1984.

Toyota v. United States, 268 U.S. 402 (1925).

Trout Unlimited. "Upper Snake River Cutthroats Chapter." n.d.

Tsuchida, John Noboya. Reflections: Memoirs of Japanese American Women in Minnesota. Covina, California: Pacific Asia Press, 1994.

Tsukamoto, Masa, and Midori Tsukamoto. Interview with the author. July 23, 1999.

Turner, Frederick Jackson. The Frontier in American History. New York: H. Holt, 1920.

Tydeman, William. "No Passive Relationship: Native Americans in the Environment." Idaho Yesterdays 39, no. 2 (Summer 1995): 23–28.

United States Commission on Wartime Relocation and Internment of Civilians. Personal Justice Denied: Report of the Commission on Wartime Relocation and Internment of Civilians. Washington, D.C.: Civil Liberties Public Education Fund, 1997.

United States Department of Agriculture. *Forest Service Manual 2300: Recreation, Wilderness, and Related Resource Management.* http://www.fs.fed.us, accessed September 1, 2006.

———. Idaho Agricultural Statistics Service. http://www.nass.usda.gov, accessed September 2, 2006.

United States Department of the Interior. *The Relocation Program.* Washington: U.S. Government Printing Office, 1946.

———. *WRA: A Story of Human Conservation.* Washington: U.S. Government Printing Office, 1946.

von Hassell, Malve. "Issei Women: Silences and Fields of Power." *Feminist Studies* 19, no. 3 (Fall 1993): 544–569.

Wallenstein, Peter. *Tell the Court I Love My Wife: Race, Marriage, and Law—An American History.* New York: Palgrave Macmillan, 2002.

Walter, Jess. *Every Knee Shall Bow: The Truth and Tragedy of Ruby Ridge and the Randy Weaver Family.* New York: Harper Collins, 1995.

Walz, Eric. "Idaho Farmer, Japanese Diarist: Cultural Crossings in the Intermountain West." *Idaho Yesterdays* 39, no. 3 (Fall 1995): 2–12.

———. "Japanese Immigration and Community Building in the Interior West: 1882–1945." PhD diss., Arizona State University, 1998.

———. "Masayoshi Fujimoto: Japanese Diarist, Idaho Farmer." MA thesis, Utah State University, 1994.

Wegars, Priscilla. "The History and Archaeology of the Chinese in Northern Idaho, 1880–1910." PhD diss., University of Idaho, 1991.

———. "Japanese and Japanese Latin Americans at Idaho's Kooskia Internment Camp." In *Guilt by Association: Essays on Japanese Settlement, Internment, and Relocation in the Rocky Mountain West,* edited by Mike Mackey. Powell, Wyoming: Western History Publications, 2001. 145–183.

Weglyn, Michi. *Years of Infamy: The Untold Story of America's Concentration Camps.* New York: William Morrow, 1976.

Wells, Merle. "The Idaho Anti-Mormon Test Oath." *Pacific Historical Review* 24, no. 3 (August 1955): 235–252.

Whitman, Walt. *Leaves of Grass,* edited by Sculley Bradley and Harold W. Blodgett. New York: Norton, 1973.

———. *The Portable Walt Whitman,* edited by Mark Van Doren. New York: Penguin Books, 1974.

Wikoff, Melvin. "Chinese in the Idaho County Gold Fields, 1864–1933." MS thesis, Texas Arts and Industries University, 1972.

Woodruff, Wilford. *Wilford Woodruff's Journal,* edited by Scott Kenney. Salt Lake City: Signature Books, 1984.

Worster, Donald. *Rivers of Empire: Water, Aridity, and the Growth of the American West.* New York: Pantheon Books, 1985.

———. *An Unsettled Country: Changing Landscapes of the American West.* Albuquerque: University of New Mexico Press, 1994.

Wunder, John. "The Courts and the Chinese in Frontier Idaho." *Idaho Yesterdays* 25, no. 1 (Spring 1981): 23–32.

Wyndham, Harald. "Spring in Pocatello." In *Where the Morning Light's Blue: Personal Essays about Idaho*, edited by William Studebaker and Rick Ardinger. Moscow: University of Idaho Press, 1994. 115–117.

———, ed. *Famous Potatoes: Southeast Idaho Poetry.* Pocatello, Idaho: Blue Scarab Press, 1986.

Yamada, Mitsuye. *Camp Notes and Other Writings.* New Brunswick, New Jersey: Rutgers University Press, 1998.

Yasui, Robert S. *The Yasui Family of Hood River, Oregon.* Published by Holly Yasui, 1987.

Yoo, David. *Growing Up Nisei: Race, Generation, and Culture among Japanese Americans of California, 1924–49.* Urbana: University of Illinois Press, 2000.

Young, Brigham. "Providence—Ignorance of Sectarian Priests—Free Agency—Recreation, Etc." *Journal of Discourses* 6:143.http://www.journalofdiscourses.org, accessed September 3, 2006.

INDEX

American Land and Life Series